Contents

Tourism Development in
Critical Environments

Cognizant Communication Corporation
New York • Sydney • Tokyo

Tourism Development in Critical Environments

Cognizant Communication Offices:

U.S.A.   3 Hartsdale Road, Elmsford, New York 10523-3701
Australia P.O. Box 352 Cammeray, NWS, 2062
Japan   c/o OBS T's Bldg. 3F, 1-38-11 Matsubara, Setgaya-ku, Tokyo

Library of Congress Cataloging-in-publication Data

Tourism development in critical environments
    / edited by Tejvir Singh and Shalini Singh.
      p. cm. -- (Tourism dynamics)
    Includes bibliographical references and index.
    ISBN 1-882345-18-5 (hard). ISBN 1-882345-19-3 (soft)
    1. Ecotourism. 2. Ecotourism--Case studies. I. Singh. Tejvir
    1930 - . II. Singh, Shalini. III. Series
    G156.5.E26T68 1999
    338.4'791-dc21   98-52536
                          CIP

Cover design: Lynn Carano Graphics
Cover photographs: Antartic: John Horniblow, all other photographs by: Michel Lippitsch.
Photographs Copyright: Planetary Coral Reef Foundation (PCRF) www.pcrf.org.

Printed in the United States of America

Printing: 12345678910 Years:12345678910

Chapter 12: Developing Tourism in the Environmentally Sensitive North West Cape Region, Western Australia 163
Ross K. Dowling

List of Figures

List of Tables

Foreword

Tourism in critical environments creates multiple intellectual challenges, as Webster's Dictionary (Neufeldt, 1988) defines critical as "designating or of a point at which a change in character, property, or condition is effected." Environments can be altered by humanly devised processes including the social, economic, and political; they can also be changed through natural processes—tectonic and erosional, the latter dominantly wind and water. In the contemporary world, these cultural and physical elements are interactive and may render an environment critical through use, misuse, overuse, and even abuse. Construction of a deep-water port to attract cruise vessels can change coastal currents and destroy the beaches that were the original tourist attraction. The use of dynamite to temporarily increase the fish harvest often destroys the off-shore reefs, with dual damage to the local economy, in loss of an indigenous industry and the potential for tourism. These convoluted issues occur and recur, with increasing frequency in relation to the demographic flow, land use, and tourism demand.

The literature in tourism took an important research turn in the 1990s, as the so-called Green Revolution and earth awareness swept the planet. To be environmentally sensitive is now politically correct, and new concepts—notably sustainable tourism, ecotourism, and ecolabeling—have emerged as important avenues of investigation. Unfortunately, the thrust appears to have been economically motivated. Is the environment "sustainable"? If so, for what purpose? Munasinghe (1993, p. 171), writing in *Environmental Challenges*, suggests that the wealthier countries are increasingly willing to trade off further growth against improved environmental quality, whereas the developing nations realize that natural resource degradation jeopardizes economic development and their goal in the alleviation of poverty. Thus, the efforts of the Bruntland Commission must be interpreted as essentially economic.

Ecotourism has been repeatedly criticized as "eco-nomic" tourism—that is, exploitation of resources to benefit tour operators. The research by Lindberg, Enriquez, and Sproule (1996, p. 543) in Belize drafts a balanced threefold definition: does ecotourism generate financial support for protection and management of natural areas, economic benefits for local residents, and support for conservation among these residents (in part, due to economic benefits)? The underlying theme is still economic but it does strengthen conservation.

Recent research has examined fragile environments, and the literature review by Harrison and Price (1996) assesses both biological and social concerns, and suggests that the term fragility denotes areas (and/or cultures) threatened by tourism in excess of the bio-social carrying capacity. As portrayed by Price (1996), these fragile environments have been primarily geographical *regions*, including mountains, the Arctic, tropics, and the indigenous inhabitants thereof. This present volume examines geographical *features*, such as coastlines and beaches that, except for small islands, are almost always limited in area proportionate to the size of the hinterland. The propensity for tourists to seek sun, sea, and sand as a prime recreation destination gives focus to the world's beaches as truly critical environments. This present volume therefore brings the role of policy, planning, and management to the ultimate stage of critical—wherein the necessity for implementation is mandatory, lest the resource base be irrevocably lost through use, misuse, and abuse.

The editors are to be commended for their recognition of this central theme, especially Tej Vir Singh, who has given his own personal concentration on mountain geography and his residence on one of the world's largest volcanic plateaus, the Deccan, whose beaches have not yet become known worldwide. The invited authors provide a wealth of experience, direction, and models for government and policymakers, as well as for professors and students, in the necessary effort to protect these vanishing recreational resources from ruin. Polluted waters, dead reefs, and tourist-dependent labor force are tragic by-products of governmental neglect and economic greed.

Valene L. Smith
California State University

Preface

In recent years, there has been an upsurge in the growth of world tourism, as if we are amidst a tourist revolution. Only within the last two decades (1970–1990) tourist volume has increased nearly 300%, despite threats of global terrorism, religious fundamentalism, energy crisis, and economic recession. There were only 25 million international tourists in 1950 but that number rose to 612 million in 1997; it is quite possible that this number will increase to 1 billion by the turn of the century. Although tourism movements are largely confined to developed nations, the developing countries are forging ahead rapidly, particularly East Asia and the Pacific region. Above all, the quest for new and inaccessible pleasure peripheries has led to discover virgin and unspoiled biospheres of tender ecologies for tourist activities—an alarming trend.

Tourism scholars and industry managers throughout the world are faced with a colossal task of managing scarce tourism resources—sustainability for the intragenerational and intergenerational needs of society. Judicious integration of *tourism* with *environment* is the biggest challenge of today's tourism, as the former avariciously consumes the latter. Mainstream tourism, with all its bust and boom, bane and blessings, seems to be inevitable as long as some workable alternative forms of benign tourism are not found. Studies in tourism impacts have established that mass tourism is the most unkind killer of the environment. Its sheer hugeness, immensity, and speed defies checks and controls, leading it to unsustainability. It often breeds like cancer and swarms like locusts, using the environment to the extent of using it up. It has, by and large, miserably failed to establish the much-needed interrelationships between people and resources, environment, and development. Wedded to the green ideology, some value-conscious tourism scholars and environmentalists seem to have found a promise in the theory and practice of "ecotourism," based on biocentric management philosophy, which can minimize predatory effects of touristic development, especially in the critical environments. Considered to be a low-impact and high-value dream, this form of tourism whatever be its name—appropriate, real, just, responsible, nature based, or green—must form a symbiosis with tourism–environment–conservation to achieve positive results. In the practice of ecotourism, the integrity of ecosystems is a prime prerequisite, made possible by respecting capacity thresholds of scale, size, speed of tourism development with positive and proactive involvement of the local people, right from policy framing, resource planning to implementation and to monitoring stages. Its main focus is on local democracy, conservation, and smallness of enterprise, which alone can ensure the genius of the place.

It is a unique though subtle economic process whereby beautiful ecosystems of nature–culture excellences can be marketed for tourism with prophylactic approaches. Success stories of Costa Rica, Belize, Ecuador, and Mexico have illus-

trated that "conservation" can also be a tourism business, creating economic
opportunities for the local citizens. Identified as a niche market segment, it is now
the fastest growing sector of the industry that the 1990s will be remembered as
the decade of ecotourism. More and more environmentally fragile and vulnerable
areas have come under its sway. In many cases, it is observed that ecotourism is
ecologically based, though maybe not ecologically sound. Ecotourism would,
indeed, be a broken promise should it yield place to "environmental opportunism."
In fact, it would be a worst case of eco-disaster because the products are too
vulnerable to be sold in the open market. To some critics, it is no more than a
pursuit of a holy grail, because even the best-organized nature tourism has a
propensity to overdevelop and assume the attributes of mainstream tourism. To
them, it appears difficult to enforce such green practices in a free society. Many
experts are of the opinion that it is better to "ecologize" mass tourism than to
search for its alternatives. However, all do agree that the long-term viability of the
industry is dependent on the maintenance of natural and cultural environments.
Ecology is a science of management, and the concept of "dynamic tourism ecosystem" shows the way for achieving sustainable development, though the task is
forbidding. Nevertheless, one would like to be as optimistic as was Robert Brown-
ing when he wrote: "a man's heaven must exceed his grasp or what's heaven for."
And there are peoples who have made a success of tourism—making it economically viable, socially responsible, and ecologically sound. The secret of this success,
and how this can be achieved and shared for the benefit of other regions, has
become the main objective in organizing this anthology.

The Centre for Tourism Research and Development, Lucknow, India some 3 years
ago, solicited theme specialists for authentic reports on successful tourism stories
in the world's high-risk zones and critical environments, viz., the far flung Antarctica, remote mountain ecosystems, secluded coastal areas, nature reserves, and
cultural heritages. Emphasis was on finding grounded realities and key factors that
made the success possible, with all the challenges and opportunities that the
proponents of green tourism faced.

This volume has a dozen contributions from known tourism personalities on the
theory and practice of holistic development—a development that makes sense, and
is sustainable despite its happening in some of the most sensitive environments.

Edward Manning and **T. David Dougherty**, in the opening chapter, elaborate on
some of the basic principles of sustainable tourism development through ecological approaches and impact assessment studies. Two problems are examined: how
best to measure systems' capacity and response to environmental changes, and
how best to represent these to decision makers for plan formulation. **Ralf Buckley**
presents a workable model of quantitative measurement of environmental impacts
of tourism in conservation reserves and fragile environments. **John Pigram** and
Peiyi Ding narrate the greening process of Australia's East Coast, particularly the
Great Barrier Reef Region of Northern Queensland, where some of the resorts are
groomed on tested ecotourism principles. **Peter Williams** and **Alison Gill** suggest
the application of growth management system for addressing development issues

in sensitive mountain environments. They argue that given the development potential of these regions, the carrying capacity of a destination should be determined by the policy statement, capital budget, and management goals and objectives of the stakeholders of the area. The Whistler case study from British Columbia exemplifies it for a better follow-up in other alpine communities in America.

Tej Vir Singh and **Shalini Singh** discuss the problem of Coastal Goa in India and argue that environmental laws and legislation are not always effective without community vigilance. Community-based tourism development affords a promise of sustainability. Ecologically conscious Goans present a living example of "Community and Conservation" through cooperative tourism. **Robert Healy** explains how soft tourism options can integrate with the coastal forest environment in Brazil.

Lest mass tourism should overtake a natural protected area and degrade its ecology, **Ray Ashton** has a comprehensive management plan for Punta Sal National Park (Honduras) and its buffer zones besides establishing park and economic authorities, which includes majority representation of local communities on the board of directors to monitor welfare of the local people. **Robert Horwich** and **Jonathan Lyon** assert that ecotourism may have its drawbacks, but can be effectively used as a tool for conserving rural resources where villagers run their own guest houses and tourism programs with local autonomy. The Community Baboon Sanctuary and Manatee Special Development Program are the best examples of experimental practices in community conservation.

Alan Lew explains how the problem of acculturation can be solved in sensitive pueblo villages in American Indian reservations through environmental cues, both overt (signage) and covert. This approach offers considerable opportunity to manage tourism in culturally sensitive settings.

John Splettstoesser builds an interesting chronicle of fairly successful tourism management in a highly vulnerable environment of Antarctica, made up of complex ecosystems, having unique wildlife. He cites the constructive role of the signatories of the Antarctic Treaty in 1950 and later the International Association of Antarctic Tour Operators in formulation of guidelines for visitors and tour operators that helped maintain the environment.

Charlotte Echtner presents three exhibits of successful tourism from African countries. Casamance in Senegal was the pioneer in practicing village-based cooperative tourism; gorilla sanctuaries in Rwanda, Zaire and Uganda are other examples of community-based tourism. **Ross Dowling** reports on the remote North West Cape Range of Australia, which adopted an effective development strategy with two options for future tourism: minimum sustainable development, and a maximum carrying capacity in its specific "tourism zones." Nature conservation and protection of community lifestyles would remain crucial to the development policy and process of this sensitive region.

A review of these reports reveals that tourism research in its evolutionary process has now stepped out of its adolescent stage. The world of scholars feels that if tourism is part of the problem, it should also be made a part of the solution. If heaven still eludes our grasp, research and more meaningful research may be the answer because tourism is complex and Nature is so mystifying in revealing her secrets.

Tej Vir Singh
and
Shalini Singh
Centre for Tourism Research & Development
Lucknow, India

Chapter 1

Planning Tourism in Sensitive Ecosystems

Edward W. Manning and T. David Dougherty

Introduction

More than other sectors of the world economy, tourism is dependent upon and
sensitive to the qualities of the natural and human environment. The reason
tourists choose a destination is strongly influenced by the cultural and natural
environment of that location. Tourists seek safe, clean, interesting, and varied
environments. The long-term viability of the industry is dependent on maintenance
of natural, cultural, and historical attractions.

Tourism involves demand for significant amounts of energy and consumption of
many goods and services. Increasingly we are discovering that, unless responsible
management practices are in place, the industry can degrade the very features on
which tourism's prosperity is based. As well, the actions of people in other economic sectors affect the quality of and access to the environment, and their
actions can degrade the environment on which tourism depends, so that tourism
management needs to be integrated with management of other economic sectors.
Thus, particularly in sensitive environments, the tourism industry can be a significant force for maintenance and improvement or for degradation. For tourism
managers these options constitute a new challenge—to manage the relationship
between tourism and the environment more effectively.

The direct links between tourism activities and environmental quality mean that
the industry has much to offer and to gain from being a leader in implementing
sustainable development. This is true particularly in developing countries, where
the industry is both a source of support for development and a vehicle for cultural
contact. The industry also has a key role in generating an informed world citizenry
and in sensitizing individuals to the benefits of a clean environment. Tourism may
be the single most important element in portraying conditions in such areas as the
Arctic or the tropical rainforest to audiences in other regions, through both direct
contact and vicarious experience. But sustainable tourism will not occur without

1

careful attention by governments and full participation by the industry and by those who serve it.)

This chapter reviews the concept of sustainable development in the tourism sector. Some basic principles of planning for sustainable tourism are examined, covering key policy instruments, planning approaches, and means of implementation. A discussion follows on how an ecological approach to impact assessment can aid the sector in identifying key values and their sensitivity to levels of use. What are the limits? How does degradation of sensitive environments affect potential tourism values? What do tourism managers need to know to plan and manage the business effectively? A practical means is proposed for identifying the key elements of carrying capacity for sustainable tourism in the site and regional planning process. Some examples of best practice are discussed that contain lessons of what is economically and ecologically sustainable, including reference to technical and managerial solutions that can limit or mitigate tourist impact. The chapter ends by discussing emerging opportunities for ecotourism—the controversy and the promise of new tourism enterprise that focuses its attention on the world's most sensitive and fragile environments.

Background

The Brundtland Commission (World Commission on Environment and Development, 1987) and the World Conservation Strategy (1980) began the popularization of "sustainable development" as a goal for human society. As it is becoming widely used, sustainable development means using natural resources and the capacity of the environment to create economic activity now without compromising the capacity to provide for the needs of future generations.

As the human population has expanded in recent centuries following the industrial revolution, the business of tourism has developed as a means to satisfy desires of people for relaxation and exploration for interest's sake. Tourism is the business of providing services to people who are traveling for the purpose of recreation. Traditionally, these services include transportation, accommodation, restaurant service, sightseeing, and recreation (sports and relaxation). The business is increasingly one of human society's largest sectors of economic activity, certainly ranking within the top five sectors on a worldwide basis. As such, tourism serves as a vital element in trade within local and regional economies, notably for small population centers, and small and island nations. Although it may benefit middle- and upper-class entrepreneurs and corporate businesses, tourism also has the potential to redistribute wealth from affluent areas to poor areas (particularly from the wealthy nations of the North to less-developed regions). For many smaller nations, particularly islands, tourism is the principal source of foreign exchange. Tourism can also provide direct flows of money from comparatively wealthy people (tourists) to poor people (providers of tourism services and local cottage industries). To perform these essential economic functions over the long term, tourism has to be conducted to ensure the continued attractiveness of the environment in which it takes place.

Ecology is the study of how living organisms interact with each other and their surrounding environment, where environment means all of the physical and biological conditions that affect an organism. The importance of ecology has increased as the rapidly expanding human population has been having more noticeable effects on its environment. Some of those effects have been ones that have affected people directly, through economic hardship, flooding, famine, or disease.

Within the discipline of ecology an area of specialization has been developed that aims at translating knowledge of ecological function into more effective management of human activities. This specialization is environmental management. Some of the key concepts used within this specialization are:

- the **ecosystem**, any grouping of plants and animals interacting within a particular physical environment;

- **environmental impact assessment**, where planners attempt to predict what effects a set of activities will have and to determine how to enhance benefits of the activities and reduce their negative impacts;

- **carrying capacity utilization**, where managers attempt to determine the biophysical limits of productivity of various natural resources and to harvest or use those resources at or below those limits, sometimes making trade-offs in the production of one resource in order to maintain the productivity of another;

- **environmental monitoring**, where planners and managers seek to test how accurate their predictions have been and use the results to determine what changes are required to achieve better results.

All of these concepts are essential to sustainable development: the ecosystem because it provides ways of viewing humans within their natural world; environmental impact assessment because of its predictive ability; carrying capacity utilization because of its emphasis on production over the long term; and environmental monitoring because of its feedback to decision makers who control economic activity. The managers of tourism, and the ecosystems that serve as destinations, need knowledge of these concepts, and of their implications for the tourism industry.

At the Globe '92 Global Conference on Business and the Environment in Vancouver, Canada, a challenge statement was prepared for the global tourism sector. This statement identified the critical steps needed if the industry was to actively seek to become environmentally sustainable. The experts present at Globe '92 agreed that many different building blocks were needed to support sustainable tourism. These building blocks included:

- actions to put in place the institutional framework for sustainable tourism, including long-term strategy development, and the creation of broader policy and planning structures;

- actions to protect the resource base that is central for the success of the industry;

- actions to establish partnerships with host communities and with private enterprise to build sustainable tourism;

- better inventory and monitoring systems for both the resource base and the actions of tourists;

- use of improved technology and design to minimize negative impacts;

- actions to take advantage of market opportunities for a greener tourism product;

- development of standards for the industry and collaboration at all levels in the development and implementation of effective regulatory mechanisms.

Together, these building blocks constitute a significant agenda for the industry to take charge of its own future—to build a more sustainable industry through better planning, better management, and cooperation to address the common concerns for the future of the sector. As a consequence of the 1992 Earth Summit in Rio de Janiero, the tourism industry at an international level has reconfirmed its commitment to environmental sustainability as a cornerstone of its own viability. In 1993, the World Travel and Tourism Council, the World Tourism Organization, and the Earth Council produced *Agenda 21 for the Travel and Tourism Industry*, identifying the strategic actions the industry must follow to assure the sustainability of the industry and the environments that the industry uses. Achievement of this agenda will help make tourism a leading industry in adopting the principles that have developed out of recent scientific and managerial advances, and a catalyst for sustainable development of destination regions. This advancement is likely to take place largely because of the growing understanding by the industry that it must act to protect the resources and communities on which its success depends and because of growing concern that the current development path may imperil the industry's own future.

Past Management Approaches to Tourism

Traditional attitudes to the environment, particularly in Western countries, have emphasized satisfaction of human demands, portraying the environment primarily as a treasure house of potential goods or services. At best, environmental consequences have been considered as "externalities"—things that are difficult to measure and for which it is often impossible to calculate costs. Our failure to recognize and incorporate the consequences of our actions is increasingly visible in the form of polluted air and water, closed beaches, inedible fish, and denuded hillsides.

Each area in which economic activity occurs has limits beyond which it can be dangerous to step. These limits are the carrying capacity of an area—the degree to which the area can be used for economic activity without degrading the environment there or the interactive harmony between sectors of the economy, groups of people, and individuals.

Recognition that tourism occurs in environments that have limits has been quite recent. We have often discovered these limits only by violating them, usually to the detriment of the tourism industry. In some cases, serious and irreversible damage has occurred to the tourism industry through the actions of tourism managers, and/or by the tourists themselves.

In the recent past, tourists devegetated some of the more easily accessible alpine meadows in the Rocky Mountains of Canada through cumulative effects of their footsteps on the very fragile plant species that tourists were coming to see (e.g., the Sunshine Meadows and the summit of Mt. Revelstoke). In many coastal and lakeside areas of North America and Europe, (e.g., the Great Lakes, the Baltic Sea, and the Black Sea) pollution from resort communities, in combination with release of untreated waste by nearby towns and industries, has rendered the water unsafe for swimming and the fish unsafe for consumption, although water-based activities were the key attractions that kept tourist resorts in business.

Emerging Management Approaches for Sustainable Tourism

A central objective of management is to sustain that which we value. If full carrying capacity utilization can be achieved, there will be maximum economic activity from the resources available within the environment. As demonstrated above, the sustainability of tourism, in particular, relies on ensuring that carrying capacity is not exceeded, while a healthy industry can exist at levels of activity below the carrying capacity.

The tourism industry can benefit from management approaches that anticipate and prevent the types of problems which occur when carrying capacity is exceeded. However, there are several obstacles to the easy detection of carrying capacities and the evaluation of the importance of differing resources (i.e., achievement of optimal carrying capacity utilization for various resources) in tourism:

- tourism depends on many attributes of an environment, such as cleanliness, presence and diversity of wildlife, access to shoreline, abundance of wildflowers, and ability to support active uses (e.g., sports), each of which has its own response to different levels of use;

- the impact of human activity on an environment may be gradual, and may affect different parts of the system at differing rates—whereas some aspects may have precipitous thresholds (e.g., habitats for fragile or endangered species), others degrade gradually in response to different use levels (e.g., water quality);

- the sensitivity of an environment to different use levels depends on the values of the users of that environment—in one site, it may not matter to anyone if a river is diverted or a breakwater built; in another site, a change in flow may be critical because downstream or further along the coast some person or species depends on that source of water;

- different types of use have different impacts (e.g., walking disturbs land less than trail biking; hunting is consumptive, whereas photographing wildlife is not).

A simple definition of carrying capacity as a single threshold value is inadequate in nearly all cases because of these factors. Instead, the identification of carrying capacity needs to reflect the sensitivity of different attributes of the environment to different types and levels of impact or use. Planning using an ecosystem-based approach facilitates achievement of this objective.

The Impact Assessment Approach

Planning for development should clearly identify the key attributes of the natural environment of the site or region. As well, it is necessary to identify the area's cultural and historical assets. These are the assets upon which tourism can be based. Environmental Impact Assessment (EIA) has emerged as a tool for identification and consideration of such attributes (although it developed for use in all aspects of development, not just tourism).

The objective in an EIA is to identify, in advance, factors that either may affect the ability to build a desired development, or the factors that will be affected by the proposed activity. The results can then influence the decision of whether or not to proceed, the choice of design and phasing, and the identification of need for mitigation of unwanted effects.

The steps involved in EIA are relatively well known, and are increasingly required for major projects in most nations. For example, the United States Department of Commerce approach to EIA (a typical approach) includes:

1. inventory of social, political, physical, economic environment;
2. forecast or projection of trends;
3. setting of goals and objectives (usually project level);
4. examination of alternatives to reach these goals;
5. selection of preferred alternative;
6. development of implementation strategy;
7. implementation;
8. evaluation.

In many jurisdictions that have begun to require EIAs, this procedure has been truncated. As a result, only a simple review process is undertaken that examines, for example, the engineering concerns of the site (drainage, soil depth, stability), and selected on-site phenomena (vegetation, fauna) that would be directly disturbed. There is no examination of alternative sites, alternative development options, off-site effects, or the social dimensions of the consequences of the project.

A fairly simple site-focused EIA can be of considerable value in identifying key biological and physical factors that developers, or those who regulate them, need to know. However, we are learning that it is often an incomplete approach and may miss many important considerations and effects. In particular, site-specific reviews will often miss impacts that occur off a development site (damage to downstream communities) and effects that are the result of many small actions, each of which appears too small to be important (the cumulative impact of pollution from hundreds of small cottages on lake water quality). Even when a relatively thorough EIA is done, if the results of an EIA are not taken into account in final development decisions significant negative impacts can develop. It does little good to have accurately predicted the effects of development if no mitigative measures are taken to improve the situation at the planning and construction stages.

Pulau Redang, a small island off the coast of Malaysia, is emblematic of a small, fragile ecosystem targeted by tourists because of its ecology. A thorough impact assessment was done prior to tourism development there. The assessment predicted that the major resort development proposed for the island would draw down the freshwater aquifer, would cause erosion of unstable slopes, and could seriously harm the reef that encircled the island. The reef environment of the island, along with its rich jungle vegetation, was the principal attraction to tourists. Limits to amount of development were recommended and strict conditions suggested for slope disturbance and means of construction.

Pulau Redang has now become a *cause célèbre* for environmental groups in Malaysia because many of the adverse effects that were predicted came true. The slopes are eroding; the siltation of the reef has eliminated many species and has clouded the water to the point where the remaining species are hard to see. The aquifer has been drawn down and salinization is evident; a 40-km pipeline is now proposed to bring water from the mainland to serve the tourist requirements. The conclusion is that, somehow, the process to integrate the results of the EIA into ultimate decisions on development have not worked effectively (Friends of Pulau Redang, 1992).

Thus, it is possible that even when environmental capacities can be successfully identified, the limits and sensitivities will not be reflected adequately in development decisions, even for large, otherwise well-managed projects. Where the form of development is one of many small changes (e.g., hundreds of cottages added a few dozen each year to a lake shore, thousands of individual fishing boats added a few dozen per season to a fishing fleet), EIAs are seldom done. EIAs are seldom required of smaller projects or dispersed activities (e.g., hiking, sports fishing) either. This lack of planning occurs even though these developments may have significant impacts on the surrounding environment. "Disaster by creeping increments" can be the result.

The Ecosystem Evaluation Approach

Although many EIA manuals are available that give planners long lists of environmental attributes which can be part of a site or regional environmental inventory, we are learning that it is essential to try to establish the links between these attributes and the benefits that are obtained from them. This step helps the planner to focus on achieving optimal results in the development process. He or she can then ask: How do the natural and cultural attributes of the environment provide opportunities for tourism development? How do environmental attributes limit the potential because of the characteristics of the site, or because of the likely impacts on the interests of others (particularly the local residents) that can occur as a result of the proposed development?

Over the past decade, work has occurred in Canada, The Netherlands, Sweden, and the United States to develop site-specific planning procedures which more clearly identify the range of ecological and cultural attributes that can be disturbed and to relate these to the benefits obtained from them. Table 1.1 provides a sampling of the key types of ecosystem functions and benefits to society. Any site may support any or all of the ecosystem functions. Therefore, any tourism activity or development may impact upon any or all of these, either on-site or in adjacent or downstream areas. In addition, many of the benefits may be key reasons why tourists may wish to visit or use the site. The functions and benefits can clearly be affected by any new development. The key for development planners is to identify early in the process which of these are likely to be important.

We need a very clear framework to address the management of the relationship between human uses and the environment. Such a framework is provided in Figure 1.1, which shows relationship between humans and their environment using an "ecosphere" approach (based on Manning, Rizzo, & Wiken, 1990) for ecosystem evaluation. In this approach, the relationship between human systems and the environment is portrayed as one of supply and demand. Thus, certain aspects of the traditional Western attitude to nature are maintained. The environment, with its biophysical characteristics, is shown as the source of all goods, services, and experiences—the base resource from which to satisfy human wants and needs, as well as the needs of other species. The many different attributes of the environment support tourism and other economic activities in particular parts of the planet.

The demand side of the ecosphere model is driven by human numbers. The total human demand on the system is the result of numbers modified by the attitudes and expectations of each person (i.e., the "footprint" of each person on the planet). Together, population and consumption demands by each person yield a "wish list" to be satisfied from the environment: food, shelter, security, education, culture, and recreation. Because the natural products and conditions of the environment are frequently not exactly what is wanted or located where it is needed, we have created a range of transformation processes to modify the supply to satisfy the demands better.

The model goes beyond traditional Western attitudes through the inclusion of a feedback loop. This loop recognizes that our actions to serve these demands have impacts, both intended and unintended, which affect the ability of the system to continue to serve our needs. It also recognizes that different cultures will have different demands and expectations. These demands and expectations yield different priorities regarding which values are negotiable and which are not.

Table 1.1. Translating Environmental Functions Into Benefits Valued by Society

Ecosystem Functions (Capabilities)	Examples of Products, Services, and Experiences Supported by Ecosystems	Examples of Benefits to Society Derived From Ecosystem Functions
Life Support		
A) Regulation/ absorption	climate regulation; absorption of toxics; nutrient cycling; water storage	flood control (lives & money saved); ꞌtaminant reduction; ꞌn water; damage reduction; ꞌealth; ꞌ control
B) Ecosystem health	nutrient cycling; food chain support; habitat maintenance; biomass storage; genetic and biological diversity	ꞏod supplies; ꞏdicinal supplies; pr　　　of pestilence; life
Social/Cultural Values		
C) Science/information	specimens for zoos & botanical gardens; natural phenomena for study	greater understanding of nature locations for study & research
D) Aesthetics/recreation	natural places for viewing; photography; birdwatching; hiking; swimming	enjoyment and relaxation; tourism
E) Culture/psychological well-being	natural places for religious uses; natural places for cultural uses; future opportunities for use	social cohesion; maintenance of culture; value to future generations; symbolic values; "home"
Resource Production		
F) Subsistence	birds, fish, mammals, reptiles, plants (e.g., canes, rushes, wild rice)	avoidance of hunger; warmth; self-reliance for communities; import substitution; maintenance of dietary traditions
G) Commercial products	foods (e.g., fish, crops); fiber (e.g., wood, straw); drugs; soil supplements (e.g., peat, manures)	avoidance of hunger; warmth; good health; jobs; income

Adapted from DeGroot (1988) and Filion (1988).

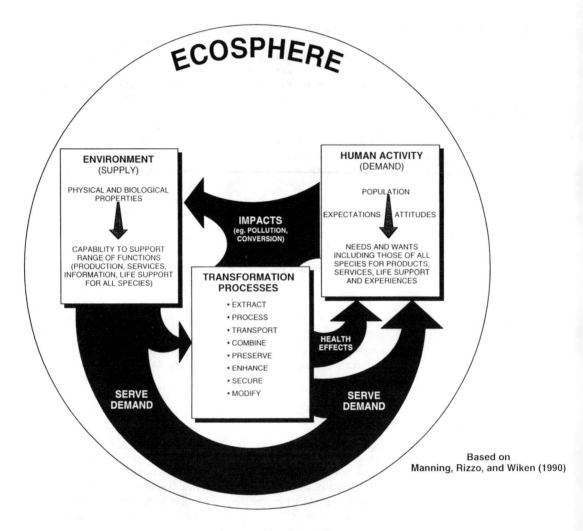

Figure 1.1. Relationship between humans and their environment using an "ecosphere" approach (based on Manning et al., 1990).

Within this framework, optimal carrying capacity utilization must be sought. The complex balance of human wants and needs with the ability of the ecosphere to serve these needs on a sustainable basis must be maintained. Our measurements of this objective must reflect:

1. the range of biophysical capacities of the environment (what are the basic physical and biological attributes of the ecosystems present?);

2. the range of values supported by each environment (who, or what, now uses this environment?);

3. the sensitivity of each part of the environment to our actions (how fragile are the ecosystems?);

4. the impacts of our actions on the capacities of ecosystems and the resulting effects on the ability of the environment to continue to support the full range of functions (what is lost to whom if we change the environment?);

5. the sensitivity of the key values to change (how much can we change and still maintain the valued parts of the existing situation?).

The biophysical capacities of various environments are only partially known at present (e.g., areas in cold climates frequently have lower rebound capability from impacts, areas with simple food webs are more easily disturbed). At times, we still get surprised by the effects of our activities (e.g., recent importation of zebra mussels from Europe in ship-borne ballast water has created very expensive problems in the Great Lakes of North America). Little is known of the potential cumulative effects of human activity on the many ecosystems. Continuing research is needed to ensure adequate knowledge of ecosystem functions.

The values of users and of residents are often not well understood because of poor cross-cultural information flow or inadequate data collection techniques. As a result, a concerted effort must be made to determine what each cohort of users wants from a particular site (e.g., more intense use may make a sandy beach more crowded, more polluted, and less favorable for swimming, but better for social gatherings). The exchange of knowledge, particularly regarding social mores and culture, is critical if successful incorporation of values into tourism management is to occur.

Further, because so little work based on this approach has been done to date, the sensitivities of ecosystems, likely effects of human activities on those ecosystems, and sensitivities of key values are not well known. This lack of understanding makes the challenge all that much more difficult. Yet, the goal is important enough to require ongoing, and even more intensive, work to improve our knowledge base.

Integrating Sustainable Tourism Into the Overall Economy

Many of the key resources on which tourism depends are managed by others or affected by the actions of others (e.g., forestry, fishing, hunting, manufacturing, agriculture). Therefore, it is not sufficient to plan for tourism in isolation from other economic sectors.

In most nations, sectoral interests like tourism are managed in different government departments from, for example, the economic planning or environmental management interests. This separation means that effective integration of tourism interests requires special attention. Some comprehensive sustainable development strategies have been developed, generally through a comprehensive consultative process (e.g., Yukon Territory of Canada). These strategies are proving very effective at identifying the interests of each sector very early in the planning process, often guiding development away from areas where its future would be threatened by other uses or by the effects on the natural environment. The challenge to tourism managers is to become a full participant in such initiatives, and to make the needs of the sector known to other decision makers.

Some promising examples of integrated sustainable development strategies that respect tourism sector interests are now in place. In Prince Edward Island, Canada, a comprehensive Conservation Strategy has become the long-term plan for the entire province, and tourism interests have an equal footing with agriculture and fisheries in its objectives and strategies. This strategy has provided tourism sector interests with access to the decision process for developments in other sectors, such as forestry or agriculture, and allowed it to advocate its interests in their planning and management activities (e.g., erosion control, maintenance of natural areas).

In the Maldive Islands, comprehensive integration of tourism planning into the environmental and development planning for each island has yielded strong control for each resort. Resorts are developed according to ecologically based site requirements that affect density of development, site plan, and impacts on shore and reef areas. The level of control in any island being developed should be comparable to urban zoning and site review.

A sustainable development strategy for Bali was completed in 1992. The strategy identified the key development constraints and opportunities for the principal economic sectors and recommended a division of the island through a form of large-scale zoning. The zoning scheme attempted to respect a very broad range of needs of each sector (forestry, tourism, agriculture, wildlife), as well as the sensitivities of the Bali culture (Gadja Mada University and University of Waterloo, 1992).

Such strategies can be difficult to put in place, particularly in the face of rapid development pressures. However, they serve to reduce negative impacts of individual developments. The advantage of the holistic approach taken in these strategies is that any regulations, subsidies, site controls, and other regulatory or incentive instruments can be made to work in concert to achieve mutual long-term goals. Such achievements can be made even where several different government authorities are involved (e.g., transport, forestry, public works, tourism, planning, economic development).

In contrast, the development of such strategies is proving very difficult where direct conflict between sectors is already occurring. For example, on Vancouver Island in British Columbia, Canada, an impasse has been reached in attempts to reconcile the demands of the logging sector to clear-cut hillsides for lumber and pulpwood with the needs of tourism operations and the demands of "environmentalists" for protection (i.e., preservation) of the forests in entire watersheds, despite attempts of the provincial government to set up a mediation process and a long-term development strategy. Bare hillsides clearly reduce the pleasure of tourists who hike the trails, cruise up the fjords, or canoe the streams. On the other hand, the total ban advocated by some "environmental groups" would keep tourists out of some of the most desired destinations on the West Coast. In Clayoquot Sound, the current center of the conflict, open hostility between loggers, environmentalists, and tourism operators has already adversely affected the tourism industry through fewer tourist visits.

The lesson from these examples is that comprehensive planning and management strategies should be put in place wherever possible before direct confrontations occur over use and management of resources. The recent World Tourism Organization (WTO) publication, *An Integrated Approach to Resort Development*, illustrates a number of the advantages of taking an integrated approach to tourism planning, particularly where the resort community is clearly identified as a planning unit. The WTO also identifies some of the advantages of having tourism development zones recognized in larger scale national or state level planning. Such zoning is particularly important for larger developments that may have significant implications for national or regional scale infrastructure or have significant influence on regional economics.

Still, it is critical to recognize that better analysis of the link between tourism and the environment will only make a difference if the institutions and mechanisms are in place to use the resulting knowledge in the decision-making process. Although the science of predicting environmental and cultural impacts is improving rapidly, a key problem is that these predictions have often been ignored or undervalued when the time comes to make the actual development decision. Even if we can predict that an ecological niche will be destroyed, a view impaired, a community violated, or an important habitat damaged, the decision maker still has the problem of weighing this against such values as job creation or capture of foreign exchange. There are no easy means to do this—the decision is ultimately determined by the national or regional priorities as are often expressed in a national plan or regional strategy document. The planning challenge for sustainable tourism is to provide the decision makers with the key information they need in order to avoid unacceptable, inadvertent damage.

What Do Decision Makers Need to Know?

In his or her role as a decision maker, the tourism manager needs some measure of carrying capacity or sensitivity in order to reduce the risk of unknowingly stepping over biological or cultural thresholds, with results that degrade the manager's own business or adversely affect others. Examples of times when tourism activity has degraded an environment to the point where it can no longer support the type or level of tourism that it was designed to support abound (e.g., polluted beaches, eroded trailsides, and degraded cultural heritage). So do examples where the actions of others have affected the ability of the environment to continue to be attractive to tourists (e.g., polluted rivers, formerly forested slopes). We may be less sensitive to the fact that the actions of tourists have also adversely affected things of value to other sectors (e.g., noise effects on wildlife and adjacent communities, sewage pollution of local fisheries).

As an example, let us look at a proposal for a 100-room hotel overlooking an alpine lake. The site borders on a peat bog and a meadow. What is the carrying capacity of the site? Will it take 100 rooms, 1,000 rooms, or more? The carrying capacity of the site depends upon:

1. what is naturally there (the ecosystem that is present);

2. who [or what] is making use of the site;

3. the type of activity proposed for the site;

4. surrounding land [and water] uses;

5. the design of the facility;

6. the values of the users (the lake may be too cold for swimming);

7. the sensitivity of the valued products and services currently obtained from the site to the proposed development;

8. proposed levels of management (e.g., nightly clean-up).

The key for the decision maker is the identification of the important values, and the rational analysis of the trade-offs. If the key values derived from a site are its unspoiled vistas, watching of wildlife, and being alone with nature, very low levels of use will be tolerable if these values are to be maintained. If any development is permitted, consideration will have to be given to scale, sight lines, and use of low-impact design. In contrast, the attractions of Cannes or Acapulco permit very high level of use of their beachfront, and the bustle of the urban setting is considered by most users to be part of the attraction. At one level of use (or type of use), certain values are sacrificed. With greater use, still more of the original values are likely to be compromised. We need to manage with clear knowledge of these trade-offs.

The bottom line for the decision maker is: What do I have to trade off to get what I want? In general, at various population densities there will be different impacts:

- at 1 person/km^2 very little of the natural functioning of the environment is likely to be lost (unless the person is using an off-road vehicle);

- at 10 persons/km^2, being alone and seeing wildlife are likely to be lost;

- at 100 persons/km^2 there will likely be little wildlife, and, unless some management is done, there will be visible pollution of the site and noticeable ecological degradation;

- at 1,000 persons/km^2 urban densities are reached, the experience is no longer a natural one, human-created values are found (even if the specific attraction is a natural one like Niagara Falls or the Cheddar Gorge), intensive management is needed to maintain the site and to remove the waste of humans.

One initiative that may aid planners at national and regional levels to better identify emerging environmental problems and to evaluate the results of their actions is the WTO Environment Committee program to develop international indicators of sustainable tourism. Begun in 1991, this initiative is designed to help provide, on a regular basis, standard data on key elements of sustainability at a national level, as well as to site-specific monitoring of hot spots and critical ecosystems. It is expected that it can act as an early warning system to reveal trends that may require timely planning or management (Manning, 1992; WTO, 1995). The initiative identifies a suite of key indicators of potential risk to the attributes of a site. Special ecosystem-specific indicators are also identified for each kind of site (beaches, mountains, ecotourism destinations). The guidebook, *What Tourism Managers Need to Know* (Manning, Clifford, Dougherty, & Ernst, 1995), has been prepared as a blueprint for the development, implementation, and regular use of indicators as a decision support system for managers of impacted destinations.

The Effects of Environmental Management

The way in which planning and management of a site can avoid the degradation and loss of valued attributes of the environment is best demonstrated by specific examples. At 10 busloads of tourists per day, the Athabasca Falls site in the Rocky Mountains of Jasper National Park, British Columbia, Canada, was showing severe degradation in the form of cliff erosion, trampling of plant species in this small and unique ecological zone, as well as danger to users who ventured too near the cliff edge to get a better view. Rather than close the site, a walkway system was built that provided viewpoints at the best locations in the site. The system was constructed of local wood and designed to take tourists on a scenic route through the site. This design also enhanced access for tourists in wheelchairs and for the growing number of elderly visitors. The system now permits a 10-fold increase in use with minimal impact on the valued natural attributes of the site. In effect, through a design improvement, the carrying capacity of the site has been increased 20-fold.

In a similar design solution, Ramada Hotels has constructed a hotel in Queensland, Australia, on ecological design principles. Built within a sensitive natural system of melaleuca trees, the Ramada Great Barrier Reef Resort used construction methods that respected the natural heritage of the site. All the trees were preserved by a construction method that avoided the tree roots and protected the trees during the construction period. Ramada executives placed a $10,000 Australian cash bond on each tree on the site and builders complied with the bonds to ensure that each tree was left undamaged. In addition, a free-form pool was constructed designed around the root systems of the trees, providing a unique experience for guests to enjoy the grove environment (Hawkes & Williams, 1993).

The largest international carrier, British Airways (BA), has recognized the global pressure to reduce CO_2 emissions, as well as to reduce noise near airports, alleviate congestion, and reduce waste. Efforts have begun to reduce the waste from flights (every kilogram not carried means reduced fuel costs). On the ground, BA has moved to electronic mail, use of recycled paper, waste reduction, and recycling of onic mail capability has reduced their paper use by 4 million pages per month). Through new scheduling procedures, BA has been able to reduce the likelihood of planes having to wait in holding patterns (planes do not have to carry as much contingency fuel as a result, which reduces fuel consumption; there is also less noise pollution and less air congestion from circling planes).

Hotel Ucliva, Waltensburg, Switzerland, is a model of how to run a small hotel following ecological principles. The hotel is constructed of simple, traditional materials and respects the design traditions of the small village where it is situated. Energy conservation is emphasized, using local fuels. Foods are nearly all locally purchased with an emphasis on organically produced foodstuffs. Most waste is recycled. Employees are all locally hired and are part of an environmental team that maintains the Hotel Ucliva Program. The design and management of the program and the small scale of the enterprise have meant that the hotel blends into the community. In fact, part of its attraction is that the hotel delivers an experience that tourists find to emulate village life. The hotel has won a number of European prizes and is nearly always fully booked.

Clovelly, North Devon, England, is a tiny picturesque fishing village on the coast. Recognized as one of the prettiest villages in the nation, it cascades down cliffs to the waterfront. During summer, over 350,000 tourists visit the village of 400 inhabitants—most descending the cobbled main street on foot. In the past, levels of congestion have made the site uncomfortable for locals and tourists alike. Privacy has been an issue, as tourists often peer into windows or wander into homes. Management of the impact has involved full participation of the village. Automobiles have been banned from the village proper, and a car park has been created nearby. One fishing cottage has been opened to the public and visitors are directed there to take the pressure off the residents' homes. A new visitor center has been created near the car park, which explains the unique location of the village and its history, and takes some pressure off the village itself. In addition, entry charges have been established, which may reduce use to some extent, but will also guarantee revenues that can aid in the upkeep and preservation of the village.

The West Coast Trail is a 100-km-long wilderness trail that allows hikers to visit the remote wild coast of Vancouver Island in Pacific Rim National Park, British Columbia, Canada. By 1990, it was clear that the wilderness experience that attracted hikers from all over the world was being compromised. During the summer season several thousand hikers could be found on the trail, overtaxing the very limited camping facilities, destroying sensitive vegetation along the trail, and creating levels of waste that were degrading the natural wilderness experience. Park managers decided to limit the numbers allowed to use the trail to a total of 100 per day. This was estimated to be the maximum capacity if the ecological values were to be maintained. At present, booking of the trail is on a first-come basis, but it may be necessary to establish a different means to allocate places. Methods considered include pricing (which may limit use to the wealthy), a lottery (which may be unfair to locals), or a combination thereof.

Other examples of new approaches to tourism management include:

- integrated conservation planning for tourism in and near protected areas in St. Lucia;

- sensitive siting of tourist lodges in wetland ecosystems in Amazonia;

- codes of practice for tourism operators in several nations, including Canada;

- the development of codes of practice for operators and for tourists in Antarctica (Pacific and Asia Tourism Association).

Each of these examples illustrates how it is possible to move toward a more sustainable tourism industry through improved planning, education, crowd control, design and management of sites, and integration of tourism into the mainstream of regional and community planning. Each helps the tourism industry to achieve its objectives in concert with the maintenance of the natural and cultural environment in which it resides. The key will be to gather more examples and learn what form of this practice is transferable to other nations and to different environmental and ecological conditions.

Ecotourism: The Controversy and the Promise

Ecotourism is a subset of the range of activities possible within the tourism industry. This subset generally involves travel for recreational purposes where:

- sensitive natural and cultural environments are visited;

- the principal activities are observation, learning, nonconsumptive and low-impact sports (e.g., canoeing, hiking);

- there is a desire not to disrupt local culture or ecology and where possible to enrich the local population, rather than have the money spent by tourists drawn away to offshore economies.

At the Second World Adventure Travel and Ecotourism Conference, held in Whistler, Canada, in the fall of 1992, ecotourism was identified by various speakers as "the way of the future," "a new source of destinations and profits," and as "a high risk both ecologically and economically."

Ecotourism has generally been used to describe tourism that is directed at natural areas (and the native cultures that inhabit them). Ecotourism appeals to those who seek to visit areas off the beaten track, and to experience little known cultures and "unspoiled" nature. Remote polar and tropical sites, mountain villages, and fragile ecological niches are commonly featured as the destination for ecotourism experiences.

A wide range of tourism activities have been labeled as ecotourism. In its narrowest use, it includes only the most rugged examples of adventure tourism in remote localities, in very small groups (e.g., by dog team across Greenland, or by kayak down a river in Siberia or Patagonia). The term has also been used much more broadly to include such experiences as ocean liner passage up the Amazon or to

Antarctica, bus tours to New Zealand's Fox Glacier or Jamaica's Blue Mountains, and even to semiurban tours to Niagara Falls or motorcade visits to animal sanctuaries on the outskirts of Nairobi. This range of use makes the term as it is currently used confusing and frequently misleading.

Contrary to some uses, ecotourism is not just "nature-oriented travel." Ten thousand travelers in a small, sensitive site can wreak havoc with the natural and cultural resources of such a site, despoiling the very things that brought them there. To be useful, the concept of ecotourism must cover both the intent of the travelers to take advantage of nature and the control of their impacts upon it.

Ecotourism should not be used as a synonym for sustainable tourism, although ecotourism is an important component of a more sustainable future for the tourism industry. The idea behind sustainable tourism development is that it is possible to have tourism development that does not damage, and in fact may help enhance the health of the environment. The achievement of sustainable tourism will depend upon more knowledgeable and sensitive management of all aspects of the industry, from overall planning, choice of type of development, levels of use, and management of the impacts and by-products of the industry.

Based on work sponsored by the Canadian Environmental Advisory Council, and standards being discussed in international fora, the following is emerging as a definition of the key characteristics of ecotourism:

- contribution to the conservation of the ecosystem while respecting the integrity of host communities (after Scace, Grifone, & Usher, 1992);

- respect for the limits and opportunities afforded by the natural environment and does not impact negatively on them (i.e., respect the sensitivity of the environment to levels and types of use);

- sensitivity to the needs and wishes of host communities;

- contribution to greater understanding of natural environments and other cultures;

- provision of long-term benefits to host nations, regions, and communities.

Ecotourism should be used to refer to small-scale, locally oriented tourism, focusing on small, often indigenous communities, rare ecosystems, and endangered or vulnerable species. In a sense, it is *tourism that focuses on the most sensitive of cultural and natural environments*. As a result, ecotourism needs to be managed even more carefully than other tourism enterprises. Limits on numbers of people who gain access to sensitive environments will be essential, as will careful design and management of facilities and activities to minimize negative impacts. Sensitive operators will be needed who will accept accountability for their own impacts. Intervention by national and regional authorities will also be required to ensure that the levels of use and nature of impact are acceptable. Such assurance will likely only come with the development of standards at national and international levels, and means of enforcement. The dispersed nature of the industry means that development of standards must involve direct participation by the industry, possibly thorough self-policing.

In summary, ecotourism is generally a positive phenomenon: a marketable new series of products that build on a growing environmental consciousness by travelers globally. Given the limits associated with the sensitivity and carrying capacity of the cultural and natural resources on which it is based, ecotourism will remain a small but important part of the market. For the market to survive, the managers of ecotourism experiences will have to become active in safeguarding the natural and cultural resource base on which their prosperity depends. Much of this resource base is managed by others (e.g., foresters, parks managers, mining firms, conservation authorities, and indigenous peoples). Active involvement of the industry and governments in the planning and management of these resources will be needed to guarantee the product continues to exist in a form that the customers desire.

Conclusion

Tourism is at the top of the food chain of human consumption. The industry is sensitive to the actions of all other economic sectors that influence the availability and quality of the product which it sells. The challenge of planning and managing sustainable tourism is an important one to the future of the tourism industry, globally and locally. Meeting the challenge will involve a greater degree of involvement in comprehensive planning and management if the industry is to meet the expectations following the Brundtland Commission and the Rio Earth Summit. The overall objective must be to manage in a way that is visibly responsible for our own impacts, and that demonstrates tourism can be part of the solution to the global concern of sustainable development.

The key to sustainability for the tourism sector is to recognize clearly the limits and capacities of the environment and to understand the relationships between that environment and the human activities that make up tourism. This chapter has shown that the tourism sector actively seeks out the Earth's treasures—the most sensitive natural and cultural environments—as the basis for the experiences it provides. As a result of insensitive development or narrowly focused management, tourism has frequently caused degradation in the resource base upon which it is built. Yet there are clear success stories where the industry has become a positive force for sustainable development, not only for its own properties but for the regions in which it operates. The success stories highlighted in the latter part of this chapter show that through efficient use of energy, through sensitive site planning, through coordinated action with other sectors, and through innovative design solutions, the industry can be a good environmental citizen. In the next century, the prosperity of tourism, both globally and locally, is contingent upon how well we learn from these lessons and continue to build sustainable solutions that benefit the tourism industry and the regions that provide the values it purveys.

Acknowledgments

Based in part on a WTO Seminar on Planning for Sustainable Tourism Development in South Asian Countries (World Tourism Organization, Kurumba, Maldives, April

1993), and presentations to the Arctic Tourism and Ecotourism Symposium (First Northern Forum Conference/Fifth World Wilderness Conference, Tromso, Norway, September 1993).

Chapter 2

Sustainable Tourism and Critical Environments

Ralf Buckley

The Evolution of Tourism

Tourism and travel is the world's largest industry sector. It is ancient in origin, but only recently has its growth been rapid and its size significant in economic terms. Historically, we could perhaps identify three phases: intrepid traveler, mass tourist, and customized package tourist.

In previous centuries, travel was often risky, often expensive, and always time consuming. You did not have to be rich, but you certainly had to be self-reliant, bold to a degree, and prepared to take considerable rough with the smooth. For great travelers such as Marco Polo or Ibn Battuta in the 13th century, for example, travel was a lifetime work.

With the advent of mass air travel, within the budget of most people in developed nations, the time it took to visit foreign lands, and the risks associated with getting there and back, fell dramatically. Thus, with a guaranteed supply of customers, the accommodation, local tour, and tourist attraction segments of the industry grew accordingly, leading to so-called mass tourism. All this, of course, is well known.

But how would today's tourism be described? There are still large and indeed ever larger numbers of people traveling within and outside their own countries. Many of those tourists still go to the same places as before and stay in equally large resorts and hotels. The difference is that there is more flexibility in packaging— there are more options. It is the difference between the first Model-T Ford, Jennings Kit-Home, or Frigidaire and the cars, houses, and whitegoods of today: they are still designed for mass manufacture, but with so many permutations on detail that they can be customized to suit different client requests.

Of course, specialized tours catering to wildlife watchers, gourmet eaters, craft buyers, or golf players fall within this category. But so too do trips where a group of Japanese travel to Australia's Gold Coast and can then choose between four-wheel-drive nature tours, river rafting, casinos, bungy jumping, motorbike tours, river cruises, and so on. The intrepid free and independent travelers (FITs) are still wandering the world on their own seeking new and different life-enhancing experiences; but less adventurous souls now have access to packaged intrepidity and life enhancement with several stars of comfort. And why not?

Environmental Management in Tourism

However we describe it historically, the fact remains that tourism and travel is a huge industry. As it has grown, so too has the importance of environmental management in that industry. Firstly, because the industry itself relies on the environment as part of its product, so that damage to the environment reduces revenue. Though often quoted, however, this argument is not entirely persuasive. It holds good, certainly, at an industry level—but less so for the individual operator, whose commercial time frame may be quite short. Immediate profits, even at the expense of the environment, can always be reinvested in other forms of tourism development, or indeed in another industry sector altogether. There is little indication that individual tourism developers attempt to minimize their environmental impacts solely to preserve a future revenue base. More commonly, it is to attract a particular clientele or simply to comply with legislative requirements.

More significant, therefore, is a general worldwide trend indicating increased public awareness of environmental issues, leading to market, media, and legal pressures for improved environmental management in all sectors, tourism included. In particular, these pressures make it increasingly difficult for tourism developers to gain approval for new greenfields tourism projects unless they can demonstrate an adequate level of environmental management or responsibility. It is this that is leading to the so-called greening of mass tourism.

Tourism in Conservation

Ecologists, environmental scientists, and conservationists concerned about global environmental deterioration have been prescribing for several decades, tools with which to reduce or combat its onset. Such tools include laws, lobbying, advertising, economic instruments, education programs, trade policies, and so on. One such tool is to persuade people to see and value unspoiled natural environments for themselves so that they themselves become increasingly concerned to protect those environments. This, of course, is one kind of tourism. So tourism has gradually been perceived as a potential tool in global conservation. Of course, this approach is unlikely to yield significant dividends from those traveling to purely urban destinations, such as gamblers or shoppers. But a surprisingly large proportion of travel does in fact include at least some nature- or culture-based component. In countries such as Australia, New Zealand, and many Southeast Asian nations this component is particularly high. And this proportion is increasing as cities become increasingly similar worldwide.

Origins and Types of Ecotourism

Over the past few decades, a number of people concerned about conservation issues have established international nature tour businesses, often targeted specifically at nonprofit associations and at influential retired people who, if they choose, have money, time, and power to affect environmental policy in their own countries. The idea is to show these people the problem and let them decide for themselves what to do about it. Gray power, it's been called.

Tour operators like these, who were using tourism as a conservation tool through environmental education and policy lobbying, came to be called ecotour operators. At the same time, however, free and independent travelers who wanted to enjoy and learn about foreign places with minimal environmental impacts were also called ecotourists, though their journeys were personal and individual rather than commercial.

Most recently, as tours run for environmental education purposes became increasingly popular, a third group has arisen as other commercial operators started to copy their itineraries and marketing strategies, but without the conservation motive. These operators also called their tours ecotours—and still do—provoking outrage from the first two groups, who see the third as using tourism to exploit nature for profit rather than using tourism to protect and preserve nature. A recent analysis of tour marketing brochures in southeastern Queensland, for example (Buckley & Araujo, 1997) found that a high proportion of self-described "ecotour" operators are in the third group. It is not surprising, therefore, that there have been such controversies over the definition of ecotourism, and the need for accreditation of ecotour operators. One way of appreciating the issues is summarized in Figure 2.1.

Definitions of Ecotourism

By the strictest definitions, ecotourism is tourism with a nature-based product, sustainable management, an education component, and some contribution to conservation (Buckley, 1994a). This definition was adopted, in paraphrased form, by Australia's *National Ecotourism Strategy* (Australia, Commonwealth Department of Tourism, 1991) and by the more recent *Queensland Ecotourism Plan* (Queensland, Department of Tourism, Small Business and Industry, 1997). It doesn't really matter, as long as it's clear what aspects are being referred to in any particular debate.

Links Between Tourism and Environment

Though it is interesting and perhaps illuminating to examine how tourism and environment have met historically, it is perhaps more important to appreciate how they are linked now. The major links are shown in Figure 2.2.

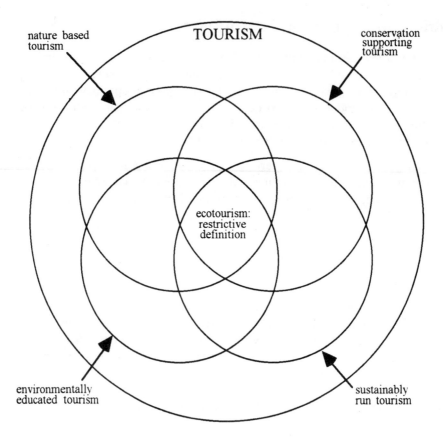

Figure 2.1. Aspects and definitions of ecotourism (from Buckley, 1994a).

Sustainable Tourism

These links provide the basis for an analysis of sustainable tourism—tourism with good environmental management.

Sustainable tourism is a less controversial term than ecotourism, because it does not involve issues such as whether an educational component or a contribution to conservation is essential. It is still hard to define in practice, however, because it is hard to define "sustainable." Indeed, it may be more useful to define what types of activity are unsustainable (Buckley, 1991a).

In any definition of sustainability the question of scale is vital—both potential scales and time scales. An individual tourist resort, for example, may produce substantial environmental impacts locally during its operating life. Regionally, however, these impacts may be negligible. But if several similar resorts operate simultaneously in the same region, the cumulative impacts may again be substantial (Buckley, 1994b). If other regions in the country concerned have little tourism development, then

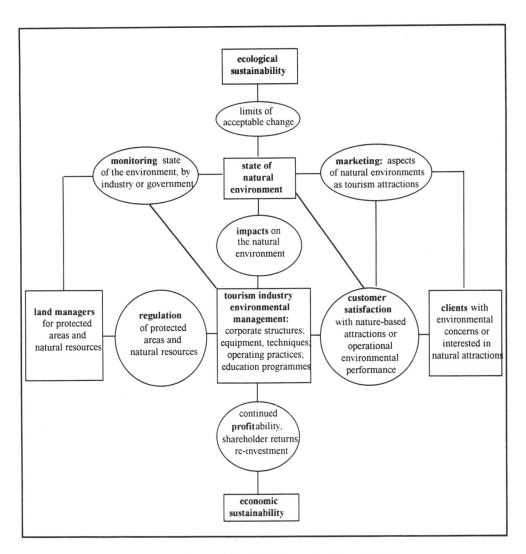

Figure 2.2. Sustainable tourism: major links (from Buckley, 1996).

overall impacts at the national scale may be small (Buckley, 1994c). But if the country as a whole depends heavily on tourism, the national impacts may be significant on a global scale. And should the impacts of tourism be considered separately from those of other industry sectors? Is it relevant that tourism is confined to one part of a country, for example, if other parts experience equal or greater impacts from agriculture, fisheries, forestry, mining, or manufacturing?

Clearly, we have several different ways to approach these issues of sustainability in tourism. For the tourism sector as a whole we need all the tools of sustainable development: new technologies, changed social behavior, new environmental laws,

Table 2.1. Major Subsectors and Environmental Management Issues

Industry Subsector	Cross-Issue Planning & Policy	Resource Conservation		
		Energy	Water	Materials
Airlines	deregulation, routes, passenger numbers	energy efficiency		reusables, recyclables, disposables
Construction of integrated resorts & non-urban hotels	land use planning, environmental impact assessment, and monitoring	integrated design, off-grid power sources	integrated water and wastewater management	use of local and/or low-impact materials
Hotels & urban accommodation	links and clashes between environmental and health constraints and client expectations	insulation, demand management	water conservation, demand management	reusables, recyclables, disposables
Operating resorts and attractions	environmental monitoring and management	demand management, energy audits	irrigation, demand management	reusables, recyclables, disposables
Environmental engineering & management	design, EIA, monitoring	energy audit, design	wastewater management and reclamation	comparing resource consumption
Motorized tours, safaris and local transport	access to conservation reserves, environmental education programs	fuel consumption per capita		reusables, recyclables, disposables
Non-motorized recreation	access to conservation reserves, hardening, environmental education	backpacker fuel choices		
Cruise boats, private motorboats	access, environmental education			reusables, recyclables, disposables
Travel agents	mediation of market demands; information and education			

Impacts on Physical Environment

| Land | Water | | | Air and Noise | Impacts on Biological Environments | | |
	Sewage	Runoff	Cleaning		Disturbance	Clearance and Damage	Weeds, Pathogens
		hardstand	bunding cleaning areas	greenhouse gases, engine design, hushkits			quarantin-able cabin wastes
landfill for remote sites, groundwater incineration	reusing treated effluent; discharge to water bodies	golf course runoff	integrated wastewater manage-ment	construction noise		habitat clearance and edge effects	weed seed & micro-organisms in soil and landscaping
			choice of cleaning products				
solid waste disposal	monitoring impacts of discharge	pesticides, fertilizers, etc.	choice of cleaning products				
solid waste disposal	integrated sewage systems	water monitoring, manage-ment	comparing cleaning products	air & noise monitoring, management			
solid waste disposal	human waste disposal		choice of cleaning products		fauna disturbance	damage by off-road vehicles	dispersal of microorgan-isms and weed seed by vehicles
solid waste disposal	human waste disposal	campsite runoff, swimming	disposal of spent cleaning materials		fauna in conservation reserves, etc.	trampling in conservation reserves, etc.	weed and pathogen dispersal
solid waste disposal	human waste disposal	engine oil	disposal of spent cleaning materials		marine and freshwater fauna	marine and freshwater fauna	weeds at campsites, landing areas

corporate environmental management tools, better planning and development control procedures, and so on. The technological requirements, for example, are summarized in Table 2.1 (Buckley, 1996).

From a legal perspective, one critical issue is the assessment of cumulative environmental impacts (Buckley, 1994b). From the corporate view, the critical tools are environmental management systems and audits (Buckley, 1995a; Buckley & Warnken, 1996) as well as new technologies. Examples include Canadian Pacific Hotels' *Green Partnership* (Canadian Pacific Hotels [CPH], 1993) and the International Hotels Environment Initiative's *Environmental Management for Hotels* (International Hotels Environment Initiative [IHEI], 1993).

Issues in Ecotourism

For ecotourism as a subset of sustainable tourism, issues are summarized in Table 2.2. One good industry example is the recent development of ecolodges as a specialist category of tourist accommodation (e.g., Buckley, 1995b).

Tourism in Fragile Environments

For ecotourism in conservation reserves and fragile environments, which is where most of it occurs, the impacts that need study are summarized in Tables 2.3 and 2.4 (Buckley, 1991c, 1991d). The rapid growth of nature-based tourism has greatly increased the demand for commercial and private recreational use of national

Table 2.2. Characteristics, Issues, and Information Needs in Ecotourism

	Markets	Products
Characteristics	green claims in advertising; environmental concerns of clients	components of natural environment as attraction to destination
Issues	market sizes, price elasticities, substantiation of advertising claims	impacts of tourism on conservation values
Information Needs	who wants to know what, who claims what, and who buys it?	what exact impacts do known numbers of visitors carrying out specified activities have in different ecosystems?

parks, conservation reserves, and other fragile environments. The environmental impacts of tourism, particularly the diffuse impacts in conservation reserves, are little studied in relation to other major industry sectors. Quantitative measurements of the environmental impacts of tourism in conservation reserves and fragile environments are therefore critical, both for nature tour and ecolodge operators and for land management agencies. We need to measure precisely what impacts are caused by known numbers of people, engaging in known activities, in known ecosystems, with known equipment, for known time periods, at known times of the year (Buckley, 1991c, 1991d, 1994a, 1996).

Types of impact include: soil erosion and compaction; vegetation trampling, cutting, and burning; introduction of weeds and feral animals; disturbance to wildlife from noise, pets, and habitat damage; litter; fire; and pollution of ground and surface waters from sewage and human waste, soap, and cleaning residues; pesticide and insect-repellent residues, etc.

There are over 150 recent studies worldwide that have quantified both the tourism pressure and the environmental response. Of these studies, 31 describe impacts on soil, 63 on plants, 32 on birds, 9 on other animals, 4 on freshwater ecosystems, and 21 on marine ecosystems. Fourteen are in cold or alpine environments, 111 in temperate zones, 16 tropical and subtropical, 13 desert, and 6 in anthropogenic habitats. For each of these, data are available on the ecosystem, geographic location, and species or community studied; the time span, mechanisms, frequency and intensity, and other relevant features of the tourism disturbance, experimental or

(From Buckley, 1994a)

Management	Money	People
minimizing operational impacts on environment	direct or indirect financial support for conservation	attitudes and behavior of staff and clients; training and interpretation programs
planning and design, resource and energy conservation and recycling	tax policies, fees and levies, park funding, purchasing practices, etc.	client expectations, quality assurance in staff training, types of program
how well can impacts be predicted, monitored, mitigated, and managed, and at what cost?	how much does tourism contribute to conservation at individual, corporate, national, and global scales?	how well do different training techniques and programs work?

Table 2.3. Environmental Impacts of Transport and Travel (From Buckley, 1991d)

Means of Transport or Travel	Vegetation Clearance or Damage	Soil Erosion of Compaction	Wildlife Disturbance, Shooting, or Habitat Destruction
Light planes, helicopters	airstrips only	airstrips only	depends on speed, altitude, frequency of flights
Bus or car on road	roads and verges cleared	compaction and erosion on unsealed roads	noise depends on traffic density; roads can act as barriers; road kills
Car or four-wheel drive on tracks	tracks cleared; tend to be widened and new tracks cut	dust, gully erosion, and compaction widespread	road kills, noise, shooting
Off-road vehicles off track	severe and extensive vegetation damage	erosion widespread, depends on terrain and soil type	widespread noise disturbance; ORVs used for shooting
Mountain bikes	less severe than ORVs	localized in heavily used areas	disturbance in heavily used areas
Horses	trampling on horse trails	localized, trails and holding paddocks	minimal, unless riders rowdy or shooters
Hiking	trampling on heavily used trails	localized on heavily used areas	generally minimal
Power boats	campsites, shoreline and aquatic vegetation	not applicable	noise, fishing, and shooting
Unpowered watercraft	generally none	not applicable	fishing only

Solid Wastes	Water Pollution	Air Pollution	Noise	Increased Fire Risk	Weed and Pathogens
empty fuel drums at remote strips			loud, but intermittent	little or none	airstrips only
litter	petroleum residues in runoff from roads	exhaust fumes	line source, volume depends on traffic density	sparks, cigarette butts	along road verges
litter	turbid runoff	exhaust fumes	as above	sparks, cigarette butts	along track verges
litter, human wastes	campsites, etc.: bacteria, soap	exhaust fumes	major impact, because ORVs can enter otherwise quiet areas	sparks, butts, campfires	spread on tires
litter, human wastes	campsites, etc.: bacteria, soap	none	voices only	butts, campfires	spread on tires
horse manure	nutrients, bacteria, dowstream of holding paddocks	none unless very crowded	voices only	butts, campfires	spread in fodder if carried
human wastes	campsites, etc.: bacteria, soap	none	voices only	butts, campfires	minimal, on boots and socks
garbage at campsites, jetsam	fuel residues, nutrients, bacteria, antifouling paints	exhaust fumes	engine noise	campsites only	campsites only
garbage and jetsam	bacteria, soap	none	voices only	campsites only	campsites only

Table 2.4. Environmental Impacts of Accommodation and Shelter (From Buckley, 1991d)

Type of Accommodation or Shelter	Vegetation Clearance or Damage	Soil Erosion and/or Compaction	Wildlife Disturbance or Habitat Destruction
Resorts, hotels: construction	site clearance	short term, during construction	habitat cleared, noise
Continuing	tracks, etc.	unsealed tracks, etc.	shyer species leave area
Fixed car or caravan camps	site clearance initially and continuing, tracks, etc.	if ungrassed and increasing with use	habitat clearance, shyer species leave area
Overnight car/4WD camps	increasing with use	increasing with use	depends on frequency of use
Horse/hiker huts	local site clearance, trampling	localized, depends on soil type, etc.	minor, localized
Boat-access shore sites	increasing with use	bank erosion	minor, localized
Often-used bush camps	localized, new tent sites	localized, depends on soil type, etc.	minor, localized
Single-use camps and bivouacs	minimal or none	generally none	temporary or none

observed, and environmental parameters measured; the degree of change in these parameters, or their value before and after the disturbances, relative to control sites where quoted; and the time when measurements were made relative to the time of disturbance. In some cases, corresponding information is available for recovery after tourism-related disturbances.

Firewood Collection and Campfires	Solid Wastes	Water Pollution	Noise	Visual
	construction rubbish, builder's rubble	sediments	construction plant	construction site and plant
collected elsewhere, if used	garbage, treated sewage	sullage, increased nutrients	machinery and motors	conspicuous buildings and infrastructure, large vehicles
large area often denuded	garbage, litter, toilets	sullage, increased nutrients, bacterial	generators, car engines, chainsaws, radios, voices	vehicles, caravans, large tents, equipment, campfires
large campfires common	litter, human wastes	bacterial, soap	car engines, chainsaws, radios, voices	cars, large tents, campfires
large area often affected, regular large campfires	litter, horse dung, human wastes	bacterial	saws, voices	huts, cleared paddocks, campfires
large area often affected, regular large campfires	litter, fish guts, human wastes	petroleum residues	outboard motors, voices	boats, large tents, fires, clearance
depends on vegetation type: large area may be affected	some paper, human wastes	bacterial, soap	voices	small tents, fires
minimal or none	generally none	generally none	minimal or none	minimal and temporary

Conclusions

Tourism relies heavily on natural environments, and good environmental management is vital to the economic as well as the ecological sustainability of the tourism industry. Tourism is an enormous industry with great potential either to harm or protect the environment; and these effects cross national borders as international tourism continues to grow. In particular, ecotourism is a rapidly growing market sector that may prove valuable in conservation. But there is a shortage of data on the ecological impacts of tourism and the economic effects of ecotourism.

Acknowledgments

Various parts of this chapter have been presented at conferences over the past 2 years and have benefited from comments received.

Chapter 3

Tourism–Environment Interaction: The Greening of Australian Beach Resorts

John J. Pigram and Peiyi Ding

Introduction

Tourism, today, is a mass phenomenon, the largest movement of peoples in human history. Its continuous annual growth, its present magnitude, and its future prospects are impressive and raise several important social, cultural, economic, political, and ecological questions.

Tourism is, to a large degree, a resource-based activity, with a capacity to initiate far-reaching changes to the physical and human environment. Many forms of tourism are seen as contributing to environmental degradation, and tending to be self-destructive. Erosion of the resource base, impairment of the built environment, and disruption of the social fabric of host communities are common indicators of the undesirable impacts that can ensue from the predatory effects of a mass influx of tourists. However, the consequences of tourism development are not always predictable or inherently destructive. Tourism certainly can contribute to environmental degradation; it also has the potential to bring about significant enhancement of the environment.

Moreover, there is growing evidence that tourism can operate in harmony with the environment, and tourism developers and operators are making efforts to achieve environmentally compatible and ecologically sustainable forms of tourism. On the international tourism scene, a number of five-star hotel corporations and major airlines are implementing environmental auditing programs in areas such as waste management, energy consumption, transport noise, purchasing policy, and staff training.

These moves reflect a global trend towards the greening of tourism and a realization that future prosperity relies heavily on the maintenance of the environmental qualities on which the tourism industry depends. Moreover, in a more environmentally aware world, green tourism not only offers new experiences and opportunities, but makes economic good sense in terms of reduced waste and lower operating costs.

In Australia, tourism developers and operators are demonstrating increased understanding of environmental concerns, and an Environmental Code of Practice has been drawn up in consultation with conservation groups, industry bodies, and planning authorities. The Code is being applied at a number of beach resorts along the east coast of Australia, several of which have been designed and constructed on ecologically sensitive principles and operate on environmentally responsible lines. Some of the best examples of the "greening" of Australian tourism are to be found in the Great Barrier Reef Region of North Queensland, where international resorts are being developed in keeping with environmental constraints, and with attention to siting, design, materials, sources of supplies, and disposal of wastes.

In a more environmentally conscious world, the tourism industry faces increasingly strident conditions on development, reflecting a concern for sustainability and the long-term viability of the resources on which tourism depends. The challenge for the industry is to justify its claims on those resources with a commitment to their sustainable management.

Studies carried out by the Organisation for Economic Cooperation and Development (1993a) report that coastal zones in member countries are under severe and increasing threat from numerous pressures and conflicts. Concerted action is seen as urgent if sustainable economic and ecological outcomes are to be achieved (Chung & Hildebrand, 1994). These concerns arise because of the impacts being imposed on susceptible natural systems by a variety of human activities and demands on the resource base. Prominent among these are tourism activities and resort developments at or close to the shoreline.

The Coastal Zone

The term "coastal zone" encompasses the marine environment, the coast itself, and a loosely defined hinterland under maritime influences. The biophysical environment of coastal areas is characterized by a variety of natural features, and flora and fauna, representing both terrestrial and marine ecosystems. Complex interactions between species and within the ambient environment are typical of coastal ecosystems, many of which are regarded as sensitive and fragile. Moreover, the coastal zone is a dynamic environment subject to incremental change through natural processes, frequently accelerated by human actions.

Too often in the past, coastal areas have been viewed as having unlimited capacity to support human activities. Vegetation has been cleared, wetlands drained, estuaries reclaimed and developed, fish and wildlife exploited, and coastal waterways and oceans used for disposal of wastes. Activities both offshore and inland have had marked effects on the coastal zone, which can truly be regarded as part of the globe's "critical environment."

Resources of the Coastal Zone

The shorelines of the world's landmasses have long held significance for human populations, and the interface between land and sea provides scope for a wide range of human activities, both marine and land based. The diverse resources of coastal zones, especially when combined with an agreeable climate and a reliable water supply, provide an attractive setting for concentrations of development and settlement.

Coastal resources are valued for a number of purposes—ecological, economic, cultural, and aesthetic—and the coastal zone has become the focus for a range of economic and social pursuits. Attributes of the coastal zone can support a number of resource functions including, fisheries, mineral extraction, transport, agriculture and forestry, wildlife habitat, urban development, and tourism.

Use of the resource potential of the coastal zone reflects the many complex natural and human interactions to be found in an environment shaped by constantly changing natural and cultural forces and circumstances. Some of these processes are strictly biophysical. Others are the result of human action or are subject to human intervention, and therefore, to a degree, they are open to manipulation and management. However, the special nature of the coastal environment raises fundamental questions of balance between natural and human forces, compatibility of particular resource functions, and appropriate planning and management techniques.

Tourism development imposes its own set of demands on the coastal environment in that, typically, it involves multiple use of water and land for a variety of activities, often conflicting over and competing for resources and space.

Space, of course, is a critical resource for tourism in the coastal zone, and competition for space occurs between tourism development and other interests seeking sites for shipping terminals, mooring areas and marinas, transport routeways and corridors, and recreation and conservation reserves. Offshore developments, too, can be a source of friction. Added to these are the demands of developers subdividing land for home sites for residential and transient populations.

Scarcity of space in the coastal zone stimulates predictable responses. High-rise development reflects claims on vertical space, whereas new forms of settlement can also emerge horizontally (e.g., reclamation of back-barrier areas for residential canal development), and even expansion seawards in some cases.

Impacts of Tourism on the Coastal Environment

Tourism facilities often seek beachfront locations and this can have repercussions on other resources and resource users. Intrusion of incompatible forms of resource use into established functional zones can occur, along with erosion of amenities (e.g., open space, light, and scenic views). Traffic congestion, noise pollution, pressure on services, and exposure to hazards are other risks. Ecological impacts can include loss of wildlife habitat and degradation of beaches and waterways.

Occupation of frontal dune systems exposes buildings and other structures, including roads, to the natural forces and processes operating in the coastal zone. This leads, in turn, to attempts at various types of compensatory action (e.g., land-fill and the building of protective structures such as groynes and seawalls). These then contribute to further aberrations in beach processes. The result can be recurrent exposure to hazardous events (e.g., storm surge) and the need for ongoing rehabilitation programs, which are not fully effective and contribute to visual scarring and degradation of the beachfront. Inland from the beach, back-barrier and wetland areas may experience similar impacts, with reclamation of estuarine margins for tourism development leading to exposure to floods, distortion of drainage patterns, subsidence, and general disturbance of natural systems.

As a major agent of environmental change in the coastal zone, tourism calls for special care and management. In many cases, undesirable impacts from tourism development stem from the failure to recognize that some attributes of the coastal environment are more susceptible to damage than others. Whereas some coastal ecosystems have useful properties of resistance or resilience, others are vulnerable to disturbance. Dune and wetland areas are especially unstable and can tolerate only a minimum of interference. Even low levels of use can promote dune blow-outs, erosion, and destruction of vegetative cover. Remedial measures are slow and frustrating, and permanent occupation of such areas can be a risk both to tourists and the environment.

Countries with significant tourism activity along their coasts report seasonal pressures that, in some cases, outstrip the capability of the resource base and supporting infrastructure, resulting in serious local or regional environmental impacts (Chung & Hildebrand, 1994). The management of tourism is of primary concern in the critical environment of the coastal zone.

Tourism and the Coastal Zone

Coastal areas clearly have great appeal for tourism, and much of this appeal can be traced to the presence of water in the marine environment. Water figures prominently in at least three aspects of tourism development:

1. The quantity and quality of available water can be major constraints in location, siting, design, and operation of tourism facilities.

2. The presence of water serves as an additional dimension to a tourism facility, enhancing the scenic quality and appeal of the setting, and contributing to the attraction and intrinsic satisfaction derived from the tourism experience. An environment rich in water forms an aesthetically pleasing setting for tourism.

3. Water is essential for the operation of the tourism industry—for drinking purposes, sanitation, and waste disposal, for cooling purposes, for irrigation, landscaping, and for the functioning of particular forms of water-related activities (e.g., swimming and boating) (Pigram, 1995, p. 212).

Mercer (1972) explains the coastal location of many tourist resorts in terms of the attraction of edges or junctions in the landscape, the coastline representing the interface between land and sea. The popularity of the coast for resort development reflects the presence of water, the inherent beauty of coastal settings, and the many opportunities for tourism experiences offered by a coastal location.

Certainly, in Australia, the attraction of the coastal zone is clearly evident, both for settlement and for tourism. Well over 90% of the Australian population lives within a half-day's drive off the coast, and vacations and tourism experiences are most frequently sited along the coastal fringe (Figure 3.1).

In the state of New South Wales, tourism visitation to coastal regions accounts for over 50% of all domestic tourism outside the capital city, Sydney (Coastal Committee of New South Wales, 1994). Figures from Queensland indicate that popular marine vacation destinations at the Gold Coast, Sunshine Coast, and Cairns attract some 3 million visitors annually (Queensland Tourism and Travel Corporation, 1993).

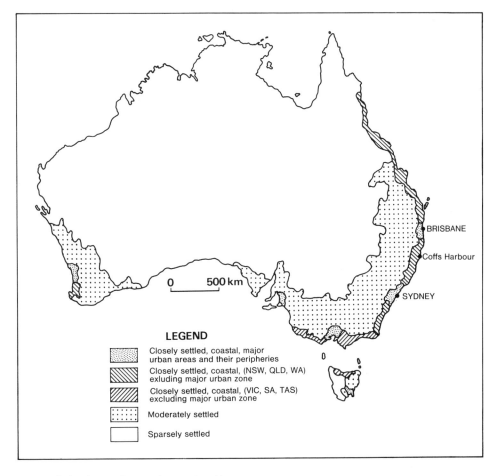

Figure 3.1. Australia settlement pattern.

The popularity of the coast for tourism activities has been matched by the growth in the development of major destination resorts along the shoreline and nearby reefs and islands. This can be seen along the coast of Queensland where the subtropical climate and proximity to the Great Barrier Reef are important attractions (Figure 3.2).

Opportunities exist for further resort development on the Australian coast. However, growing concern for the environmental implications for the coastal environment has led to closer scrutiny of resort proposals, and the imposition of rigorous requirements for environmental management. In Australia, resort developers and

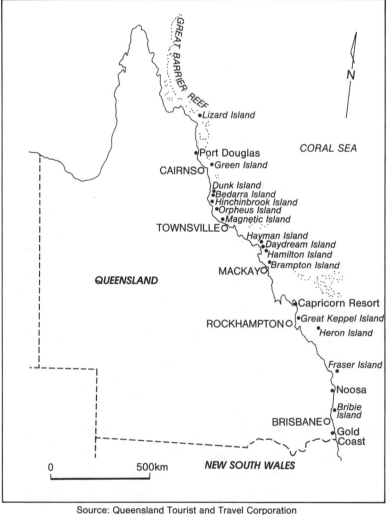

Source: Queensland Tourist and Travel Corporation

Figure 3.2. Queensland resorts and resort islands (source: Queensland Tourist and Travel Corporation).

operators are demonstrating increased appreciation of this concern and implementing steps to achieve more environmentally compatible and ecologically sustainable forms of tourism. Subsequently, reference is made in this chapter to beach resorts along the east coast of Australia that reflect this "greening" trend.

Beach Resorts in the Coastal Zone

The term "resort" is used in many contexts and is subject to conflicting definitions. The early coastal resorts of Britain, Europe, and North America were really special-purpose forms of urban development, and their morphological characteristics have emerged in other parts of the world, including Australia (Pigram, 1977).

More recently, resorts have come to mean purpose-built facilities, or groups of facilities, providing accommodation, shopping outlets, restaurants, recreation, and entertainment, on the one relatively self-contained site. These "destination" resorts are meant to cater for people seeking relaxation and enjoyment for more than just an overnight or weekend stay. However, there is little consistency, in Australia or elsewhere, in the way that resorts are defined (King & Whitelaw, 1992).

According to Helber (1985):

> A true resort must be, in a sense, an integrated community—one that not only includes all the facilities and activities that cater for the visitors . . . but also for those people who will work as employees within the resort. (p. 37)

Helber sees a resort as a self-contained community, almost a "new town," though in a nonurban, natural setting, and with all necessary support services and infrastructure. If these attributes are accepted, it is easy to see why the coastal zone is so frequently chosen as the site for integrated, destination resorts of this type. The challenge in resort development is to preserve the site's natural environment and special features, and to develop additional components to enhance the inherent attractions. Coastal resorts face particular difficulties in meeting this challenge.

Some observers remain convinced that, "in the long run, tourism, like any other industry, contributes to environmental destruction" (Cohen, 1978, p. 220). In susceptible environments such as the coastal zone, the potential of resort development for degradation of marine ecosystems has been recognized. In the Mediterranean region, Stachowitsch (1992) sees the most serious threat as coming from increased organic material and nutrients from tourism development along coastlines. Other negative effects include:

- destruction of coastal ecosystems to provide tourism infrastructure;

- damage to coral reefs and seagrass beds from anchoring of pleasure boats;

- disturbance of wildlife habitats and refuges;

- littering of beaches;

- depletion of fish stocks by recreational anglers;

- collection of marine organisms as souvenirs. (Stachowitsch, 1992, p. 30)

Stachowitsch makes the point that not only does tourism contribute to these problems, it is also among the first industries to suffer from ecosystem deterioration. In some situations the problems stem from the pressure of numbers beyond a critical threshold or saturation point. In others it is not so much numbers, as the characteristics of visitors and their activities that lead to deleterious consequences for the destination area.

Nonetheless, the consequences of tourism development are not always predictable or inherently destructive. Tourism certainly can contribute to environmental degradation, but it also has the potential to bring about significant enhancement of the environment.

Several modes of expression of tourism–environment interaction are possible (Pigram, 1989), and Cohen (1978) concedes that at least four major factors can affect the rate of decline (if any) in environmental quality. The factors identified are:

- intensity of tourism;
- resilience of ecosystems;
- time perspective of the developer;
- transformational character of the development.

These factors take on added importance with resort development in the coastal zone. Beach resorts typically represent relatively intensive development on restricted sites, with the probability of sensitive and vulnerable natural features being exposed to disturbance. Economic imperatives and the need to generate a rapid monetary return may also receive priority, despite recognition of the benefits of environmental conservation in the longer term. Resort development, too, is essentially "transformational" in character, and special care is necessary to create a resort in harmony with its environmental setting.

Despite the risk of negative outcomes, there is growing evidence that modification of the coastal environment for resort development need not destroy natural and cultural values and, in fact, can contribute to an aesthetically pleasing landscape. However, some would argue that environmental benefits are only in the short term. An S-curve model of resort evolution is presented by Meyer-Arendt (1990) to describe the development of coastal resorts. According to the model, stages in resort evolution culminate in the "maturation" level, after which a coastal destination resort loses its attractiveness. Despite initial inordinate attention to aesthetics, it is postulated that, in time, environmental degradation becomes dominant and economic returns decline.

As with similar models of resort development (Butler, 1980), there is nothing inevitable about the sequence of evolution, or the ultimate stage reached. Such models work best in an unregulated economy where resort development proceeds spontaneously. In most countries of the industrialized world, government intervention is the norm and an array of regulatory procedures must be satisfied before

development can take place. Public agencies can draw upon a range of
encourage compliance with environmental constraints in resort development.
Prominent among these is environmental impact assessment.

Whereas assessment of likely environmental impacts and prediction of possible
long-term environmental degradation are necessary and useful procedures prior to
approval of new tourism developments, postdevelopment assessment, or auditing,
also are now seen as an important aspect of the ongoing monitoring of environmental performance. Environmental auditing offers an effective management tool
for tourism to reinforce initial impact assessment and help offset progressive
environmental decline.

Environmental Audits

The concept of environmental audits is still relatively new and there are many
interpretations of exactly what is meant by the term (Buckley, 1991a). In its
common form, environmental auditing is a process whereby the operations of an
organization are monitored to determine whether they are in compliance with
regulatory requirements and environmental policies and standards. The essential
purpose of environmental auditing programs is to ensure compliance with environmental management planning; that commitments made are implemented; that
environmental standards are met; and that relevant procedures are in place and are
being followed (Australian Tourism Industry Association, 1990). In this sense,
environmental auditing is, or should be, a necessary part of tourism management.

In the context of sustainable tourism the principal objectives of environmental
auditing are to identify and document the environmental compliance status of
tourist developments and operations, and to provide an effective means of monitoring the sustainable performance of the tourism industry. Environmental audits
provide a useful picture of the environmental status of a tourism facility and a
ready means of self-regulation of its environmental performance.

A well-conducted environmental auditing program could be expected to:

- increase the overall level of environmental awareness in the tourism industry;
- assist tourism management to improve environmental standards through
  "benchmarking" against proven performance;
- identify opportunities to reinforce positive environmental interactions;
- accelerate the achievement of Best Practice Environmental Management in the
  industry, endorsed by tourist operators and regulatory agencies, and supported
  by the community.

Environmental Audits in the Tourism Industry

On the international tourism scene, a number of five-star hotel corporations and
major airlines are implementing environmental auditing programs in areas such as
waste management, energy consumption, transport noise, purchasing policy, and

staff training. These companies and groups have produced their own environmental management manuals. Canadian Pacific Hotels and Resorts, for example, has undertaken the development of an environmental program called *The Green Partnership Guide* for all of its hotels in Canada (Troyer, 1992). The main objective of the program is to institute the highest possible standards of environmental responsibility throughout the hotel chain in order to identify environmental improvements that, at the same time, could result in lower operating costs. The corporation also undertook an internal environmental auditing program, the aim of which was to identify those areas of hotel operations that could be changed to induce more environmentally benign practices and products, and to determine the level of support for environmental initiatives among its employees (Checkley, 1992).

Another example of self-monitoring is British Airways' internal environmental auditing program in which the main aims are to make the airline "a good neighbour," concerned for the community and the environment (British Airways, 1992). The airline places the emphasis of its monitoring program on the following main areas: noise, emissions and fuel efficiency, wastewater, energy, materials, and congestion. It also recognizes the importance of sponsorship, recycling, staff training, and environmental responsibility. Through these activities, the airline has increased its awareness of the importance of identifying and ensuring compliance with environmental regulations affecting the environment.

In Australia, the Inter-Continental Hotel in Sydney adopted the international corporation's *Environmental Reference Manual* as its internal environmental auditing guidelines. The aim was to increase awareness of environmental concerns, to provide direct responses for application in the hotel, to reduce pollution to a minimum, and to be environmentally sensitive in all aspects of hotel operation.

Again, in the international scene, the role of environmental audits has been highlighted by the International Hotels Environmental Initiative, which produced *Environmental Management for Hotels: The Industry Guide to Best Practice*. The manual provides a most useful reference and blueprint for improving environmental policies and procedures. It is believed that in the future, more and more major hotels and international tourism groups will become increasingly involved with environmental auditing programs.

Such programs demonstrate a worldwide trend towards the greening of tourism reported to the Globe '92 International Conference on Business and the Environment (Hawkes & Williams, 1993). The tourism industry is realizing that future prosperity relies heavily on the maintenance of the environmental qualities on which it depends. Moreover, in a more environmentally aware world, green tourism not only offers new experiences and opportunities, but makes economic good sense in terms of reduced waste and lower operating costs.

The Greening of Australian Beach Resorts

As noted earlier, Australian tourism developers and operators are demonstrating increased understanding of environmental concerns, and the Australian Tourism

Industry Association (1990) has drawn up an Environmental Code of Practice in consultation with conservation groups, industry bodies, and planning authorities. The Code is being applied at a number of beach resorts that have been built along the east coast of Australia. Some of these are fully integrated resorts offering five-star hotel accommodation, with luxurious residential properties, and a range of world-class recreation facilities. Several resorts have been designed and constructed on ecologically sensitive principles and operate on environmentally responsible lines.

Some of the best examples of the "greening" of Australian tourism are to be found at beach resorts in the Great Barrier Reef region of North Queensland. Two exclusive resorts on Bedarra Island off the Queensland coast are among Australia's most environmentally friendly tourism developments. The structures represent a different approach to resort architecture, using local materials and nature-responsive design. The approach is to offer visitors the chance to retreat from the outside world and recharge themselves through close contact with the surrounding island landscape and rainforest.

Further north, Green Island near Cairns has been redeveloped in keeping with environmental constraints, and with attention to siting, design, materials, sources of supplies, and disposal of wastes. Said to be Australia's first five-star "ecotourist" resort built on a coral cay, Green Island offers luxurious accommodation under the rainforest canopy, with structures suspended to protect the delicate ecology of the forest floor.

The redevelopment of Green Island is subject to strict controls imposed by Cairns City Council and the Queensland Department of Environment and Heritage regarding:

- the layout of the resort;

- design details including materials and finishes;

- waste disposal;

- construction methods.

A Code of Environmental Practice has been drawn up by the developers and given to all site staff and contractors to convey an environmental conservation philosophy to all those involved in development and operation of the resort. The Code explains the fragile nature of the island and provides practical advice on:

- avoidance of the spread of weeds, exotic plants, and diseases;

- maintenance of ecosystems, fauna, and flora;

- the importance of the groundwater aquifer to survival of native rainforest;

- cultural heritage, both European and Aboriginal;

- national parks and marine parks;

- tourists, visitors, and other leaseholders on the island.

The Green Island Resort represents an impressive (and expensive) approach to resort development in harmony with nature and the beauty of the tropical island setting.

A further example is Ramada Reef Resort, on the mainland. The resort is implementing many of the environmental initiatives currently being undertaken by Ramada hotels and resorts throughout the world. From its inception, the Reef Resort was designed on ecologically sensitive principles, with buildings and facilities harmoniously integrated into the surrounding natural environment. Extra precautions have been taken to ensure that individual trees are fully protected, even to the extent of a unique, free-form swimming pool created around the root systems of rainforest trees. The Ramada Reef Resort is rapidly earning a reputation as one of the most environmentally responsible hotel developments along the Australian coast (Kelleher, 1993).

Despite these examples, proposals for further resort development on the Queensland coast have encountered strong resistance from conservation groups. The planned Port Hinchinbrook resort development at Cardwell, south of Cairns, was delayed because of fears that it would affect nearby World Heritage Areas. Despite approval by the Queensland State Government, the federal authorities intervened after initial site clearing had begun. The multimillion dollar project has now been allowed to proceed following further environmental assessment, and amendments to the scale and operations of the resort.

Further south, the Coffs Harbour region, on the New South Wales coast, north of Sydney, has seen rapid expansion of tourism in recent years. In 1990, a conference was organized at Coffs Harbour around the theme of "The Green Resort." The purpose was to examine and formulate design principles for resort developments along the Australian coastline. Concepts such as environmentally compatible methods of waste disposal, more energy-efficient design and operations, including solar power, and sensitive and aesthetically pleasing resort architecture were discussed (Oppenheim, 1990, unpublished workshop papers).

The Coffs Harbour region is an established focus for tourism on Australia's east coast. The area has a remarkable diversity of scenic attractions ranging from pristine sandy beaches to spectacular rainforests a few kilometers inland. The climate is rated among the best in Australia, with a mean summer temperature of 28 degrees and 22 degrees in winter. Visitors can choose from a variety of activities including surfing, sailing, ocean and estuary fishing, whitewater rafting, ballooning, and following nature trails on foot or horseback.

A wide choice of accommodation styles is also available to tourists visiting Coffs Harbour. The area has long been an attractive location for second homes, but short-term visitors can utilize apartments, motels, caravan parks, and campgrounds. In recent years, a number of sophisticated resorts have been created along the coastline north and south of the city.

These offer international style facilities with a full range of sporting and recreational activities, entertainment, beach access, and a setting compatible with the natural environment. In many respects, these establishments reflect the "greening" of beach resorts along Australia's coast. Typical of this trend is Aanuka Beach Resort.

Aanuka Beach Resort

Located six minutes from the center of Coffs Harbour City, Aanuka Beach Resort is set in four hectares of landscaped grounds on the beach front. Aanuka is a relatively small, secluded resort created in a natural rainforest setting with direct access to a safe surfing beach. It has won awards for the best resort in Australia and best resort design for a setting reminiscent of an island in the South Pacific. The emphasis is on the attractions of native fauna and flora in a subtropical environment. The developer boasts that just six trees had to be removed to create the resort, but 20,000 trees have since been planted on the site. Furthermore, construction companies were required to agree to a bond of A$3000 for any tree seriously damaged during development of the resort.

Construction materials, architectural design, and landscaping are in keeping with the inherent appeal of the site. No expense has been spared in fitting out the resort for the comfort of guests. A large outdoor rock pool has been created with waterfalls, a cave with jacuzzi, and a swim-up bar. The 48 suites are designed as buré style, low-rise units in harmony with the natural environment and offering complete seclusion and privacy. Each suite is fully equipped with luxury facilities and a two-person spa and atrium. Open space, low density, environmental sensitivity, and a casual social setting set the tone for the resort.

Some of the best facilities offered to tourists in Australia are available at Aanuka Beach Resort. However, the beachfront site does present some disadvantages. Maintenance costs are high with corrosion of metal fittings, repeated cleaning of glass surfaces, constraints on plant types, and heavy demands on upkeep of the grounds. The resort is also exposed to occasional strong winds, and infrequent cyclonic disturbances and storm surge.

Great care has been taken to keep Aanuka compatible with and buffered from surrounding land uses. An important development in this respect is the construction of Aanuka Beach Village adjacent to the Resort. Once again, the intention is to maintain the integrity of the setting and provide harmony between architecture and nature. Beachside residential villas are offered for sale or investment for longer term visitors, to underpin the commercial viability of the resort itself.

Operation of Aanuka Beach Resort incorporates many features of best practice environmental management in the tourism industry. Comprehensive programs for recycling and management of wastes, energy and water conservation, and protection of the natural environment are features of resort operations. Advertising programs feature the "greenness" of the resort and its management. The success of Aanuka Beach Resort is perhaps a good indication of the marketing advantage to be gained from environmentally sensitive tourism development in the coastal zone. Moreover, the demonstration effect of the successful appeal to tourists of a nature-based resort is already being reflected in the promotion of neighboring "green" beach resorts in the Coffs Harbour region.

Aanuka also provides convincing evidence of the benefits of monitoring environmental performance, and the role of self-regulation and environmental auditing. The resort has detailed procedures in place for detecting and correcting any environmental impacts that occur, and for checking on levels of compliance with operational procedures. The primary responsibility for sustainable management of beach resorts presumably rests with regulatory authorities and planning agencies. However, an important component of environmental monitoring programs should also be self-regulation.

The adoption of in-house auditing procedures to monitor the setting and observance of appropriate standards of environmental excellence, as is the case at Aanuka Beach Resort, serves as a useful benchmark for other tourism developments in the coastal zone. The experience at Aanuka and similar resorts is important, because the example of large-scale international corporations, mentioned earlier, may not translate readily to the level of individual resorts. The challenge is to devise an effective, user-friendly environmental auditing system for tourism undertakings and demonstrate its benefits for specific sectors of the industry at defined scales of operation. Development of such a process is the objective of research focused on beach resorts in the Coffs Harbour region, and reported in Ding and Pigram (1995). This work complements other steps being taken to endorse and implement auditing of environmental performance in the tourism industry.

Implementation of Environmental Auditing

At a conference on ecotourism in Australia, the case was argued for the development of environmental management plans, incorporating monitoring mechanisms, as part of a broad environmental management system for tourist resorts (Anderson, 1994). This reflects a global trend towards environmental stewardship, a key element of which is environmental auditing and the perceived benefits to be gained from an active audit program (Cornwall & Burns, 1992). These benefits include:

- cost savings, through reduced reliance on raw materials, elimination of wasteful practices, and avoidance or minimization of legal liabilities for breaches of regulations;
- enhanced public image from consistent environmental performance and demonstrated sound corporate citizenship;
- incremental improvements in operational practices emanating from routine auditing procedures;
- enhanced environmental awareness within and beyond the workplace.

Despite these benefits, implementation of an industry-wide environmental auditing system for tourist resorts may not be easy because of marked differences in the scale of operations. As noted earlier, the term "resort" has different meanings and can refer to large integrated establishments, individual components in a corporate group, or small, independent "Mum and Dad" enterprises. Convincing such disparate elements of the resort sector to move "beyond passive regulatory compliance" (Anderson, 1994, p. 9) may call for a range of incentives, and possibly sanctions.

Industry groupings (e.g., motel chains and motoring organizations) could play an important part in convincing their members to endorse environmental codes of practice, adopt the means of auditing compliance, and monitor their performance in implementing such codes. Part of this approach could include awards and incentive schemes for superior environmental practice, and identification of industry leaders for "benchmarking" to compare performance. Sanctions might involve downgrading in ranking, or cancellation of membership of the organization.

Peer pressure, too, can be influential as support and enthusiasm for "greener" tourism to gather momentum. Pressure from within the resort sector for operators to lift their "environmental game" could well be reinforced by market forces. It is not inconceivable, in a more environmentally aware world, that visitor preference might be directed towards those resorts that can demonstrate a respectable environmental track record. It is here that auditing can assist in substantiating consistent and successful procedures for ensuring compliance with accepted levels of environmental performance.

Future visitors to beach resorts, for example, could well prefer, and be willing to pay extra for, an environmentally compatible product—an establishment located, designed, and constructed in keeping with the ambient environment, and operated along environmentally "friendly" lines. The emergence of a generation of more environmentally concerned tourists could reveal neglected market opportunities arising from greater economic understanding of environmental values in the resort industry. Perhaps the current systems used to rate hotels, in terms of comfort and facilities, will ultimately be replaced by "green diamonds" to indicate the degree to which a resort measures up to best practice environmental management.

> With a significant number of consumers translating their environmental concerns into purchasing decisions . . . "green marketing" is a viable marketing option. (Townley, 1995, p. 165)

One of the more promising ways in which a higher order of compatibility can be achieved between tourism and the environment that nurtures it is through education and communication. It is not enough merely to inform those involved of the consequences of resource misuse. They need to acquire and demonstrate a sense of social responsibility and concern for environmental quality. Resort developers and operators not prepared to adopt a more enlightened approach to tourism–environment interaction are likely to be forced to conform by combined pressure from industry organizations, market forces, and regulatory agencies.

Conclusion

The beach resort phenomenon is well established along the Pacific coast of Australia and some outstanding examples can be found of establishments developed and managed at the highest standards of environmental excellence. In maintaining these standards, systematic monitoring of environmental performance should be the norm, as in other sectors of the Australian economy. Anderson (1994) advocates "environmental co-regulation" as the preferred option towards achieving the goal of sustainable tourism development. This implies collaboration between the resort sector and government in a more relaxed regulatory regime that liberates, rather than inhibits, initiatives in pursuing higher environmental standards. Environmental auditing can be a most useful management tool in this process, and the critical environment of the coastal zone will benefit as a result.

In a more environmentally conscious world, the tourism industry faces increasingly stringent conditions on development, reflecting a concern for sustainability and the long-term viability of the resources on which tourism depends. The challenge for beach resorts is to justify their claims on the resources of the coastal zone with a commitment to their sustainable management.

As global demands on space and resources grow with increased population, technological change, and greater mobility and awareness, pressure will emerge for the tourism industry to implement appropriate steps for monitoring its environmental performance. The task ahead is to put in place effective, self-monitoring procedures to promote greener, more environmentally compatible forms of tourism development, and avoid the imposition of sanctions to satisfy mandatory compliance measures.

Chapter 4

A Workable Alternative to the Concept of Carrying Capacity: Growth Management Planning

Peter W. Williams and Alison Gill

Introduction

Tourism pressures on mountain regions have escalated in recent years. This phenomenon has drawn considerable attention from planners, managers, and researchers concerned about the escalating effects of growing concentrations of travelers in mountainous regions around the world. In the Alpine regions of Europe dialogue, research, and management policy have, to a large extent, centered on the effects of mounting levels of nontraditional economic activity (including tourism) transforming the environment and economies of the region (Bridel, 1984) Similarly, excessive tourism development (e.g., mountaineers and trekkers) in the Himalayas has led to management concerns for not only the fragile alpine environment, but also the cultural integrity of local inhabitants (Singh & Kaur, 1985). In North America, widespread concern has been expressed about tourism's social and environmental impact on mountain communities (Culbertson, Jackson, & Kolberg, 1992; Price, 1985; Stillwell, 1987).

There is widespread acknowledgment of the relationship between increasing numbers of tourists and escalated degradation of environments and cultures (Butler, 1980; D'Amore, 1983; Doxey, 1975). Embodied in this relationship is the concept of carrying capacity, which suggests an approach to management that permits growth within acceptable limits (Hawkins, 1987). Consequently, it is not surprising that it has been intuitively supported by land use planners and resource managers in many tourism regions. Despite its seemingly clear and rational intent, the concept of carrying capacity as a management tool creates ongoing controversy and frustration (Wall, 1982). On the one hand, it appeals to a recognized need to limit and control tourism development that may threaten the sustained use of limited resources. Simultaneously, it runs at odds with other desires for maximizing opportunities for growth, and realizing the potential benefits associated with increased visitor use.

As a more practical and viable alternative to the concept of carrying capacity management, this chapter recommends the application of growth management planning approaches for addressing tourism development issues in mountain environments. In particular, it summarizes the key conceptual foundations on which previous tourism and recreation carrying capacity strategies have been based, provides examples drawn from a mountain community to illustrate the range of management tactics that can be employed to address tourism growth issues, then suggests the common overriding themes that should be incorporated into the development of any growth management strategy for mountain tourism destinations.

Tourism Carrying Capacity Management

Varying perspectives on carrying capacity as a tourism management tool exist. In its most traditional sense, the concept refers to the maximum number of tourists or tourist use that can be accommodated within a specified geographic destination (O'Reilly, 1986). As such, it conjures up images of a specified "limit," "ceiling," or "threshold" that tourism development should not exceed. In a North American context, most strategies to manage tourism growth have been in controlled recreation settings such as parks and river corridors (Askey & Williams, 1992). In Europe, recent efforts have focused on the control of mountain tourism expansion especially in the Alps (Zimmerman, 1992), and the management of coastal resort development in Spain and nearby island resort areas (Inskeep & Kallenberger, 1992). These studies and others propose a wide variety of carrying capacity indicators that describe optimum or benchmark thresholds of tourism and recreation development in volume, density, or market-mix terms. Difficulties with these numerical carrying capacity indicators arise when efforts are made to link them directly to the management of specific tourism impacts. Little evidence exists to suggest that by simply changing a specified carrying capacity standard, predictable changes in tourist impact will happen. Instead, the key appears to lie in how change is managed.

From an environmental perspective, carrying capacity management involves maintaining a balance between physical/ecological and visitor requirements associated with a destination area. In this context it refers to "the maximum number of people who can use a site without an unacceptable alteration in the physical environment, and without an unacceptable decline in the quality of the experience gained by visitors" (Mathieson & Wall, 1982, p. 21). This implies some prior designation of preferred or desired conditions upon which levels of acceptable tourism impact can be judged.

For others, tourism carrying capacity is market driven (Butler, 1980; Plog, 1991). Critical carrying capacity thresholds appear to occur when tourist numbers approach levels that strain the capability of the destination to provide quality tourist experiences. Key indicators of encroachment upon these capacity ceilings have been traditionally related to identifiable changes in market demand. Any number of physical, economic, social, environmental, psychological, or political reasons can trigger tourist apathy towards a destination. However, it is frequently assumed that when visitor perceptions of desired on-site conditions are not met, declines in tourist demand occur. Depending upon the appropriate conditions established by destination decision makers, actions may be taken to expand the ability to absorb tourism and rejuvenate visitor interest in the destination; or conversely constrain the detrimental dimensions of tourism activity so as to reduce tourism's effects to more appropriate levels.

From a community perspective, carrying capacity relates to a destination area's capability to absorb tourism without unacceptable negative effects being felt by local residents (D'Amore, 1983; Doxey, 1975). Levels at which these inappropriate impacts occur are based on values determined by the community as opposed to the visitor. Operationalizing this perspective requires considerable consensus building among community stakeholders (e.g., residents, developers, operators, governments) to determine the desired conditions for a destination area, and how to most effectively manage tourism towards those ends. In this context, it is important to recognize that community perspectives on desired conditions may change over time and in response to different planning and management approaches (Martin & Uysal, 1990). Consequently, a regular review of what is considered to be desirable and acceptable is a critical part of managing tourism from a community perspective.

New Management Directions

Carrying capacity management's traditional focus on attempting to determine explicit use limits has made it a particularly difficult tool to use in a tourism management context. There appear to be too many limiting factors that hamper its use. In particular, the concept has not been fully operationalized due to:

- unrealistic expectations (i.e., a technique exists which can provide a magic number that identifies "how much is too much");

- untenable assumptions (i.e., a direct relationship between tourism use and impact exists);

- inappropriate value judgments (i.e., conflicts between the views of "experts" as opposed to destination stakeholders concerning what conditions are appropriate for an area);

- insufficient legal support (i.e., the lack of a formally recognized institutional process to ensure management strategies are implemented and enforced) (Gill & Williams, 1993).

However, those aspects of the concept that focus on establishing desired conditions or outcomes appear to have practical value for the management of tourism in a mountain tourism context. This is particularly the case if they can be incorporated into broader planning processes associated with sustainable development and growth management.

When applied within planning systems that focus on managing growth for desirable and acceptable change, some components of the carrying capacity management concept offer potential. Knowledge of the consequences of exceeding desired impacts can be used to direct management policies and practices in keeping with a more sustainable tourism. This implies the development of management guidelines that support forms of tourism which emphasize:

- architectural character and style sensitive to an area's heritage and environment (Dorward, 1990);

- preservation, protection, and enhancement of heritage and environmental resource quality (Braun & Winston, 1986);

- improvement to the quality of life for local populations (Pigram, 1990).

Growth Management Systems

In mountain tourism management situations, there are frequently several groups with often divergent views concerning tourism growth. They include tourists, developers, local residents, existing and proposed business operators, and the public agencies responsible for managing the environment within which all groups must operate. Depending on the specific circumstances of a mountain community (e.g., stage of tourism development, community economic conditions, or past tourist–resident encounters), the needs of one group may take precedent over those of the others in growth management decisions. It is not uncommon, for example, to see the needs of the tourist and developer take priority over the requirements of community residents during early stages of development (Lawrence, 1990). Although in the short term this helps stimulate growth, long-term sustainability of the tourism industry may suffer if the quality of life of residents who require affordable housing, schools, and community facilities is not adequately addressed. However, once most of the tourism infrastructure is in place, the role of the developer may diminish and the needs of local residents and visitors may take precedence. The real possibility of such changes in priorities is what makes the establishment of fixed long-term capacity limits a particularly challenging task, and creates the need for a more flexible, systems-based approach to managing tourism growth.

In a growth management systems context, notions of carrying capacity are linked to the "desired conditions" that best meet the goals of the area being managed. Although sensitively managing an area's unique natural and cultural resources is frequently central to a mountain destination's competitive advantage in the tourism marketplace, the resource base does not determine carrying capacity. Rather, it is a function of the management goals and objectives established by the community's stakeholders. If their main objective is to stabilize population growth patterns in the community, tourism's capability to contribute to that objective

becomes the key growth management concern. Indicators of population stabiliza-
tion might include changes in emigration and migration levels, age and gender
structure. If job creation is identified as the community's priority objective, then
indicators of the types of employment to be generated (e.g., seasonal, year-round,
front-line, supervisory, management) by tourism development become the growth
management focus. The establishment of goals and objectives determines which
indicators of change become the focus of growth management and monitoring.

General goals give broad direction to the planning and management of the mountain conditions desired. Objectives offer more precise statements of the mechanisms by which the desired conditions are achieved (Heath & Wall, 1992). A
general goal might be to manage the rate and quality of mountain development in
order to achieve and maintain a diversified community economy. Objectives
associated with this might include monitoring agricultural and tourism development to determine whether an appropriate balance between these two land uses
is being maintained, or managing residential reserve areas in an attempt to ensure
that employee housing supply keeps pace with this demand (Resort Municipality
of Whistler [RMOW], 1993).

A suggested systems approach to incorporating desired destination community
conditions into practical growth management practices involves:

- developing tourism goals and objectives that mesh with the broader comprehensive plan for the region and/or destination;

- establishing a set of performance indicators reflecting the expected objectives
  of tourism development;

- implementing management strategies that direct tourism toward the achievement of the stated goals and objectives;

- monitoring the performance of tourism development with respect to these
  indicators;

- evaluating the effectiveness of the management strategies in influencing the
  performance of tourism with respect to these indicators;

- developing refined and/or new tactics for managing tourism based on the
  effectiveness of these techniques (Getz, 1982).

The growth management systems approach offers a distinct perspective in that it:

- involves no identification of an ultimate limit to the number of visitors;

- relates tourism growth and development to its effect on destination goals and
  objectives;

- employs indicators of desired conditions to trigger either the implementation or
  adjustment to growth management strategies;

- reviews and modifies goal and objective priorities as destination circumstances
  change.

Growth Management Planning

In a North American context, tourism carrying capacity concerns can be incorporated into the comprehensive planning agendas of most mountain tourism destinations. Key to the success of such initiatives are growth management plans. Based on a destination's ability to articulate a vision of what community conditions and expansion rates it would like to encourage, growth management plans offer a potentially useful "guidance system" for implementing that vision (Schiffman, 1989). These plans include policy statements, capital budgets, and specific improvement programs that guide decision making concerning tourism expansion. Practical instruments to support identified programs encompass public investment strategies, land use regulations, and fiscal incentives or disincentives. They go beyond strictly land use planning by incorporating control mechanisms influencing tourism and other activities within the destination.

Many tourism-dependent communities (e.g., Stowe, VT; Lake Tahoe, CA; Park City, UT in the United States; Languedoc-Rousillon, France; S'Agaro, Spain; Cancun, Mexico; Niagara-on-the-Lake, Ontario, Canada) exhibit some aspects of a well-developed growth management plan. However, there appear to be few comprehensive applications of these approaches (Williams, 1993).

These techniques are most fully applied in two contemporary North American mountain tourism destinations. Both Aspen/Pitkin County, CO in the United States and Whistler, British Columbia in Canada exhibit what may be considered "state-of-the-art" growth management planning systems.

Most recently, Whistler B.C. has overhauled its growth management policies and illustrates the most current and comprehensive tactics for managing tourism effects in North American alpine communities (RMOW, 1993). Because of its incorporation of the best practices occurring in other mountain jurisdictions (including Aspen/Pitkin County) and its experience with past growth management planning efforts, its approach to growth management is discussed here.

Whistler Case Study

Growth Management Context

Whistler is located 120 kilometers from Vancouver, British Columbia, Canada. Nestled in the Pacific Range of the Coast Mountains, at an elevation of approximately 668 meters, the municipality encompasses an area of 12,630 hectares. Within its boundaries are found six major lakes, several environmentally sensitive areas, a variety of parks and recreation sites, a village core, and surrounding residential, commercial, and to a lesser extent industrial land uses. The population of Whistler is comprised of approximately 5,000 permanent residents, 2,000 seasonal residents, and a substantial year-round flow of tourists that use the area's stock of commercial hotel, condominium, bed and breakfast, and campground accommodations. The municipality sits at the base of two of North America's most highly rated and largest ski mountains, Blackcomb (2,284 meters) and Whistler (2,182 meters).

Whistler has evolved from a small, water-focused summer recreation area in the 1960s to an emerging four-season mountain tourism destination in the 1990s. However, this evolution has been marked by several critical planning events. In 1975, a special act of government incorporated the community as the Resort Municipality of Whistler (RMOW), and at that time the first Official Community Plan was established. The Whistler Village Land Company (WVLC), a wholly owned subsidiary of the RMOW, was established in 1978 to guide the development of a new village core. This placed control over the pace and direction of growth largely in the hands of the municipality's elected Council. Their philosophy and intent with respect to growth in this mountain region was clear: to achieve the goal of creating a mountain destination of international standard. Significant facility and amenity expansion designed to meet the demands of tourists was encouraged and approved. However, the municipality's plans and activities were derailed in the early 1980s, when a severe recession led to the bankruptcy and eventual restructuring of the WVLC. As part of this restructuring process, the British Columbia government took back development control of all provincially owned lands and facilities in Whistler Village. This served to reduce the level of community input into Whistler's development and also led to an unprecedented level of tourism facility expansion. To reach the critical mass needed to have an impact in the marketplace, minimize taxation effects, support wide range of resort amenities, and recover the large public investments in infrastructure incurred in the prerecession days, rapid growth was encouraged. As a result of these activities, by the mid-1980s Whistler was firmly established as a major ski destination in North America. However, there was a growing recognition that new challenges had to be addressed.

Concerns over an uncertain vision of the eventual size of the resort, the protection of the quality of the environment, and the overall ability of the destination's infrastructure to handle the ever growing levels of tourism traffic led to the development of the RMOW's first Comprehensive Development Plan (RMOW, 1988). The CDP was designed to act as the strategic planning guide for the development and planning of this mountain resort community. It became the policy statement of the RMOW and played a key role in influencing the content of the municipality's development regulations as expressed in the Official Community Plan and its related bylaws.

In the process of its creation, the resolution of other issues emerged as being critical to Whistler's long-term success. These concerns included the development of facilities and services that would permit the destination to become an all-season tourism destination, as well as the provision of housing and community-oriented services for a growing permanent and seasonal labor force vital to the resort's operation. Based on a perceived priority need for additional summer facilities and services necessary for a truly competitive international all-season resort destination, the CDP allowed additional development rezoning and expansion in exchange for these provisions by the developers. These modifications boosted the "ceiling" of development to 52,600 bed-units, of which 30,000 were built as of late 1992. However, the most challenging issue not directly addressed in the CDP from a growth management perspective was determining how Whistler would manage existing and future commitments to expansion without a clear appreciation of the effects of this development growth on the environment, community, and the overall quality of the resort.

After the British Columbia government returned full responsibility for the alloca-tion, development, and management of these lands to the RMOW in 1992 and Whistler was firmly established and recognized as a year-round mountain tourism destination, a more locally based and specific approach to growth management has emerged. This approach is articulated in the RMOW's newest Comprehensive Development Plan (RMOW, 1993). In many ways, the plan's policies and goals related to growth management issues are seen as the most important factors in determining whether the fundamental goal of the CDP (i.e., maintaining and enhancing the quality of the resort and the community) will be achieved (RMOW, 1993).

Changing Goals for Growth

Prior to the development of a growth management policy, the primary goal guiding development in Whistler was to achieve a level of development that would ensure a viable position in the international mountain resort destination market. Priority was placed on attracting investment to develop infrastructure and facilities serving tourists' needs. As noted in Whistler's initial CDP, the community's approach to managing growth and development was a reflection of the unique characteristics of the area at a particular time (RMOW, 1988). The resort has now evolved from that stage and the challenge has now moved from developing primarily tourist amenities to providing services for residents and protecting the environment, while maintaining the quality of the overall experience for visitors. Although some development of tourist facilities is necessary, the municipality will focus on the essential task of maintaining environmental quality, protecting the viability of the resort economy, and securing community services as opposed to more grand commitments to resort amenities and development (RMOW, 1993).

The general goals specified in the most recent CDP are to:

- balance the environmental, economic , and social needs of the community and resort;

- maintain the high quality of the natural and built environment;

- encourage kinds of economic activity compatible with the resort;

- guide the RMOW's activities to manage growth in the resort and broader region.

Programs and Mechanisms

With reference to each of these general goals, related growth management policies and programs have been articulated. Examples of these serve to illustrate how growth management strategies have been incorporated into the plan.

Growth Management Policy
Concern has been expressed about what changes will occur to Whistler as its current capacity grows from 30,000 bed-units to its committed size of approxi-

mately 52,600 bed-units. These limits are loosely related to the capacity of the water and sewage systems. They are not absolute limits as greater capital expenditures on technical support systems could expand the development capacity. Eventual "build out" is largely a question of what the RMOW deems to be desirable, given the community's goals. What is different from past circumstances for the RMOW is that the municipality, through its CDP, is now addressing the issue of growth management in a comprehensive fashion. The emphasis has shifted from managing numbers to addressing impacts.

At present there appears to be little need for further increase in the size of Whistler, as the mountain community already has considerable remaining approved capacity for all forms of development. By 2002, total development is forecast to be in the range of 45,000 bed-units, with the only remaining capacity to be in commercial accommodation. This situation affords some all-important "breathing room" to address questions about the long-term effects of Whistler's current tourism growth patterns. The CDP outlines a wide variety of growth management policies and programs designed to manage future growth towards community goals. Some of these are outlined in the following paragraphs.

Environmental Quality

Increasingly, tourists are expecting resort destinations to be set in natural environments with superior air, water, scenery, flora, and fauna attributes. Permanent residents are drawn to such locations for similar reasons. Whistler's CDP (RMOW, 1993) includes policy directives which recognize that the community's mountain environment places unique limitations on development. The municipality's policies with respect to land use, transportation, servicing, and other aspects of community development are consistent with the goal of protecting environmental quality. Examples of the types of growth management instruments being implemented to address environmental issues include:

- the adoption of a Municipal Environmental Strategy designed to encourage programs that focus on reducing solid waste, water consumption, wastewater production, private automobile use, toxic chemical use; encourage solid waste recycling and composting procedures; promoting education programming that encourages resident and visitor resource conservation practices;

- the design and implementation of water and wastewater treatment systems that maintain and enhance the quality of watercourses within the RMOW and its neighboring regions;

- the development of land use planning guidelines and coordination systems that protect visually sensitive areas (e.g., mountainsides, highway approaches, entrances) that are critical to the residents' and visitors' resort experience;

- the introduction of zoning, bylaw, and design approval processes to restrict or prohibit upper mountainside or other natural area development in locations identified as being environmentally or visually critical to the overall quality of the community;

- the incorporation of a habitat protection and improvement program to maintain and encourage the presence of wildlife in the area;

- the implementation of design measures to reduce noise levels associated with transportation systems into the RMOW (e.g., aircraft overflights and highway industrial traffic);

- the adoption of a tree protection bylaw to regulate the cutting of trees throughout the RMOW;

- the use of a project approval process to prohibit activities involving the use of risk-generating toxic or hazardous substances that can cause soil, water, or air contamination;

- the use of research programs to upgrade knowledge concerning areas within the RMOW that have significant development constraint and environmental sensitivities (e.g., watercourses and wetlands, etc.);

- the implementation of outdoor illumination guidelines that avoid diminishing the ability of residents and visitors to clearly view the night sky.

Community Facilities

Development approval policies implemented in previous planning periods by the RMOW have ensured that the community received its fair share of recreational amenities. These development contributions have enhanced the quality of life for permanent and seasonal residents as well as for visitors. However, because the previous focus was on developing facilities and services that were primarily a prerequisite for attracting tourists, Whistler currently lacks some of the facilities that are necessary for a complete and stable community. The current CDP has incorporated many of these community requirements into its policy directives. Some of the instruments that are in place or being considered to ensure that the RMOW's future growth adequately addresses these concerns include:

Affordable Housing: ensuring that a range of housing types and prices is available through an Employee Service Charge By-Law designed to provide an ongoing fund for subsidizing seasonal housing development; providing publicly owned lands at below market value for affordable housing development, encouraging employers to develop employee accommodation; applying a regional employee housing and transportation focus to meeting affordable housing requirements, including affordable housing in new residential development designations and approvals within the Official Community Plan. (Culbertson & Kolberg, 1991)

Local Transportation Infrastructure: providing a convenient local transportation system that places emphasis on alternative modes of transportation to the private automobile through the implementation of road layouts and standards that promote safety and the quality of the travel experience as well as reflect the special mountain resort character of Whistler; the continued implementation of bike routes and lanes as well as pedestrian routes and walking trails; the consolidation of air transportation service nodes at a location accessible to the community and free of significant noise impacts; the improvement of existing public transit services at times and locations suited to the needs of local residents.

Parks and Recreation Facilities: developing and maintaining a parks and recreation system that places a high priority on improving and expanding pedestrian and cycling trail systems; integrates historical and cultural elements; includes a greater diversity and variety of experiences; as well as protects and monitors natural habitat areas.

Other Community Facilities: expanding the community's identified cultural, educational, public safety, health and social services, heritage, and administrative capacities through the identification of projects that reflect the long-term needs of the community and resort, and the ability to generate the revenues to pay for them. For example, some community needs that have been identified in the CDP policy that have been developed include a community recreation center and new medical, police, and library facilities.

Monitoring and Evaluation

As opportunities for further expansion and the potential cumulative effects of development increase within the RMOW, the need for effective monitoring systems that gauge the effects of tourism on the area escalate. Consequently, as part of the ˙CDP's growth management policy, and Official Community Plan, a initial comprehensive community and resort monitoring system is now established. Although still in an early evolutionary stage, this monitoring system now provides feedback to elected community decision makers, private sector operators and developers, and other community stakeholders concerning what changes in the resort and community have occurred as the numbers of bed-units, residents, and visitors have increased. Incorporating a wide variety of community involvement and public input techniques to ensure as full a consultation process as possible is a central operating principle for this monitoring process. Other critical elements included in this system are:

- using information gained from a wide variety of existing agencies and organizations associated with the RMOW as the baseline data sources for assessing changes to the area;

- collecting information concerning not only changes to the natural environment, but also the "built," social, and economic environments of Whistler;

- communicating the findings emanating from the monitoring process in an annual public report, as well as at yearly town meetings in order to ensure the widest possible understanding of the changes happening in the RMOW;

- incorporating the community responses to the monitoring report into an annual review of the RMOW's growth management policy.

Common Lessons Concerning Tourism Growth Management Strategies

The growth management concerns addressed in the preceding discussion relate to issues of growth and development found in many typical North American communities. The need to balance the needs of the community and visitors in a mountain environment is what makes growth management particularly challenging in

Whistler. In this regard, certain distinctive features stand out as being particularly critical to the successful implementation process. These include the diversity and ever-changing priorities of stakeholders; the evolutionary stage of the tourist community; and the importance of maintaining a high-quality resource base. What strategies are implemented typically represent the meshing of political and social requirements with technical and administrative realities (Pigram, 1990). This is particularly the case in mountain resort destinations such as Whistler, which face growing demands for tourism development.

Stake Holder Diversity

Community involvement in establishing desirable conditions is perhaps the single most important element of growth management. Developing appropriate mechanisms to incorporate divergent views is critical for successfully establishing appropriate resident–visitor relationships (Cleveland & Hansen, 1994). A basic distinction can be made between residents and visitors, but in reality there are much finer distinctions with respect to attitudinal differences towards development (Lawrence, Hafer, Long, & Perdue, 1993). In many tourist towns, there is a significant second-home resident population as well as seasonal employees. Each of these resident groups has very different needs in terms of housing and service amenities. Although input into the planning process from permanent residents can be accomplished through traditional means such as public meetings, incorporating the viewpoints of these other community groups is more problematic. Alternative mechanisms, such as more informal small-group meetings, have been used in some instances (e.g., Whistler, BC and Park City, UT). In conjunction with this process, active community information and publicity programs (e.g., via radio talk shows, newsletters, etc.) are often necessary to ensure that the perspectives of more transient and/or recent residents of the community can be incorporated into the growth management process (Gill, 1992).

In addition to residents' attitudes, it is also important to conduct surveys of visitors in order to understand why they have decided to visit the destination and how well their expectations are being met, and what can be done to make their stays more enjoyable (Williams & Dossa, 1994). Maintaining a balance between the needs of tourists and those of all residents is critical. As many residents of tourist towns choose to live there because of perceived lifestyle and amenity factors, programs designed to allow local use of tourist-focused attractions, facilities, and services through more favorable resident pricing structures can be employed to reduce friction between residents and visitors.

Development Stage

Resort communities are extremely dynamic in character. In the early phases of development, a high investment in tourist facilities and infrastructure is necessary to reach a "critical mass" of attractions, services, facilities, and visitors in order that the destination can sustain a tourism economy (Pearce, 1989). Unfortunately, tourism demand is frequently unpredictable and subject to such problems as seasonality and aggressive competition. Development activities often entail considerable investment risk. Consequently, encouraging investment is often the primary objective in the early stages of development and destinations have often compromised the needs of the resident community to achieve this support. Although in the short term this seems an appropriate course of action, there may be negative repercussions at a later date. Examples of this can be found in most tourism towns that have evolved without an employee housing policy. Whereas the cost of providing employee housing acts as a disincentive to early investors, failure to do so has created serious problems in many communities once land values have increased (Gill, 1992).

Environmental Quality

Many tourism regions are resource dependent. Maintaining the quality of their resources (natural and cultural) is critical to the continued success of their tourism industry. As a consequence, resource management standards and guidelines are frequently higher than those necessary in other settings. For instance, the capability of the sewage and water systems must be able to meet the peak loadings that characterize service use in many tourist communities. Similarly, building and landscape design guidelines frequently reflect more stringent aesthetic goals (Dorward, 1992). Identification of the desired conditions to be associated with an area's critical tourism resources is also important in establishing priorities in the event of conflicting goals. For example, in the Lake Tahoe region of California and Nevada, highest priority is given to the lake water clarity and quality, as it is the resort's most essential tourist resource. Establishing desired conditions for the resource base is an essential step in growth management. This includes consideration of natural, cultural, and scenic resources in surrounding areas that may not necessarily lie within a municipality's borders, but still affect the overall quality of the area. It is important to decide how residents and visitors feel about the desired quality of such resources prior to determining what kind of management will be necessary.

Conclusions

Research suggests that traditional approaches to carrying capacity management have met with limited success in application. This situation exists primarily because of unrealistic expectations, untenable assumptions, inappropriate value judgments, and insufficient legal support systems. As a result, the concept is discussed considerably but used infrequently in a tourism management context.

Given the inability of traditional carrying capacity management concepts and techniques to be operationalized, an alternative approach is suggested. Its focus shifts from past concerns over establishing use limits, to issues of identifying environmental, social, and economic conditions desired by a community, and the creation of growth management strategies for managing tourism's carrying capacity challenges in mountain settings. In the case of Whistler, the RMOW has established a maximum ceiling index or number for growth within its boundaries; in recent years its focus has changed from managing the number to addressing the existing and potential effects of growth. Many of its growth management strategies are in the early stages of their development or implementation, and only time and monitoring will attest to their utility. However, the RMOW has chosen this approach as a workable alternative to the use of traditional carrying capacity strategies, because it allows the community to direct growth towards goals and conditions important to the community. Whistler's growth management strategies reflect the kinds of actions that can be implemented to ensure the sustainablility of our mountain tourism environments.

Chapter 5

Coastal Tourism, Conservation, and the Community: Case of Goa

Tej Vir Singh and Shalini Singh

Issues

Oceans, the world over, are showing marked signs of deterioration. Endangering of fish fauna, erosion of marine diversity of life, and climatic changes have been reported by both the media and academia. A recent World Watch study reveals that the three quarters of the total pollution that enters the oceans comes from human activities on the land. Shipping, oil spills, and ocean dumping alone account for 22% of ocean pollution.

The coastal zones support some of the most vulnerable stages of ocean life. These sea-land interfaces are complex and highly dynamic zones of great economic and environmental significance. Of late, these fragile and sensitive habitats have come under severe stress by increasing pressures from urbanization, pollution, and tourism development. Fisheries, offshore and onshore recovery of hydrocarbon, and mining have become other paradigms of coastal development. Unfortunately, the coastal terrain is polluted and often physically destroyed by human settlements. Nine out of the ten largest cities in the world—almost half of the world's population—are situated in coastal zones. Rapid development of mass tourism has brought high densities of people in direct contact with wetlands, coral reefs, and other fragile resources. These pressures are likely to increase, having significant implications for all who enjoy the coast.

The issues associated with coastal tourism are economic efficiency, environmental protection, and conservation besides issues of equity and regional development (Organisation for Economic Cooperation and Development, 1993b).

Indian Situation

India has a 7500-km coastline (including islands), distributed over nine states and two union territories. Its coastal ecosystem constitutes, perhaps, the largest living laboratory in the world with its wide range of subsystems, ranging from tropical, subtropical, arid and semiarid zones in the Western Sea Board and deltaic systems of major rivers, estuarine resources, mangroves, and related vegetation and flora (Swamy, 1993).

The coastal areas of India are in the midst of economic development subject to varied uses: ports, cities, large industrial belts, rural regions with fisherman settlements, exploitation of minerals, agriculture, and tourism. Six metro cities in the coastal belt, with tourism as their important function, account for one sixth of the total population of the country, and are responsible for urban and industrial waste that threatens the fragile aquatic ecosystem besides causing considerable economic and recreational loss. The malaise of environmental degradation further worsens by badly managed beach tourism development all along the Western Sea Board (WSB) and the Eastern Sea Board (ESB). Some of the beach resorts are reported to have overdeveloped beyond their carrying capacity, accelerating the waste-generation syndrome further. Mahabalipuram in the ESB hosts more than 100,000 tourists annually when the resident population (including the four surrounding settlements) is only 70,000. Goa, in the WSB, has visitors equal to the size of its total population, which has caused serious concern among the indigenous population for the protection and conservation of resource amenity, strongly pleading for tourism to develop as a community-based industry. In fact, the case of Goa's tourism movement vividly exemplifies the fact that a socially responsible and environmentally viable tourism cannot be fostered without a dialogue constructed and controlled along indigenous needs and in indigenous terms (Johnson, 1990).

Using Goa's example, it would be worthwhile to examine how the host community's awareness and peoples' involvement can be helpful in making tourism development sustainable.

The Case of Goa

Goa, the former Portuguese colony, is the most colorful state in its land and people. Situated on the west-central coast of India, it spreads over an area of 3,702 km², having a population of 1.2 million. Administratively, it is divided in two districts of North Goa and South Goa with 11 *Talukas* (subdivisions). Of them Pernem, Bardez, Tiswadi, Marmugao, Salcete, Quepem, and Canacona face the Arabian Sea. About 65% of the state's population is settled within the coastal talukas. Tiswadi, because of its early history, is better developed by having the additional advantage of inland waterways of the Zuari–Mandovi–Cumbarjua system.

Geographically, Goa has to the east the green mountain environment of the Sahayadries rising up to an elevation of 3827 feet (Sonsagar); the central part is an undulating plateau landscape, punctuated by river basins of the Mandovi and Zuari rivers. Close to the shoreline are the world famous beaches, interspersed with dark brown and blackish bluffs with thick plantation of majestic coconut trees. Culturally, it has hospitable people with all their richness in art, craft, dance, and music;

religious edifices, churches, temples, and monasteries form other tourist attractions. Goa expresses its rich architectural heritage in its human settlements.

The coastline of Goa covers a length of 106 km of which 65 km consists of extensive sandy beaches. The coastal landscape of Goa is scenic alternation of bays and headlands, significantly broken by the large estuaries of the Mandovi and Zuari rivers, interspersed with minor estuaries. Of the bays, the Baga, Calangute and Colva are extensively curved stretches with almost white sands. The headlands have played an important role in Goa's history as sites of forts and landmarks for marine and coastal navigation. Aguada, Reis Magos and Chapora, and Cabo de Rama (in the south) have been important strongholds in Portuguese colonization.

Generally, the beaches on the north have steep slopes with sediments larger than the south beaches. The foreshore of Calangute is much more steep (8°–10°) than that of Colva (5°–7°) (Veeryya, 1978). From north to south the coasts of Goa present the following features:

- The coastal area of Pernem, between the Tiracol and Chapora rivers consists of primarily open sandy beaches, interrupted in a few cases by hills.

- Northernmost part is the hill with fortification of Tiracol.

- The coastal area of Bardez, between the Chapora and Mandovi rivers, presents a variety of features, typical to Goan coast line. From Chapora Fort to Baga village, the terrain rises for sandy bays bounded by hills such as Vagator and Anjuna beaches. Further to the south to Fort Aguada, the beach is extensive, typical of the Goan open coastal landscape.

- The coastal area of Tiswadi, flanked by the two main rivers of Mandovi and Zuari, is generally narrow, associated with hilly terrain inland and Cabo Raj Niwas, a steep cape, facing the ocean.

- The northern coast of Marmugao, along the Zuari river, is mainly used for maritime activities, boat repairs, and other activities.

- The most extensive and rich sand beach extends from Dabolim in Marmugao to Mabor, the southernmost coastal area of Salcete.

- The rest of the coast to the south is hilly with a few pockets of sandy bays.

The coastline of Goa is fairly stable. Beaches, in most cases, are smooth to the sea and are safe for swimming and other water sport activities. Because of the climatic advantage Goan coasts enjoy 250 days of sunshine through the year. Being a well-protected coastline, winds are generally mild. The coastal region also experiences the land-and-sea breeze phenomenon. During October–November the sea breeze normally grows weak and mean wind speed ranges from 4 to 5 kmph. However, the average wind speed observed is of the order of 20–22 kmph, which can rise up to 35 kmph.

The highest wave activity is found to approach the shore during the South West monsoon period, rising to a height of 6 m. In the remaining period of the year, waves approach generally from the northwest with maximum height of about 3 m. The predominant wave periods during the southwest monsoon season are 5–7 seconds and during the remaining season of the year are of the order of 5–10 seconds (National Institute of Oceanography [NIO], 1977).

Given such a magnificent coastline of bays and beaches and sun and sand, tourism was destined to flourish. Quite early, the fact-finding Committee on Tourism (Jha, 1963) was quick to identify the rich resource potential of Calangute as one of the 20 target destinations to developing tourism for foreign markets. Interestingly, the drifters from the west, the so-called hippies, were the first to discover the charm and the fascination of these virgin beaches of Bardez taluka. Soon after, Anjuna, the small fisherman's village sprang to fame as a "hippie ghetto." The first batch of visitors came around 1963; then followed the "freaks," the "flower children," and the "junkies," who indulged in nude bathing (sun and sea) and moonlight orgies. Albuquerque's (1988) punchent remark is worth quoting, "interestingly the white skin came in search of sun while home tourists came in search of white skin."

In due course, hordes of visitors from all over the country converged on the golden sands of Anjuna, Calangute, and Colva, placing Goa foremost on the national tourist map of India. Tourism has now emerged as Goa's major industry, contributing directly and indirectly, through trade and commerce, as much as 16.45% of net domestic product (Town & Country Planning Goa, 1987). It is estimated that about 20% of Goans earn their livelihood, directly and indirectly, through tourism (Kamat, 1996). Growth of tourist traffic to Goa has been dramatic in recent years, particularly after the 1980s. The number of tourists visiting the country has now increased from 775,212 in 1985 to 1,107,705 in 1995 (Table 5.1). The World Tourism Organization report (WTO, 1989) places a target of 2.5 million visitors by the turn of the century.

Today the size of the visiting community is about 1.1 million, almost matching Goa's total resident population. According to Goa Tourism Development Corporation, the state offers over 21,000 beds including 4,770 beds in the star category. More and more hotels are springing up in the land and sea interface area. According to the Directorate of Tourism Goa, about 77% of the hotels have come up in the coastal belt with 73% of total bed strength (Kamat, 1996). It is also observed that about 77% of domestic travelers and 95% of foreigners prefer to stay in the coastal belt.

In 1995, 229,218 foreigners visited Goa and the majority of them came from the UK (58%) and Germany (10.7%), followed by Finland and Switzerland. The ratio of domestic vs. foreign is 90:10.

The tourist boom of Goa, particularly after the CHOGM Retreat in 1983, spurred the spirit of consumerism, resulting in uncontrolled and badly managed tourism development along the coastline. Some structures were not only incompatible with the character of the area but had a tendency to move closer to the beaches, aggravating erosion and preventing access of the people, besides polluting adjacent areas by effluents or emission (WTO, 1989). Integrity of sand-dunes was

Table 5.1. Tourist Arrivals in Goa 1985–1995

Year	Domestic	Foreign	Total	Annual Growth (%)
1985	682,545	92,667	775,212	—
1986	736,548	97,533	834,081	7.6
1987	766,846	94,602	861,448	3.3
1988	761,859	93,076	854,935	-0.7
1989	771,013	91,430	862,443	0.9
1990	776,993	104,330	881,323	2.2
1991	756,786	78,281	835,067	-5.6
1992	774,568	121,442	896,010	7.3
1993	798,576	170,658	969,234	8.2
1994	849,404	210,191	1,059,595	9.3
1995	878,487	229,218	1,107,705	4.5

Source: Directorate of Tourism, Goa.

undermined. The sanctity of "No Development Zone" was violated and the conservation line (500-m setback) was ignored by tapping underground water. This haphazard development to the detriment of local people, who treated beaches as a commons for their traditional pursuits, created new social problems. Goa's Tourism Master Plan, which had envisaged soft, integrated and community-based development of the coastline by creating 13 Tourism Development Areas (TDA), 5 Tourism Resort Areas (TRA), and Tourism Village Areas (TVA), did not see the light of the day. The Goa Regional Plan 2001 AD was amended to suit the interest of tourism industry. This situation created unrest among the local people who owned the resources and were aware of the irreversible damage that mainstream tourism was bound to cause. They cried out for a robust, well-defined, and sustainable policy for the protection and conservation of their precious coastal habitats, having some of the best beaches found any where in the world.

Conservation: Issues and Approaches

Fortunately, the initiative for the conservation and protection of India's coastal zones came from the Prime Minister's Office, when Mrs. Indira Gandhi, in 1981, sent directives to all the Chief Ministers of the Coastal States to keep beaches free from "artificial development, pollution, industrial and urban waste and to see that our lovely coastline and its beaches remain unsullied."

Following this clarian call, the Department of Environment on September 1, 1982 prepared guidelines for sustainable development of coastal belts. Based on these guidelines, Goa set up a body of Ecological Development Council (EDC), which shall regulate construction within 500 m of high tide line (HTL). Goa also set up an Ecological Control Committee (ECC) to function as a technical arm of the EDC. Of paramount significance was the Environment Protection Act (EPA) in 1986, applicable to the whole country. The Act, under section 5, grants power to close down industry (hotels), stop supply of electricity or water in case it was found violating the provisions of the Act. Standards of emissions or discharge of environmental pollutants have also been laid down. Goa got these powers, under this Act, as late as September 22, 1988.

Coastal Regulation Zone

Another hallmark event in the history of coastal environment security was Coastal Regulation Zone (CRZ) notification that came into effect on February 19, 1991, under Environment Protection Act of 1986, which prohibits some activities and regulates others on all coastal stretches of sea, bay, estuaries, rivers, and backwaters that are influenced by tidal action.

CRZ is certainly the most laudable effort to integrate development with environment. Without these sets of regulations the Goan sea beaches would not remain unique and beautiful destinations of the world, so different from Spain or Florida beachscapes that have been spoiled by massive construction on the waterfronts.

It would be relevant to elaborate some of the highlights of CRZ in the Goan context, because the question of "setback" has posed problems, particularly between the tourism promoters and the environmentalist, which needs reconciliation for wholesome development of the coastal areas.

According to the Ministry of Environment & Forests (MEF) notification, the coastal stretches within 500 m of the HTL of the landward side are classified into four categories. Category 1 includes areas that are ecologically sensitive, such as national parks and sanctuaries, and are likely to be inundated due to rise in the sea levels, consequent upon global warming. No construction is permissible up to the 500-m setback in this zone.

Category 2 refers to areas that have already been developed up to or close to the shoreline. In CRZ II, no further construction or building is permitted either on the seaward side of the existing roads or proposed roads in the Coastal Zone Management Plan. However, reconstruction without change in land use can be permitted but the design and construction of buildings shall be consistent with the local architecture and style.

In CRZ III are included areas that are ecologically undisturbed and do not belong to either category 1 or 2, and are classed rural areas, developed and undeveloped. In this category a "no development zone" has been demarcated up to 200 m from the HTL, and no construction is to be permitted, except repairs of existing structures.

However, villages can expand in keeping with traditional rights. Vacant plots between 200 and 500 m of HTL may be permitted for construction of hotel/beach resorts for temporary occupation of tourists with the prior approval of MEF and subject to conditions laid down in the guidelines. No construction shall exceed two floors. Maximum height of a building should be less than 9 m.

Category 4 includes the coastal stretches in the Andaman and Nicobar, Lakshdweep, and 13 other small islands, save those designated as categories 1, 2, and 3.

Annexure II of the notification provides more specific guidelines for the development of beaches, resorts. and hotels in the designated areas of CRZ. It does not permit any project component like fencing or any other barrier within 200 m on the landward side from HTL and within the area between the LTL and HTL. The ground water shall not be tapped within 200 m of HTL. However, within 200–500 m it could be tapped with the approval of the Central or State Ground Water Board. No extraction of sand, leveling, or digging of sandy stretches would be permitted within 500 m of HTL.

In Goa, all along the sea fronts, a width of 200 m from the HTL has been marked as "No Construction Zone" since 1984, though in certain cases it has been relaxed to 90 m. In the case of lands fronting estuaries, creeks, and rivers this control was not being exercised. The CRZ notification is applicable to the area up to the limit where tidal action and salinity ingress is felt. The development control within the 500-m setback is, indeed, the first line of defense against despoliation of sea coast and beaches. Goa, perhaps, is the first state in India to submit its Coastal Zone Management Plan (CZMP), though it still awaits final approval from the Centre. It is hoped that this Plan is related to spatial aspects like integrated development of beaches and coastal areas through proper land use planning and development with statutory backup. In fact, there is imperative need for detailed knowledge of coastal areas, base maps, identification of HTL, impact of sea level rise, and the like without which, obviously, no CZMP can bring about the desired results.

Breaching the Conservation Line

Despite specific conservation measures, notifications, regulations, and acts (EDC, ECF, EPA, CRZ), the coastal areas cannot remain inviolate and invulnerable to environmental violation by tourism promoters. Hoteliers seem to have an obsession for breaching the conservation line (90–500 m), obviously for the fascination of coastal scenery and proximity to magical quality of waters. The sacrosanct 200 HTL zone, which was to be the "No Development Zone," witnessed many environmental trespasses, especially from hotel developers, viz., raising of fencing, depriving public access to beaches, raising of structures on beaches in some cases up to 24 m (when the prescribed limit was as low as 9 m), sand extraction from dunes for industrial purposes, tapping of ground water within the conservation line (whereas EPA imposed a ban on all such activities).

Tourism development forces seem to have powerful sway on higher authorities and, surprisingly, in November 1985 the Prime Minister Office issued a notice relaxing the ban on construction on beaches from 200 to 500 m (Alvares, 1993). Strangely, many hotel projects were approved despite inadequate Environment Impact Assessment (EIA)—a precondition for hotel project sanction. In fact, the entire politics of coastal development revolves around the demarcation of CRZ II. If large areas of the coastal states are placed in this category in the state plans and the MEF clears the plan, it will accelerate the pace of development, causing damage to coastal ecology. Most controversial, indeed, is the draft amendment of November 11, 1993 to the earlier notification of February 1991 that seeks further relaxation of HTL from 90 to 50 m, which shall definitely prove disastrous to precious estuarine and riverine flora. The hoteliers want to use the relaxation for rocky headlands and promonotories, although it is anticipated that they would extend their activities to all coastal stretches. This has caused serious resentment among Goa's Green Groups, who have been at war with the tourism industry and the public sector on these sensitive issues of protection and preservation of their prized land and sea interfaces (Singh, 1994).

A brief narrative of these antitourism grassroots movements of Goa would be pertinent to understand how zealously the *Goenkars* possess and protect their precious resources, particularly their coastal lands and beaches.

The Community

Socioculturally conscious and ecologically aware, the people of Goa are proud of their natural and cultural heritage and would not suffer the idea of its erosion or disruption at any cost. Not that they are ignorant of benefits that development of tourism can bring to a society that has limited resources for raising the living standard of its people, but that they had a different idea of the development ethics than what the mainstream tourism usually perpetuates. Certainly, they had aspired for "benign tourism" or "real tourism," where development increases peoples' control over resources and strengthens community identity, and that this is compatible with the maintenance of essential ecological process and biological diversity, besides being economically efficient.

The tourism boom factor unsettled them altogether as they witnessed unbridled luxury tourism taking the hardpath of modern technology, ignoring the most concerned, especially the marginalized and politically voiceless groups, viz., the traditional fishermen, toddy tappers, and the farmers who were not consulted and were dismissed as uninformed and malicious if not actually deserters from the cause (Jungk, 1979). Right from the Hippie invasion on their beaches in the early 1960s to the assault of the golden hordes of the 1980s, the indigenous people found that this form of tourism is not only *bad* but also *ugly* and should at once be cried to a halt. Laxity of morals, acculturation, xenophobia, drug abuse, nudism, prostitution, and crime, besides many more sins, were attributed to modern mass tourism. The resentment of the people ranged from ethical consideration of social concerns to question of physical amenity, viz., degradation of beaches and coastal environment, water shortage, and power crisis (Lea, 1993). This gave rise to tourist activism and grassroot movement against further development of coastal tourism. Soon it gathered momentum and assumed the proportion of mass movement, joined by hundreds of militant groups of Goan youth, workers, students, professionals, and individuals who called themselves *Jagrut Goenkaranchi Fauz* (JGF) or Vigilant Goan's Army. JGF is a secular group whose struggle emerges from its socioeconomic and sociocultural analysis of the phenomenon of modern tourism. They encourage local action at village and town level for empowerment of people on issues of development democracy. They firmly hold, "We have a right to decide our economies, our occupation, our environment and our culture." JGF, in order to protect Goa's fragile traditional economy from leisure-oriented economy, came out with a Five Point Declaration against uncontrolled expansion of Goa's five-star resorts.

Community Protest

The JGF will mobilize the people of Goa in cities and villages to fight for: (1) a total ban on any new five-star hotel, (2) a freeze on the expansion of existing hotels, (3) the withdrawal of the declaration of tourism as an industry by the government of Goa, (4) a strict code of conduct to be observed by hoteliers with regard to their advertising Goa in a manner that is detrimental to Goan culture and women, and (5) the governments' noncollusion with hoteliers by organizing and sponsoring infrastructure required for five-star tourism. The JGF warns the government that if these demands are not met immediately the JGF will paralyze the functioning of the government and its tourism program (Srisang, 1987).

This declaration marked the culmination of community unrest, what Alito Siqueira (1991) vividly describes in his thought-provoking article, "Tourism and the Drama of Goan Ethnicity." Apart from JGF other indigenous groups who vehemently oppose mass tourism are: The Goa Foundation, Citizens' Concerned About Tourism (CCAT) and Bailancho Saad (B.S.). The Goan Foundation (1986) is committed to environment protection and enhancement of Goan quality of life through empirical research and publication for sustainable development. Recently, the Foundation filed a few writ petitions against the construction and expansion of a number of hotels and resorts on Goan beaches, viz., Dalmia Resort, Leela Beach Resort, Majorda Beach Resort, and the Taj Holiday (Alvares, 1993).

Citizen's Concerned About Tourism (CCAT) is mainly concerned with the damage done by tourism to Goan ethical and cultural values. CCAT monitors backpackers' activities on the beaches that threaten the fabric of Goan society adversely. It successfully campaigned against the notorious Flea Market in Anjuna. With a mass signature campaign (1989) they appealed PMO to set up an antinarcotic squad and a branch of Narcotic Control Bureau in Goa, and asked to impose a ban on nudism on Goan beaches. Mention should be made of the Women Collective Organisation called Bailancho Saad (BS), which strives for a just and humane society. They have strongly protested, along with a contingent of Roman Catholic nuns, against the practices of nudism on Goan beaches. They strongly registered their resentment against child abuse and prostitution. The BS resents commercialization and commoditization of their culture for tourism promotion.

For a long time these coastal areas have served the sociocultural needs of the local people. Hindus and Catholics hold their periodic rituals and ceremonies on these shores. Hundreds of elderly village folks assemble along these shorelines for therapeutic use of salt water and sand for the cure of chronic ailments. For centuries small land holders have kept these areas green by their sustainable indigenous activities (planting paddy, coconut, and cashew); toddy tappers prepared the popular *Fenni* and fisherman carried out their humble pursuits without disturbing the pristine landscape. After the liberation, this bucolic scene has been changing, succumbing to tourism development, although many beachheads resemble a glorified urban slum. The recent threat has been the proposal of golf courses along the coastline to serve Japanese clientele. The Pernem Coastal Peoples Welfare Action Committee (1993) resisted such a move and observed "World No Golf Day" by holding a *morcha* (agitation) on April 29, 1993 in Panjim.

These community groups give full vent to their feelings against rapid and uncontrolled tourism development and its adverse impacts on the sociocultural aspects of the host community, through mass movement and media coverage. These indigenous groups have also been successful in seeking international support, specially from Southeast Asia, Western Europe, and the United States for the cause of righteous tourism. The Roman Catholic church has been waging war against mass tourism on ethical grounds by organizing a series of international symposia in the 1980s besides setting up the Ecumenical Coalition on Third World Tourism (ECTWT) in Bangkok. They have also put out a quarterly tourism newsletter, *Contours*, that focuses on the Third World tourism and invariably carries articles on the Goan problem of tourism. *Equations* (Equitable Tourism Options), in Bangalore, is active against promotion of mass tourism, focusing on the breach of Goa's conservation line in their newsletters. *Tourism Concern*, from London, highlights the ecocultural problems of Goa tourism in their widely circulated bimonthly, *Tourism in Focus*.

With all this antitourism literature accumulating on the negative impacts on Goan society, it remains by far highly subjective and qualitative in its statements. At best, it sounds an angry note of alarm and a voice of resentment. Some matter of substance with quantitatively definable impacts on the theme is still desired. Because of this lack of objectivity, the protourism lobby, who have some tangible facts to prove tourism's positive benefits, particularly in the field of state and national economy, have often been found calling these activists an "unholy brew of opponents who snipe at success" (Gantzer, 1991). Some of them have questioned the involvement of church in such antitourism activities and have been scathy of their old association with the erstwhile colonial power (Lobo, 1991).

While this debate on tourism development in Goa, *for* and *against*, goes rife, the environmentalist groups have been able to assert that full involvement of local communities in the tourism sector not only benefits them and the environment in general but also improves the quality of tourism experience. Experience has shown that projects imposed from outside and motivated by the pursuit of rapid economic growth often override local needs, conditions, and resources and result in unacceptable environmental, social, and cultural costs (Barnett, 1992). Perhaps one of the most significant responses to the problem of tourism is the emerging participation of indigenous peoples studying, discussing, and devising strategies to control or capture control over the development decision-making process (Johnson, 1990).

Certainly, the dream of building a community-led tourism industry in Goa remains far too distant, but there is no gainsaying that the persistent struggle of these tourist activists has not gone in vain. Decision makers now are agreeably inclined to frame sustainable tourism policy for ecodevelopment, a concept hitherto considered merely academic. Industry managers also view green tourism as a new product that has a niche. This is, indeed, a paradox of ecotourism that the perceptions of the industry and of local people are at variance. What appears to be green to product sellers does not appear to be so green to resource owners who consider it a marketing ploy for selling their precious environment. Table 5.2 explains how conflicting are the views.

No tourism development, however ingeniously conceived, can foster sustainability that fails to respect needs and aspirations of the local people. Doxey's concept of local attitude changing with the *scale* and *form* of tourism development holds good in the case of Goa. Goan activists feel that luxury tourism flowing from the affluent West may bring some economic gains for the society but eventually affects the milieu adversely, both ecologically and culturally. Recreation management should be concerned with reducing conflicts between visitors and the community. It should endeavor to *conserve* rather than *consume* resources that constitute heritage of the region.

Concluding Remarks

Informed and able citizens and conservation groups should be encouraged to participate in the decision-making process regarding the development and future of their community. Care should be taken that ecological, cultural, historical, and

Table 5.2. Green Tourism: The Conflicting Views

Resorts	The Image (What the Brochures Say)	The Criticisms (What Local People Say)
Taj and Fort Aguada holiday complexes	"Relaxed . . . laid back . . . beautifully and peacefully positioned." (*Inspirations India*)	Local people denied beach access and access to water pipeline.
Leela Beach Hotel	"Walk about in the extensive grounds and the predominant noise is birdsong." (*Inspirations*)	Refuses to rent out coconut trees to tappers, damages trees, illegal wells built, villages displaced from land, beach access denied.
Cidade de Goa Hotel	"Lovely, beachside setting . . ., comfort, elegance and friendly service." (*Cosmos*)	Beach access denied by wall, sewage dumped, court orders taken out against it.
Dona Sylvia Hotel	"Excellent location . . . alongside a wonderful beach." (*Sunworld*)	Illegal fence built, dunes damaged to give guests seaview.

Source: Tourism Concern (1993).

aesthetic values in the coastal zone, which are essential for the well-being of all citizens, are not damaged or lost. Conservation is seen as the wise use of resources and is concerned with harmonizing the use of different resources with minimum conflicts (Murphy, 1985). Management plans should ensure that all forms of development are adequately controlled and that changes in land use are in sympathy with the milieu and ecological value of the coastal areas (Inskeep, 1994). Tourism in any case should not be allowed to destroy the composition of nature through reformation of ecosystems, cliffs, riverbanks, and beaches (Miller, 1987).

It is, indeed, in the interest of overall development that tourism and other traditional occupations like fishing, pisciculture, toddy tapping, and agriculture of the workforce in the sea–land interface coexist and a balance between the two is achieved. It is also essential that special areas are earmarked for these occupations and their proper growth and development.

A plausible suggestion is that the entire coastline, comprising the whole of the revenue village, should be taken as a unit of planning as against the present 500-m setback from the high water mark in order to help retain the rural character and to integrate all development activities within the village settlement (Tourism Master Plan: Goa, 1987).

There is an urgent demand for planned, rational, and concerned efforts, jointly performed by the central, state, and local governments, to prevent the inherent harm and an uncoordinated and piecemeal development of the shoreline. The concept of Cooperative Tourism, where all parts of tourism systems become party to and share responsibility for policy decisions is also worth trying.

Considering Goa's high quality of landscape and vast stretches of unspoiled and undeveloped nature of shoreline and with increasing tourism development pressure, it would be worthwhile planning for the Coastal Heritage, a concept that England and Wales have successfully practiced with the positive cooperation of voluntary organizations, landowners, farmers, and fishermen in promoting conservation of their precious coastline. It is just caring for the undeveloped coast now that will benefit future generations. However, heritage coast remains as areas in which recreation and tourism occur alongside habitats and communities that retain their ecological intrinsic appeal (Edwards, 1987). Important is the realization of the fact that Heritage Coast Policy is dependent on voluntary agreement made in good will with the local people. The careless use of the Heritage Coast concept for tourism promotion may well lead to the loss of this good will and the subsequent demise of the Heritage Coast.

Acknowledgment

The authors gratefully acknowledge financial support provided by the United Nations Environment Program in preparing this chapter.

Chapter 6

Tourism in a Critical Environment: Brazil's Atlantic Coastal Forest

Robert G. Healy

Introduction

Brazil's Amazon forest is generally considered the country's most critical environment. Yet the Amazon is an enormous area, much of it is still inaccessible by road, and about 80% of the original forest cover remains intact. Much less known, but more endangered, is Brazil's Atlantic Coastal Forest. It once stretched along almost the entire Brazilian coast, a linear distance of over 3,000 km, and extended inland in some places several hundred kilometers (Dean, 1996). However, the historical settlement of Brazil began along the coast, and today most of Brazil's large urban centers continue to hug the coast. As a result, much of the brunt of historical land use change was borne by the Atlantic Coastal Forest.

The combination of agricultural clearing, forest harvesting, and urbanization has reduced the Atlantic Coastal Forest to an estimated 8.8% of its original area. Along the 1,500-km stretch of coast in Brazil's northeast, only small fragments of the original forest remain. Most was long ago removed in the course of establishing sugar cane cultivation. The portions that remain, primarily along Brazil's central and southern coast, occur on steep slopes or areas without road access. They are often surprisingly pristine, even though many lie quite close to major urban centers.

The Atlantic Forest, even in its present much reduced state, contains an unusual concentration of biological diversity. Of 207 species of Brazilian fauna officially listed as endangered, 152 live within the Atlantic Forest Domain. Many of these are endemic to Atlantic Forest habitats and do not occur elsewhere (Fundacao SOS Mata Atlantica, 1992). Among these are 10 species of primates (monkeys, marmosets, and tamarins), jaguar, giant otter, maned sloth, sea turtles, yellow-throated caiman, and 13 kinds of parrots. So unexplored are parts of the Atlantic Forest that Brazilian scientists have recently discovered a previously unreported species of primate (the black-faced lion tamarin) on the island of Superagui and the adjoining mainland, only 250 km by air from the huge city of Sao Paulo.

The Atlantic Coastal Forest is also exceptionally diverse floristically. Recently, scientists from the New York Botanical Garden and Brazilian colleagues discovered 450 distinct species of trees on a single hectare (in Southern Bahia). This surpassed the previous record of 300 tree species per hectare, recorded in Amazonian Peru in 1986 ("Cientistas descorbrem," 1993).

Nearly all of the remaining areas of Atlantic Forest, particularly those over 1,000 hectares, have been protected either by their rugged terrain or by the fact that they are on low-fertility coastal floodplains isolated from inland cities by mountains and from beachside settlements by rivers and wetlands.

Defining a Study Area

Even given that the present area of Atlantic Forest is drastically reduced from its current extent, the size and scattering of the remaining forest fragments is so broad that any serious discussion of tourism must focus on a subregion. For purposes of analysis, I have chosen to study tourism in a band of forest extending approximately 300 km along the southern Brazilian coastline from Peruibe (State of Sao Paulo) to the northern edge of the state of Santa Catarina (see Figure 6.1) and extending approximately 100 km inland at its greatest extent.

The area contains a major part of the largest remaining area of Atlantic Forest (although it does not include adjoining areas in the northern part of Sao Paulo state and southern Rio de Janeiro). This forest is for the most part a contiguous expanse, particularly along the mangrove-bordered coastline and the mountain ridges. However, the landscape is dotted with clearings for banana plantations and cattle and water buffalo ranches, and bisected on the inland side by BR-116, the major highway that connects Sao Paulo with the cities of the south.

Styles of Tourism

Although the study area lies within a few hours' drive of approximately 25 million people, much of the forest has been little affected by tourism. How is this possible? The answer is simple—Brazil is a "beach culture." Each weekend, and for months during the Christmas to Carnaval summer vacation period, millions of urban Brazilians descend on the narrow littoral zone, which boasts extensive and attractive sandy beaches. Residents of Sao Paulo (18 million) and Curitiba (1.5 million) journey to the coast in buses and automobiles, clogging highways and producing massive crowds at their destinations. Modern highways connect the cities directly to the major beach destinations, passing by viaduct and tunnel the forest-covered mountains that separate the cities, which lie on a plateau at elevations of about 1,000 m from the coast. Large remnants of Atlantic Forest cover these mountains—they are passed by beachgoers, but are not their destination. Moreover, the mountains are so steep and infertile that agriculture has traditionally passed them by.

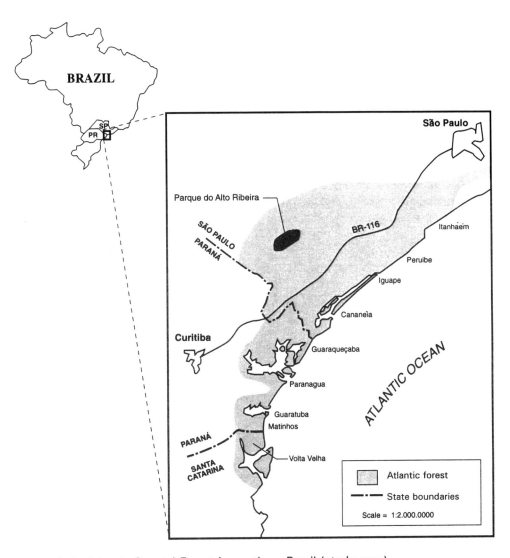

Figure 6.1. Atlantic Coastal Forest in southern Brazil (study area).

In order to serve beach visitors, a string of resort towns has sprung up in the study area, including Peruibe (Sao Paulo state), Matinhos-Caioba (Parana state), and Guaratuba (Parana). Each boasts high-rise condominiums, many hotels, seafood restaurants, clothing and souvenir shops, and video arcades. In each case, and in some smaller towns, public authorities have developed beachside promenades along the most popular areas. There is also a large number of resort towns on the coastline north of Sao Paulo, which lie outside of the study area discussed in this chapter. These towns are subject to most of the problems identified here and are also in some cases adjacent to Atlantic Forest fragments, including state and national protected areas.

During the beach season, the population of the coastal towns swells far beyond the number of permanent residents. In Peruibe, for example, an important destination for Sao Paulo residents, the permanent population (32,959) can reach 300,000 during the height of the season. Guaratuba (17,987), a favorite resort for Curitiba residents, can grow to 500,000.

In order to cater to these visitors, a wide range of accommodations is offered. There are deluxe hotels and guesthouses for the most affluent visitors. Middle-class Brazilians are likely to patronize the many campgrounds, or to rent rooms in the homes of local residents. This latter phenomenon extends to the small villages outside the limits of the resort towns, where farmers may simply open up a pasture and post a sign offering "camping." Local people also operate food and drink stands, which line roads both in populated areas and on dirt tracks that stretch to undeveloped beaches. A popular item is *caldo de cana*, the fresh juice extracted by crushing sugar cane in a hand-cranked press. Stands also sell souvenirs and local agricultural products, such as cheese.

Although the destination for most visitors is the beach, increasing numbers are visiting alternative destinations within the Atlantic Forest. In some cases they visit publicly owned outdoor recreational sites long developed for fairly intensive tourism. In others, tourists pursue extensive recreation—hiking, camping, rock climbing—with little or no control over their use of natural resources.

One example of an intensively visited recreational attraction is the Graciosa Road in the State of Parana. This is an old colonial road, later upgraded to a two-lane paved highway. It winds up and down the mountains between Curitiba and the well-preserved colonial town of Antonina. A highly popular form of recreation is to drive the scenic highway, stop for a picnic or at a roadside waterfall, and hike numerous side-trails, many of them parts of the cobblestone road put down by slaves hundreds of years ago. There is also a train excursion from Curitiba over the forest-covered mountains. The train runs daily during the summer and on weekends throughout the year and is among the attractions most heavily promoted to visitors to Parana. The train stops at several places as it traverses the mountains, allowing hikers access to trails. However, for many tourists, the train excursion is an end in itself and the Atlantic Forest is merely a scenic backdrop.

Another developed site is the Caverna do Diabo (Devil's Cave) in the State of Sao Paulo. The cavern is in the Parque Estadual de Jacupiranga, part of a complex of state parks in the Valley of Alto Ribeira, about 3 hours' drive from Sao Paulo. The Caverna do Diabo is highly developed for tourism, with interior lighting, paved walkways, and a large restaurant. For decades, it was operated by a state-owned railways company (apparently a matter of administrative convenience), but in early 1994 administration was changed to the Sao Paulo Department of State Parks. About 50 km away, another cavern, Caverna de Santana, offers trails, but no interior electric lights. Visitors, who are led through the cave in small groups by guides, wear helmets with an attached carbide torch, an eerie sight in the darkness of the cave.

The developed caverns exist in the context of two other kinds of natural resources. First, the two developed caverns are among literally hundreds of "wild" caves, cut into the limestone topography. Some are regularly visited by caving groups, often using climbing equipment. Others are not fully explored. Second, the caverns exist within much larger areas of protected forest. For example, Caverna de Santana is surrounded by the Parque Estadual Turistico do Alto Ribeira, with an area of over 35,000 hectares. Many trails begin at the cave entrance, leading to other caves, waterfalls, and scenic walks through the exuberant tropical forest (Secretaria do Meio Ambiente, 1991).

Another type of intensively visited recreational site within the Atlantic Forest consists of natural swimming pools in the numerous streams. The most popular of these often feature sliding rocks and waterfalls. In a few cases, there is obvious evidence of overuse of these sites. One popular pool, in the Jureia ecological park, near the coast, is visited by several thousand people on summer weekends. The result is eroded trails, a proliferation of food and souvenir stands, and water pollution.

Most visitors to our Atlantic Forest study area are passive consumers of the landscape—drivers on their way to the beach, sightseers on the Graciosa Road or on the Curitiba-to-coast train. A much smaller number have a particular destination in mind, such as the caverns and swimming holes. However, there are also visitors who spread out through the forest to engage in various activities that one might term "nature-oriented tourism."

One specific subgroup is the rock climbers, who visit a variety of sites in the mountains. They blaze trails to popular climbing sites, and a few of them work as guides for visitors. Another group is sport fishers, who frequent the many estuaries within the Atlantic Forest's littoral zone. There appears to be a great deal of room for expansion of the number of sport fishers, though catches are hampered by overfishing by both commercial trawlers and the large number of artisanal fishermen.

Another group of tourists, whose number augments considerably during the summer, consists of persons who seek undeveloped beaches for swimming or camping. Although part of the littoral zone is highly developed, there are scores of kilometers of sandy beaches accessible only by water, and hence largely deserted. Tourists arrive at these beaches either by private pleasure craft or make arrangements with local fishermen. The most popular destination, Ilha do Mel (Island of Honey), is operated as a state ecological park and is served in the summer months by regular ferry service from the mainland.

These last three groups of tourists—climbers, fishers, and seekers of deserted beaches—have definite destinations in mind, although they do spread across the landscape to a greater degree than do the developed site recreationists. What of the forest itself, already mentioned as a site of incredible biological diversity? To what extent is it frequented by nature-oriented tourists or "ecotourists," a type of tourism growing extremely rapidly in other tropical forest regions throughout the world?

The answer is that there is at present very little of this type of tourism, but that the potential for its development is great. The study area has the potential to draw many more tourists from the nearby states of Sao Paulo, Parana, and Santa Catarina. Together, these states contain 44 million people, and their level of economic development is the highest in Brazil. The vast majority of the residents of these states live in urban agglomerations within a few miles of BR-116, which is the major north–south highway in southern Brazil and which bisects the study area. Numerous roads, some paved, others dirt tracks, lead off BR-116 to mountain and forest areas.

Much of the present ecotourism development is related to state and national parks and reserves. The study area contains seven federally protected areas, with a total extent of 946,000 hectares and 13 state areas, totaling 1,126,000 hectares. They are operated under a bewildering variety of management categories (state park, ecological station, area of touristic interest). In a few cases, the area is clearly demarcated, park guards are in evidence, and there is a reception area for visitors. In others, the boundaries are not marked, and it is unclear how much of the land is publicly owned and how much is private. Over all of these specific management systems is a national Law of the Atlantic Forest, which sets strict federal controls (often ill-enforced) over the clearing of forest and extraction of forest products.

At least a few of the parks and reserves in the study area are actively managed for ecotourism. For example, the state government of Sao Paulo operates the Ecological Station of Jureia-Itatins, stretching along the southern Sao Paulo coast beyond the place where intensive beach development ends. During the season, personnel of the ecological station conduct hikes into the forest and conduct environmental education activities. Similar trips are offered at the Ilha do Cardoso State Park, along the coast to the south. At Ilha do Cardoso, package excursions including hiking and beach visits are sold by Sao Paulo-based tour operators, and simple accommodations and guide service are made available by local fishermen (Diario do Grande ABC, 1994).

A form of ecotourism that is small numerically, but potentially of great importance, is use of the Atlantic Forest by scientists. On Ilha do Cardoso, the state of Sao Paulo operates a research station called the Center for Applied Research on Natural Resources (CEPARNIC). It provides accommodation for 40 scientists or students, laboratories, and an auditorium. There is also a Center for Marine Studies, operated by the Federal University of Parana. Although located at Pontal do Sul, at the edge of the developed part of the Parana beaches, the Center is well-sited to be the jumping off point for research in the Bay of Paranagua, just to the north.

Scientists have several important functions relative to ecotourism. First, they are a form of "pioneer tourist" who blaze trails, explore the area, and provide initial economic benefits for local residents. Second, scientists publish books and papers, both scientific and popular, that attract future ecotourists to a given site. Third, scientists serve as unpaid forest guards, protecting the resources they study from poaching or other damage. Indeed, one might argue that scientists are among the best guards, as most prefer to spend their time in the forest itself, rather than at park headquarters.

In addition to ecotourism that depends on government-protected lands, the study area contains two interesting privately owned natural areas, linked to tourism. Private, tourist-supported tropical forest reserves, which are also found in Costa Rica and Ecuador, among other locations, provide a way of protecting resources without government support or intervention (see Alderman, 1990; Healy, 1988). In the case of the Atlantic Forest, the private reserves are Volta Velha, located in Santa Catarina state, just over the border with Parana and Salto Morato, near Guaraquecaba. (A third private reserve, near Morretes, is operated by the director of Curitiba's Municipal Botanical Museum, Dr. Gerdt Hatschbach. It contains both natural forest and cultivated plants, and is occasionally visited by tourists.)

The Volta Velha reserve originated several years ago, when an accountant from Curitiba purchased 1,000 hectares of pristine Atlantic Forest, with the idea of raising cattle upon his retirement. The accountant's son, a university-trained biologist, persuaded his father that preservation of the forest was both worthwhile and potentially profitable. The land, which remains privately owned, has been voluntarily put under the protection of the Brazilian National Environmental Agency (IBAMA), and has since 1992 been operated as a site for biological study and for ecotourism. Facilities capable of housing a dozen researchers have been constructed on the site, and trails and sample plots have been laid out.

The family has also constructed a small hotel (attractive cottages and a restaurant) along the coastline, about 20 miles from the nature reserve. The hotel is promoted as a site for "ecotourism and leisure." Guests can enjoy water sports, a swimming pool, and visits to the historic town of Sao Francisco do Sul, as well as the possibility of visiting the nature reserve. The owners have hosted groups of students from Antioch College (USA), who stay in the hotel facility while pursuing environmental studies in the reserve.

Salto Morato is a major waterfall in the Guaraquecaba region of Parana. Although nominally protected by law, the area between the main access road and the falls was operated as a cattle ranch, with visible clearing of land and no facilities for visitors who wished to see the falls. In 1993, the Boticario Foundation, a Curitiba-based nonprofit that is supported by a successful toiletries firm, purchased the 1,716-hectare ranch as a Private Natural Heritage Reserve. Trails have been constructed, access is clearly marked, and a visitor center with exhibits on the Atlantic Forest has been opened. Initial scientific studies by the sponsoring organization indicate that the area protects 45% of the state of Parana's avian species, 48% of mammals, and 20% of the reptiles (Fundacao O Boticario, 1996).

Private reserves in Brazil are being encouraged by a new federal program for Private Natural Heritage Reserves, which offers owners exemption from the rural land tax, priority for credit from state finance institutions, and technical and management advisory support (Instituto Brasiliero para Meio Ambiente e Recursos Naturais [IBAMA], 1996)

Problems of Biodiversity Protection in the Atlantic Forest

The forest and coastal resources on which present tourism depends and on which the future development of ecotourism must rely are under a number of serious and immediate threats. Tourism itself threatens the resources (see below) but its impact is minor compared to other influences.

Perhaps the most important threat to the Atlantic Forest, both in the study area and elsewhere, is the large amount of land being deforested by private owners for agricultural pursuits. For example, in the Guaraquecaba region of Parana, which is designated as a federal area of environment protection, large tracts of lowland forest have been cleared for grazing water buffalo, an Asian animal recently introduced into southern Brazil. In Sao Paulo, other areas of protected Atlantic Forest have recently been cleared for banana plantations. Even when land is not cleared, a great deal of extraction of forest products, such as wood, palm heart, and wildlife, is taking place. This degrades the inherent quality and diversity of the forest, even though overall forest cover remains.

Another threat to the forest is real estate speculation. On the island of Superagui, which contains the 20-km Praia Deserta (Deserted Beach) and which is accessible only by water, it is said that real estate agents have laid out several hundred thousand lots, presumably for sale to affluent urbanites.

The Law of the Atlantic Forest, a series of federal decrees meant to protect the forest, has proven to be quite problematic for the "caicaras," local people who live within the forest and draw their livelihood from forest and marine resources. There are an estimated 6,000 caicaras in the Guaraquecaba area of Parana—and perhaps two or three times that number in the study area as a whole. These people are in general of Portuguese and other European descent, though some are Tupi-Guarani Indians and others are of mixed ancestry. Isolated and generally poor, they are essentially country people who have evolved distinctive methods of fishing, canoe making, food preparation, and even a characteristic dance, the fandango (for information on caicara culture, see Alvar & Alvar, 1979; Roderjan, 1981). By creating uncertainty and encouraging illegal activity, the Law of the Atlantic Forest has actually tended to delay the vital task of finding ways in which local people can coexist sustainably with their world-class forest resources.

The dependence of the caicaras on the forest is indicated by the following quote from Roderjan (1981): "The [native] of the coast makes [for himself] all implements necessary to his survival, retaining elements of his own environment" (p. 49).

These include the dugout canoes used for fishing, the simple wooden machines employed to process manioc into flour, and even the homemade musical instruments used in the fandango. Other locally made products include artisanal foodstuffs, particularly manioc flour (farinha), cacacha (a fiery drink distilled from sugar cane), and heart of palm (palmito). For those living immediately adjacent to the coast, or along rivers, the most important economic product is seafood, including both fish and shrimp.

The livelihood of the caicaras depends on the forest in several ways. First, the forest supplies raw materials for various articles of production. Hearts of palm are gathered by cutting the living trees, generally at about age 7–10 years. Cupiuva (*Tapirira guianensis*) and caroba (*Jacaranda puberula*) are among the woods used for making dugout canoes. Caxeta (*Tabebuia cassinoides*) is a light, easily carved wood used for making a variety of household articles and artistic carvings, as well as musical instruments. Vines and bamboos are also collected from the forest for use in basketmaking.

Second, the forest provides the land used for small-scale crop cultivation. Soils are sufficiently fertile in some parts of the lowlands so that true swidden (shifting) agriculture need not be practiced, and most farming takes place near residents' houses. Nevertheless, any expansion of area under cultivation comes from clearing nearby forests.

Third, the montane forest protects the quality of water entering the estuaries, whereas the coastal mangroves provide a nursery area for fish and shrimp. These marine products provide the livelihood for substantial numbers—probably the majority—of the rural people living in the study area.

Attempts by the Brazilian government to protect the Atlantic Forest have had the unfortunate tendency to make traditional extractive activities illegal, while failing to provide the caicaras with an alternative source of livelihood. As a result, a great deal of furtive and illicit extraction continues.

Relating Tourism to Environmental Protection

Tourism occupies an ambiguous position with regard to the Atlantic Forest. On one hand, it is a contributor, albeit localized, to the forest's degradation. On the other hand, controlled ecotourism promises to provide an economic rationale for forest protection. These benefits can give landowners and the government an incentive to keep primary forest intact, and can, if carefully distributed, offer local caicaras compensation for loss of the ability to freely extract forest products.

Reducing Negative Environmental Impacts of Tourism

Tourism offers a number of potential threats to the environment, many of which are now being felt in the Atlantic Forest. One problem is the aesthetic blight associated with facilities in developed beach resorts that are either ill designed or simply out of scale with the surrounding community. For example, the small beach town of Peruibe, in Sao Paulo state, which consists mainly of one- to two-story homes and shops and which borders an important nature reserve, is dominated by a 16-story condominium complex. This development could easily have been made more attractive by reducing its height and bulk. Yet there are minimal, if any, zoning controls governing coastal development. One interesting policy, put in place in parts of Santa Catarina state, requires that future high-rise developments rise in tiers away from the beach, with those in the row closest to the beach being only two stories in height, the second row four stories, then eight, etc. (Doris

Ruschmann, personal interview, 1994). This allows the construction of high-density tourist facilities, but in a more attractive pattern, and with less chance of casting shadows on the beach.

water

Another problem is the lack of urban infrastructure in many, if not most, of the region's tourist resorts. The most obvious problem is lack of sanitary sewer systems, leading to water pollution. Tourist facilities contribute to this pollution, and the resulting pollution becomes a problem for tourists. The extent of this problem can be gauged by the following observation: on a single summer day (February 17, 1994, just following the Carnaval peak of beach visitation) the quality of water at popular beaches throughout Sao Paulo state was measured by the state environmental agency. Of 81 beaches sampled, 47 had "inadequate" water quality; only 23 were rated "excellent" (Folha de Sao Paulo, 1994).

Real estate development along the coast is related to tourism in that most of the lots and dwellings are marketed as second homes. Such development causes demand for new road access to previously remote areas, and can present the problems of visual degradation and lack of infrastructure that are associated with mass tourism. Speculative lot subdivisions are particularly insidious, as they commit land to future conversion and deforestation, yet can occur in large number with no immediate physical effect, and hence do not engender the public outrage. Ilha Comprida, for example, has been extensively subdivided, but there is little actual development there.

The opening of new roads to and along the coast during the last two decades has been extremely important to the development of tourism and to land speculation. A proposed major highway linking Sao Paulo with Curitiba (BR 101) would cut through Jureia Ecological Station and cross the Parana border through the Parque Estadual do Jacupiranga. This would make it much easier to get to currently remote parts of the shoreline and would make it possible to develop thousands of already subdivided lots in such now pristine locations as Ilha Comprida. A proposed bridge connecting Ilha Comprida to the mainland near Iguape would have a similar effect—and is being supported by the municipality and by land dealers (Harry Bollmann, personal communication, 1994).

Tourism as a Contributor to Sustainable Regional Development

Among the most difficult problems in ecotourism is finding ways for its benefits to reach local people (Brandon, 1993). Healy (1994) offers a typology of three general ways in which local benefits can be generated: (1) fees can be collected from tourists, which are directly distributed to local people or used to support development projects; (2) local people can provide services to tourists, including guide service, transportation, food, and housing; (3) local people can sell handicrafts, foodstuffs, and other tangible goods (tourist merchandise) to visitors.

Each of the above alternatives might be considered in the study region. With regard to fees, virtually none of the protected areas collect entrance fees from visitors. An exception is the developed caves in Sao Paulo state parks, Caverna do Diabo and Caverna de Santana, where a modest fee is levied. In Brazil, parks are typically supported from state and national budgets, rather than being self-financing. On the other hand, there is some precedent for looking at parks as sources of economic development. In Sao Paulo state, the Parque Estadual Turistico do Alto Ribeira (PETAR) is not only the largest employer in its region, but also has a new revenue sharing plan, in which 30% of entrance fees to the caverns will go to local government and 70% will remain in the park. The new revenue sharing would increase the main municipality's revenue by 316 times (Clayton Lino, personal communication, 1994). In another Sao Paulo park, Jureia, a park-sponsored economic development project is helping seven caicara families, living deep within the protected zone, to manufacture banana candy, which is then packed in 5-kg containers and sold in Sao Paulo.

With regard to tourist services, local participation varies greatly from place to place. Towns such as Guaraquecaba, Iporanga, Cananeia, Peruibe, and Paranagua all provide food, lodging, and transportation for tourists who then venture within protected zones. Small communities within the parks, such as Ilha do Mel and Superagui, offer simple food and lodging to visitors, sometimes in private homes. There appears to be unexploited potential for sport fishing, which would be an excellent complementary activity for the hundreds of artisanal fishermen who work in the waters of the region.

The third option, sale of tourist merchandise, also offers possibilities. Unfortunately, under the current Law of the Atlantic Forest, most products are extracted illegally. Research is now being performed to determine how such products as heart of palm and caxeta can be harvested sustainably, with an eye to developing systems of use that the government might legalize (for heart of palm, see Orlande, Laarman, & Mortimer, 1994). An interesting possibility for adding value to local products is a labeling system for artisanal foodstuffs implemented by a state agricultural extension agency in Parana called EMATER. The agency extends technical assistance to producers of various foodstuffs, then provides labels that offer consumers some assurance that proper sanitation procedures have been followed. There is a significant opportunity for using the existing EMATER labeling system to guarantee the sustainability of consumer products extracted from the forest. Properly implemented, such a system could make products more valuable to tourists, both in direct producer-to-tourist marketing and in weekend and holiday markets held in coastal tourist towns.

Conclusion

Brazil's Atlantic Forest is one of the world's most threatened ecosystems, important both because of its high degree of biodiversity and the fact that more than 90% of its original area has been removed. A large remnant section of this ecoystem, totaling over 1 million hectares, and with contiguous extent of over 500,000 hectares, still exists in the southern states of Sao Paulo, Parana, and Santa Catarina. Protected by steep mountains and poor road access, this remnant forest has remained remarkably intact, despite its proximity to large urban centers and to a flourishing beach-oriented tourist industry.

Most of the remnant forest has been "protected" by inclusion in a complex system of national parks and reserves. However, these areas contain a large amount of private land, and are subject to considerable pressure for logging and conversion to agriculture or grazing. There is also a threat of real estate development along the extensive coastal sections. Although some parks, such as the state parks of Sao Paulo, are well bounded and well protected, others exist only on paper. The national government has attempted to protect the entire forest with a sweeping set of decrees called the Law of the Atlantic Forest. However, the primary result of this policy has been to threaten the livelihood of several thousand caicaras living in traditional communities dependent on the forest and adjacent waters.

The Atlantic Forest is just beginning to be affected by a growing domestic and international demand for nature-oriented tourism, which includes hiking, rock climbing, camping, caving, amateur nature study, and professional and educational research. Thus far, such tourism has been confined to a small number of sites. Careful expansion of this type of tourism holds promise of providing resources for improved park management, as well as opportunities for the caicaras to use forest resources legally and in more sustainable ways.

Acknowledgments

This research was supported by the U.S. Forest Service, Forestry Private Enterprise Initiative. I deeply appreciate the hospitality and information provided by scores of Brazilian colleagues, including park and reserve managers, university faculty at the Federal University of Parana, the Pontifical Catholic University of Parana, and the University of Sao Paulo, and the comments of Harry Bollmann, John Pye, and Erin Sills.

Chapter 7

Working for a Successful Ecotourism Story: The Case of Punta Sal National Park

Ray E. Ashton, Jr.

Introduction

Sustainable tourism, if it is to succeed, must be a profitable business. This requires capital and investment in such things as advertising, booking systems, program development, and insurance (Ziffer, 1989). Successful travel programs also require minimum volumes of tourists to be economically feasible. Because of these requirements, very few indigenous people are able to operate tourism programs simply because they do not have the capital or minimum volume of tourists to be profitable. This indeed, is considered to be the "great broken promise" of ecotourism (Ashton & Ashton, 1993).

The first step to overcoming obstacles to successful tourism is to consider all tourism as potential ecotourism. If the proper infrastructure is put in place to develop the appropriate carrying capacity, a relatively large volume of tourists can visit a protected area (Ashton, 1991). If planned and managed properly, communities willing to enter into the business can receive economic reward for their efforts. Not surprisingly, many areas near ecotourism sites have already reached a stage of mass tourism. Tourism programs in Costa Rica and Belize have demonstrated that ecotourism develops into mass tourism within a period of 15 years (Ashton & Ashton, 1993). The key to making it a success lies in examining the impacts of tourism developments on protected areas and the community in order to ward off undesirable consequences on the resources for which conservation is sought. It is, therefore, important that the workers in the field of ecotourism should not ignore, but work carefully with, the community representatives and protected area administrators to develop tourism plans. Such an approach affords promise of a sustainable ecotourism.

This chapter discusses the Tela Ecotourism Project and is designed to demonstrate the methods of incorporating all forms of tourism into ecotourism. In particular, it will illustrate the efforts required to prepare the local communities for the possibility of mass tourism, and outline actions required to ensure the "enfranchisement" of local people in all levels of policy making and management of protected areas and to provide political free will of local communities from government agencies to redevelop protected areas and handle financial management. The Tela project attempts to address key ecotourism issues including raising funds from tourism and reinvesting of those funds into protected areas in lieu of the national general fund (Lindberg, 1991). This presentation is not a case study showing a successful project. Instead, it is a case study designed to demonstrate an attempt to develop, in one project, all the criteria that define ecotourism.

Punta Sal National Park

For 2 years, the author with his team, was associated with a project known as The Tela Ecotourism Project, sponsored by the Institute of Honduran Tourism. This project was funded, in part, by the UNDP and a debt swap program of the International Development Bank between Mexico and Honduras. Tela lies on the north shore of Honduras, and is one of the major Caribbean ports. To the west of Tela is the newest protected area in the country, Punta Sal National Park (PSNP) (see Figure 7.1). This park is comprised of more than 100,000 square hectares of lowland rainforests, fresh- and saltwater lagoons, and a great diversity of tropical ecological communities. Scattered in the park's buffer zone are 16 communities including Rio Tinto, Miami Beach, and Tomabe. All together, there are approximately 13,000 people living inside the park. Some of these people have lived there for generations whereas others migrated in as soon as it was learned that the area was being considered for protected status. Most of the migrants hoped that the government would have to pay them for the land they moved to and cleared.

The Task

It was our job as the project's ecotourism consultant, in part, to do the following:

- Establish the Protected Area Policy for PSNP and protect its biodiversity.
- Establish a policy of home rule for the protected area.
- Develop a way in which tourism would pay for the protection of the park.
- Develop a system where local communities and their citizens would benefit from tourism development.
- Develop a management plan for PSNP and tourism to ensure sustainability.

Method Approach

Method approach to accomplish this task included collection of ground data, reviews of existing laws and regulations, interviews, and organization of workshops.

A number of researchers (Baez & Ashton, 1992; Drake, 1991) who have studied tourism impacts on local cultures clearly point out that a major problem in devel-

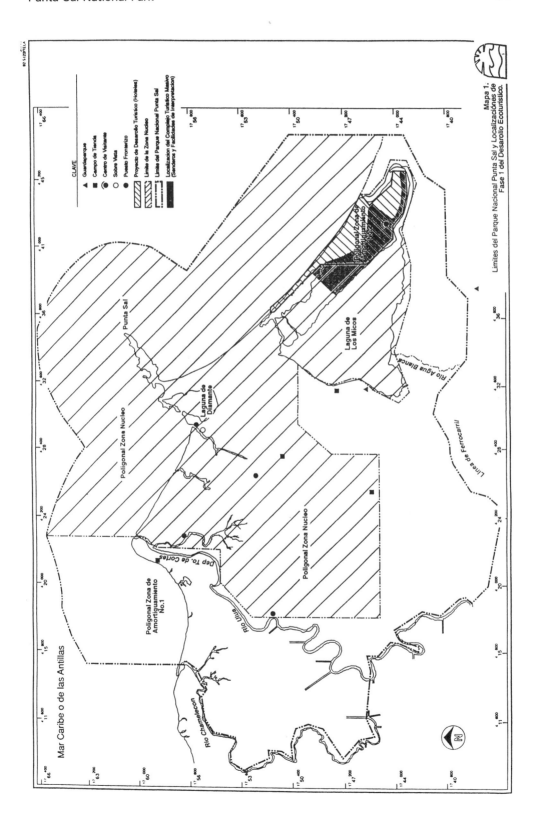

Mapa 1.
Límites del Parque Nacional Punta Sal y Localizaciónes de Fase 1 del Desarollo Ecoturístico.

oping a functional relationship with a community is identifying the key individuals within the community (Patronatos). To overcome this potential obstacle, one researcher was deputed to stay in the Tela region amidst the PSNP communities to learn about them and also to identify important community members who could be involved in the program. This informal observation of the people helped in ascertaining who they were and how they perceived the project. In this process a lot of valuable information was gathered.

A review of Honduran law was undertaken both at the Yale University Library and in meetings with government lawyers in Tegucigalpa. The focus of the research was on protected area laws and regulations as they pertain to people and communities living within protected areas. Laws relating to land ownership rights were also reviewed. The purpose was to recommend regulations in keeping with the current laws such that the newly proposed regulations would be recognizable with the preestablished norms and traditions.

A questionnaire, containing a brief on the project, was also developed and distributed randomly to the members of each community. It was managed by the patriarch of each community. Approximately 90% of the questionnaires were returned.

Individuals Interviewed

Based on the information collected during the 2-month effort and information provided by Tatiana de Pierson, meetings were held with key individuals from the buffer zone communities, the municipality of Tela, business leaders, established tourism businessmen, and other community leaders. The meetings were informal and were designed to facilitate sharing of information concerning the development of PSNP, the ecotourism project, and the potential impact of these changes. The goal was to learn about expectations, anticipated needs, and problems that may develop later on. Another goal was to learn more about current conditions. From these meetings, a series of recommendations emerged that would form the basis for the PSNP management plan and park regulations.

Interviews were held with the head of the Honduran Corporation for Forest Development, Corporation Hondurena de Desarrollo Forestal (COHDEFOR) protected areas, Ciro Ahmed Navarro, Wildlife, Gloria Zelaya, members of FONATUR, Martha Garate, Arturo Saavedra, Juan Noriega, Jesus Palma Gutierrez, and Moises Flores Ventura, the Mexican group developing the site plan for the tourism project, the chief ecologist in charge of the biological survey, Carlos D. Cerrato, and the director of the Honduran Institute of Tourism (IHT—Instituto Hondureno de Turismo), Maria Antionetta de Bogran. These meetings were held to summarize the problems, needs, and criteria for acceptable recommendations for park management and regulations.

The project sociologists organized an all-day workshop for the community leaders to determine basic community needs such as education, water supplies, health services, and others. Also, during this process, the reasons why these needs have remained unmet were discussed. The ecotourism staff attended the meetings and recorded responses.

The ecotourism project staff held a meeting with the Advisory Committee of PROLANSATE, the regional conservation organization responsible for managing PSNP for the past year. The advisory committee constituted various COHDEFOR regional staff, Executive Director, President, and Peace Corps Advisor of PROLANSATE, business leaders, and military and community leaders. During this meeting, a list of regulatory areas, requiring recommendations, were discussed and the committee's recommendations were noted.

A similar workshop of community leaders was organized from the buffer zone, Tela municipality, and representatives of key groups as identified by the ecotourism project staff. During the full-day workshop, key issues were discussed and recommendations were put forth by the group. These issues are briefly outlined.

Key Issues

The key issues identified as those requiring consideration for the PSNP include: hunting, fishing, land tenure, land use, deforestation, pollution, watershed management, population growth, and political support.

The community leaders and the PROLANSATE advisory committee discussed the primary issues, with the recommendations made to our team summarized below.

Hunting

A. Nuclear zone: total prohibition of all hunting in the PSNP nuclear zone.
B. Buffer zone:
    1. Divide the buffer zone into two areas:
        a. *Intensive use zone:* where there is heavy farming and where large numbers of people live.
        b. *Restricted zone:* this is between the nuclear zone and lands that the government owns or lands where no clear ownership of land exists.
    2. Determine "untouchable" zones, giving technical assistance to protect these areas and increase wildlife.
    3. Permit hunting in specific zones—subsistence hunting or only hunting for food.
    4. Prohibit all commercial hunting in the buffer zone.
    5. Respect the prohibition of hunting for protected species.
    6. Permit only hunting by residents of the buffer zone by issuing permits.
    7. Establish hunting seasons to ensure that the numbers of hunted species are sustained.
    8. Establish programs for farming or ranching oriented to reproduction and domestic consumption (iguanas, guaturas, etc.) and to restock wild populations in the buffer zone.
    9. Regulate types of arms permitted in the buffer zone.

Fishing

Recommendations were made for controls on fishing:

1. Eliminate the use of nets that have mesh less that 3 inches in diameter.
2. Eliminate the use of trawling nets and all commercial fishing within 3 miles from the shore of PSNP.
3. Allow sport fishing only with the catch and release system.
4. Prohibit all spear fishing because this was not a traditional method of fishing by residents.
5. Regulate and limit diving for fishing (lobster) purposes in marine zone to specific areas and local residents.
6. Establish a moratorium on all commercial fishing or the take or harassment of endangered and threatened species and all marine mammals in the park.
7. Establish use zones in marine environment of PSNP to protect reefs and bird rookeries.
8. Establish fishing seasons and increase surveillance during these periods.
9. Establish an authorized and resident identification system and use of permits for fishermen in the park.

Land Tenure

A. Nuclear zone:
    1. Eliminate human habitation in the nuclear zone, or reduce it to subsistence level in very limited special areas.
    2. Identify land owners who have title; establish a census.
    3. Establish a plan to remove all nontitle holders from all zones within the park within 5 years. People who recently moved into the park, within the past 2 years, should be moved immediately. Others should have 3–5 years to move or be relocated.
B. Buffer zone:
    1. Implement census to define the present population and proper ownership of all land in the buffer zone.
    2. Allow agricultural and cattle activity on private property. No overgrazing or expansion of farms will be permitted.
    3. Those without legal ownership will have to be moved as those within the nuclear zone.
    4. Technical assistance and education should be provided to stabilize agricultural and grazing activities to sustainable level and to protect water supplies and the land.

Land Use

Recommendation were given for the following uses:
A. Agriculture
    1. No agriculture of any type should be allowed in the nuclear zone.
    2. Confine domestic animals to the buffer zone and report any incident involving endangered wildlife species in order to avoid the elimination of these species (jaguars, crocodiles, etc.). No one is permitted to shoot jaguars.

3. Provide technology and economic support (to campesinos) in order to improve conditions and to develop sustainable farming practices.

B. Grazing
   1. No grazing in the nuclear zone or off private property.
   2. Provide technical assistance for developing better pasture to eliminate clearing of additional forests.

C. Forestry Exploitation
   1. Develop a sustainable forestry plan for the buffer zone.
   2. Develop tree farms and encourage land owners to plant fast-growing native species.

D. Tourism
   1. Develop specific regulations for the establishment and operations of tourism in all areas of the park.
   2. Communities should have a right to choose whether or not to be involved in tourism and should have some say in how tourism affects life in the park.

E. General recommendations
   1. Specific additional regulations will be required for fishing, pisciculture, species reproduction use, and prohibiting introduction of exotic species.
   2. Private land cannot be subdivided, broken up among family members, or sold.

Deforestation

A. Nuclear zone:
   1. No deforestation should be permitted in this area.

B. Buffer zone:
   1. Develop forestry activities in a sustainable way. Get technical assistance to plant native trees where farming should not be taking place.
   2. Establish a 200-m legal buffer zone (between nuclear and buffer zones); reforest the area along the Laguna de los Micos.
   3. Study the housing situation on the Laguna de los Micos shore. Replant with fruit trees, and work around community there.
   4. There should be enough funding from ecotourism to pay for enforcement, training, and other programs in the buffer zone.

Pollution

1. Prohibition of any nutrient discharge in the Laguna de los Micos.
2. Recommend systems of recycling and treatment for sewage in all local communities.
3. Establish mechanism for disposal of solid waste. Tourism complex should pay for its waste disposal.
4. Develop a contingency plan for oil spills in the Bay of Tela. Work with military authorities who have expertise in these manners.

Watershed Management

1. Establish a cooperative mechanism with governmental institutions to stop pollution and siltation into the watersheds that drain into the Laguna de los Micos.
2. Recommend construction of oxidation lagoons for oil palm factory and plantation wastes that drain into the park.
3. Keep a 100-m forestry conservation zone along the watersheds and do not permit grazing in or around streams.
4. Supervise the ecotourism facilities proposed for construction in the buffer zone of the PSNP to ensure that any type of waste is not drained into the watersheds or lagoon.

Population Growth

1. Make a human management plan for the PSNP's buffer zone.
2. Relocate or evict those persons with no legal rights to land in the park property. Provide ample time for relocation.
3. Private property in the buffer zone cannot be subdivided, neither can new deeds be written. This is to help curtail population growth in the zone.

Political Support

1. It is necessary to define the management structure that will provide resources for the park's protection.
2. It is recommended the COHDEFOR sign an agreement assigning responsibility to a local authority for the management of park resources.
3. It is necessary to develop an action plan at the governmental level to implement a "rejuvenation" system for the Laguna de los Micos.

These results of the meetings were used to develop the recommendations on regulations and management plans for PSNP. These recommendations and conversations with key individuals also led to the proposed development of PSNP Authority and Trust.

Results

Following all the input from the various meetings, workshops, and discussions, the ecotourism team discussed various aspects as to how regulations should be developed. The two most important elements addressed in this chapter are development of a management team and a trust to control and maintain the park's finances outside of the government budgeting processes.

The first element is the formation and functioning of a park authority that would be acceptable to the national government, and that allows local communities, conservation organizations, private tourism organizations, COHDEFOR, and the IHT to manage the PSNP. This element must also provide both a financial plan permitting adequate income generation from visitation, and the authority to use the income for the park instead of government use through the general fund or the COHDEFOR general budget. The precedent has already been established in Honduras for the management of protected areas by recognized Non-Governmental Organizations (NGOs). The development of a proposed PSNP Management Plan and Park Regulations was developed as well. The regulations set forth in the proposal were based on recommendations of various stakeholders.

Punta Sal National Park Authority (PSNPA)

Several alternatives were considered for the development of an NGO that would be responsible for the management of PSNP. The first was to turn this responsibility over to the regional conservation NGO—PROLANSATE. This organization has carried out this role along with IHT. After careful review of the organization, organizational health, and recommendations of the various stakeholders, it was decided that this organization could play a more important role as an advocate for conservation issues as a member of a governing board, and to carry on as an advocate for conservation in other conservation issues.

The other alternatives were similar in nature and focused on developing a corporate style of management for PSNP. Ultimately, a two-level authority organization was recommended—a board of directors that would form the Punta Sal National Park Authority, and the second level comprised of individuals sitting over the Authority called the PSNP Trust. The PSNP Trust was made responsible for fiscal operations of the park. It was designed from the development of the National Ecotourism Council established under the Paseo Pantera Program and a similar structure developed in Costa Rica under the same program.

The primary goal was to allow local communities, along with the primary central government authorities, to operate the park and its budget and control development within the buffer zone.

Structure

There are two levels of Authority membership: voting members and associate members. Voting members are those representing the 16 communities within the buffer zone, Tela municipality, two members of the tourism private sector, the president of PROLANSATE, COHDEFOR protected areas director, IHT director, and the directors of PSNP and Lancetilla Botanical Gardens (Figure 7.2). The Associate members are made up of people who represent other groups that may wish to participate in or are involved in various aspects of park operations. The actual makeup will be determined by a steering committee, which will be organized in the very near future.

Role of the Authority

Once approved by COHDEFOR and IHT, the PSNP will be responsible for the conservation on Punta Sal National Park. Through a set of bylaws, the Authority will govern the park by establishing policies and regulations and reviewing impact assessments of uses or changes in use within the park. The Authority will have a

Table 1
Autoridad del Parque Nacional Punta Sal

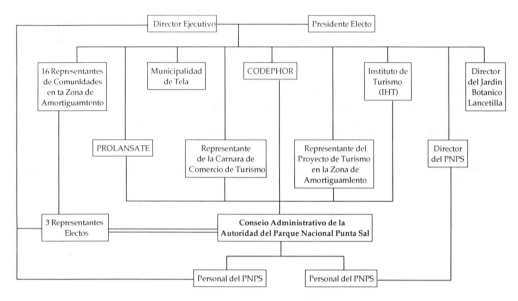

Figure 7.2. Structure of Punta Sal National Park Authority.

staff including an executive director responsible for carrying out the Authority's responsibilities. COHDEFOR and the IHT will have representatives on the Authority. The Authority will also be involved in the hiring of the park director and other professional positions.

A major function of the Authority is to provide input and communication among the 13 communities surrounding the park, the park staff, and the central government. As requested, the local communities wished to have a role in the decision-making process that could directly affect them. The council allows involvement of the other key stakeholder groups including tourism, local municipalities, and PROLANSATE, who represents regional conservation interest.

The Authority will be responsible for acting as an advocate for the protection of PSNP. This includes addressing outside issues that may negatively affect the park. Currently there are many such problems that affect both wildlife and buffer zone communities. These include siltation and pesticide contamination from large farms located upstream, legally permitted deforestation in watershed areas, and artificial drainage systems into the park. The Authority will coordinate efforts to address these issues, contacting the appropriate regional and national government agencies.

PSNP Trust

The PSNP Trust is essentially the board of directors of the PSNPA. The Trust is designed to provide a balanced representation of the Authority at a functional size to routinely handle the park's financial matters. Its ultimate authority will be determined by the Authority steering committee. The primary function of the Trust is to handle the fiscal responsibilities of PSNP. It must, by current COHDEFOR regulations, develop an annual budget for COHDEFOR's approval.

Budget Control

The Trust will be responsible for setting and collecting park fees. Because PSNP is designed to operate on funds generated solely by tourism fees, the Trust must develop a budget that adequately develops and maintains the infrastructure and facilities necessary for both tourism services and protection and preservation of park resources.

The first step in developing the required tourism facilities is to determine the investment requirements for people investing in the new tourism complex located in the north buffer zone. The feasibility studies for this area indicated that good facilities, which allow easy access to the park, are paramount for successful marketing of the area. Based on this information, investors should also develop the required trails, outposts, observation points, and other facilities needed for the park. Additional funds for this project can be borrowed against expected revenues from entrance and user fees to be generated from a particular hotel or operator.

One of the major problems with tourism support for protected areas is that the fee structures are set well below budgetary requirements of the areas. The Authority will have the responsibility of establishing a balanced budget that includes entrance fee amounts, user fee amounts, operator taxes, wildlife farming or ranching fee amounts, and other sources of income. Fees will be tiered based on park use because it may be unconstitutional to set fees based on whether an individual is local, regional, or foreign.

One of the PSNP Trust's goals is to develop excess funds that will go into a revolving fund in COHDEFOR to help with budgetary shortfalls in other parks. Based on current and projected tourism figures into the area (as high as 400,000), this should not be difficult.

Park Staff

The Trust will be responsible for hiring the park's professional-level staff. These positions include the director and two assistant directors, one for business and the other for park ecology. Moving the responsibility of hiring park staff from COHDEFOR to the Trust should accomplish two goals. First, the Trust can attempt to hire the most qualified people for the positions. Tourist-generated park fees will accommodate higher salaries that usual, enhancing hiring opportunities. Second, the Trust is in a position to establish a system for hiring and training local people for advancement within the park staff.

Community Support

The proposed park regulations call for the PSNP Authority to fund projects in the buffer zone communities that will enhance the conservation of the park. These projects include sewage treatment, siltation control, and education, among others.

The application for and approval of these projects will go through the Authority and will be funded by the Trust, based on available funds. Also, projects relating to providing tourism services or to developing wildlife ranching or farming programs for local needs or restocking may be financed.

Conclusion

Punta Sal National Park is the first attempt in Central America to establish tourism as the base for developing a totally integrated method of supporting conservation through park financing and local community support and self-rule. What makes this possible is the recognition by the project of the needs and uses of the park by all forms of tourism, from wildlife viewing to cruise ship passengers, to the extent of 85,000 local visitors. Without this consideration, PSNP would not have the appropriate infrastructure to protect if from the expected use (carrying capacity). PSNP's 1994 operating budget is not adequate to pay for gasoline for the parks patrol boat, let alone staff and construction of even the most basic tourism facilities. The current park staff is not qualified or trained in wildlife conservation, park management, or tourism. Without adequate funding, from various fees, PSNP would erode from overuse as tourism grows in the region.

The development of the Authority provides the means for a dialogue between the park and the communities affected by both the park development and the influx of tourism development in the area. Unlike some park authorities, which are run by conservation NGOs, this one is developed to provide a balance in input and management. Because the well-being of the park is paramount to that of the surrounding communities, conservation takes on a different meaning than that of a conservation group.

Problems are expected to occur. The development of the Authority will require carefully planned and carried out interim agreements between COHDEFOR, IHT, and local interests. Already, PROLANSATE expressed displeasure on not being recommended to control the park and the Authority. There is a need for careful direction and guidance in the development of the Steering Committee during implementation of the Authority. Our surveys indicated that local communities do not grasp the potential impacts of increased tourism. This scenario requires carefully planned community education programs to avoid poorly planned schemes to get into the tourism marketplace. Such efforts are already underway.

Over the long term, the Authority will have to make many park management decisions requiring experts in ecology and tropical biology. A system must be established to provide funding for consultations with biologists when such issues arise. Appointing an ecologist director position with an ecologist assistant director is one of the Authority's goals.

Finally, the major problem will lie with the PSNP Trust and the means by which it maintains the fiscal well-being of the park. Not only does success lie in its decisions, but in the Trust's ability to handle COHDEFOR's budget approval authority as well. PSNP's potential income is quite large compared to other protected areas and the budget of this agency. There will be a desire by COHDEFOR to siphon off money from PSNP before its budgetary needs are met. An understanding by both COHDEFOR and the PSNP Trust is necessary to ensure that the facilities and services required to protect the park, and the provision of tourism services to maintain high-income levels, are provided and maintained.

Finally, the development of such a plan, just like other attempts at developing sustainable development, relies on methods and plans created by one culture that are used and implemented by another. This particular attempt at achieving sustainable development provides considerable opportunities for local people to develop and operate the protected areas in their community. However, the structure still is based on a corporate and government structure different than what has ever been operated in this region. Decisions made over the next 3 years will be critical to the success of this experiment and will, hopefully, be worthy of future evaluation as a model for other protected areas.

Acknowledgments

The author gratefully acknowledges valuable field research assistance provided by Kelly Heaton and Lorna Solis of Water and Air Research Inc., Gainseville, FL.

Chapter 8

Rural Ecotourism as a Conservation Tool

Robert H. Horwich and Jonathan Lyon

Introduction

Ecotourism has become the battle flag for organizations and individuals working to preserve environments and peoples from the inevitable waves of mass tourism and its associated pressures. Unfortunately, definitions of ecotourism are often so vague (Alderman, 1990) and academic that the goal of helping to protect natural areas through tourism is rarely achieved at the local and ground level. Benefits from ecotourism rarely connect directly with the local people, communities, and environments that the goals of ecotourism dictate. Indeed, there is often a tendency for reserves to accentuate an economic disparity between the reserve and local communities, often with the consequent losses of uses of the natural resources to the community (Western & Henry, 1979 in Alderman, 1990). Often local participation and control is only a peripheral component of the ecotourism (no local guides, insensitivity to cultural traditions, etc.).

Many definitions of ecotourism are satisfying if there are no adverse effects on the natural resources (Alderman, 1990). It is our contention that the long-term viability and successful integration of ecotourism projects should be gauged by assessing the extent to which ecotourism efforts actually enhance the environmental or cultural atmosphere that is the focus of ecotourism programs. Ecotourism must be responsive to changing cultural, economic, environmental, and social conditions. Ecotourism must also respond to local, regional, and foreign pressures on the resource. Flexibility and responsiveness to local peoples and changing environmental conditions must be an essential component of any program hoping and striving for sustainability.

Despite our use of ecotourism for both conservation and community development, it is a tool that has a number of defects (Horwich, Murray, Saqui, Lyon, & Godfrey, 1993) and any tourism program must be monitored continually so that it does not destroy the natural resources it seeks to preserve (Alderman, 1990; de Groot, 1983). However, it can be a mechanism used to provide a secondary supplemental income to rural farmers, which can allow them to stay on the land (Moulin, 1980).

In this chapter we describe five projects touting ecotourism goals that are rooted in different environments and cultures (Figure 8.1). Furthermore, the five projects have very different land ownership regimes: purely private lands, purely public lands, and a mix of private–public lands, as well as different blends of community and government liaisons. We describe how ecotourism programs developed for the five projects use ecotourism as a method to help ensure conservation of the various resources. We stress the need to match ecotourism potential with day-to-day operations and to consistently strive to empower local peoples through all social, cultural, economic, organizational, and governmental avenues possible.

The Community Baboon Sanctuary, established in 1985, was one of the first experiments in community-based conservation. The project, now managed by a local committee, has engendered local pride and empowerment and, through example and publicity, has stimulated many communities to begin their own ecotourism and resource management programs. These community programs encompass a variety of management systems that span from private lands to private cum public lands to full public lands. We have initiated or attempted to guide some of these programs, which will be discussed in this chapter. They represent a progression of interaction and coordination of communities with district and national government, with the expressed purpose of encouraging communities to manage their own lands for local control and economic benefit.

Ecotourism and Conservation

There are two levels at which ecotourism has functioned to generate interest in conservation within a country or area (Boo, 1990; Lindberg & Enriquez, 1994): governmental and community. These levels of interest seem to coincide with temporal progression and economic levels, governmental level coming first and being more associated with higher economic level of tourism. Both levels show similar patterns, first connecting natural resources with economic benefits and later developing a fuller conservation land stewardship ethic. These levels, accentuating an economic division, often do not work together but instead create a paradox as they have in Costa Rica (Hill, 1990) between "alternative" and mass tourism, between city and rural, between locals and foreigners, and between governments and their people.

Initially, as ecotourism was introduced into Belize, conservationists were able to point to it as a potential industry for the developing country. Politicians saw the possibilities of attracting foreign capital with low expenditure and a small infrastructure resulting in low impact on their country and its natural resources. This potential provided an economic justification to politicians for the protection of certain national areas (Boo, 1990) including the Cockscomb Basin. In a relatively

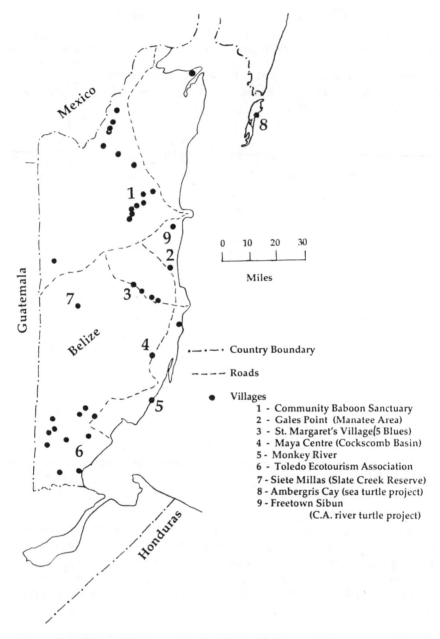

Figure 8.1. Map of Belize, indicating Belize Projects and towns mentioned in the text as well as other orienting map features.

short while, ecotourism had made an impact on the whole Belizean tourism industry and had radically increased foreign income into the country. However, most of the income generated came into the cities, and larger as well as more affluent hotels were built, and most of the income remained in the cities. This first influx of development also resulted in private reserves being created primarily by more affluent Belizeans and foreigners. This first wave of tourism was very important because it convinced politicians, affluent investors, and politically powerful individuals of the importance of preserving the natural resources as an important economic resource. However, although an important first step, natural resource preservation in some or many cases may be so directly tied to profits that a drop in tourism (potentially a flighty industry) might quickly result in other uses of the lands.

Although important, this initial tourism development in Belize merely began to accentuate the rift between more and less affluent people and between rural and urban people. In nearby Mexico as well, tourism in Quintana Roo has resulted in conflicts between authorities and villagers with the general consensus that they, the villagers, are not getting any advantages despite their interest in tourism (Daltabuit & Pi-Sunyer, 1990). In Belize, rural people who had traditionally been living on the land began to see the possibilities of participating in this ecotourism boom. However, their lack of investment capital has made it difficult for them to break into the ecotourism industry. This problem is compounded by the populated cities becoming the centers for both the ecotourism industry and the conservation community. In the United States, these urban/rural divisions have existed for a long time. In the Kickapoo River Valley of Wisconsin, urban conservationists blocked the building of a rural dam, which rural residents perceived as a project that would bring tourist dollars to the area. This created enormous controversy in the area for over 20 years and left a tremendous distrust of politicians and environmentalists (Sinclair, 1983).

The Community Baboon Sanctuary (CBS) in Belize introduced the potential to other rural Belizeans how they might become involved in the ecotourism industry. This project has stressed ecotourism that is concordant with the rural lifestyle and economic level: traveler adventurers, researchers, and students. It has attempted to create additional economic opportunities by encouraging visitors to stay overnight instead of only a day visit with just an admission fee. It has also encouraged day tour groups to purchase meals prepared by villagers, local crafts, farm goods, and local services such as guiding.

The CBS also stressed the difference between local management empowerment and locals working for outside tourism concerns (Figure 8.2). Large profitable ecotourism agencies develop their own infrastructures and systems for bringing tourists to a given site. A key problem is that locals have little or no control or influence over this large external process. When given more responsibility, people respond with more involvement, although it may be a very slow process. As with the government level of ecotourism previously discussed, villagers initially perceive the wildlife and forests mainly as an economic resource. For example, due to the popular publicity of the Community Baboon Sanctuary in Belize, howlers have become a resource that many people want and protect for their economic potential. When we were translocating monkeys from the CBS to the Cockscomb Basin

Figure 8.2. Rueben Rhaburn, local guide, lectures tourists on natural phenomenon.

for conservation reasons (Horwich, Koontz, Saqui, Saqui, & Glander, 1993), there were rumors at the CBS that the translocations were solely for encouraging tourism in the Cockscomb at the expense of CBS tourism. Thus, we made special efforts to negotiate which troops should not be moved because of their tourism value. Despite villagers' fears, research indicates that the howler population is increasing in the CBS at a very rapid rate and howlers reinhabit vacant areas easily. Conservation attitudes in the CBS are linked closely both to the intrinsic value of the monkeys as well as the economic value for tourism (Bruner, 1993). As tourism to the area increased, competition between CBS villages also increased. This increased villager economic expectations of the ecotourism/conservation program (Bruner, 1993; Hartup, 1994).

The Community Baboon Sanctuary:
Private Landownership—No Government Involvement

Much has been written about the CBS and thorough reviews of its initiation and development are provided elsewhere (Bruner, 1993; Hartup, 1989, 1994; Horwich, 1990; Horwich & Lyon, 1988, 1990, in press). In this chapter we will describe those salient points and project aspects that focus on linking ecotourism with natural resources.

The Community Baboon Sanctuary began as an experiment to protect one of the most viable populations of the black howler monkey (*Alouatta pigra*) within its limited range on the greater Yucatan Peninsula. Because this population inhabited the private lands of subsistence farmers and ranchers, an innovative approach had to be devised to work with these private landowners. Thus, the CBS became a model for creating a sanctuary entirely on the lands of a large number of private landowners. In the process, it became apparent that the monkeys thrived in the secondary forests disturbed by agriculture on land holdings large enough to permit continual forest regeneration. We utilized the focal species approach while keeping the whole ecosystem in view as we worked on management plans with villagers. We later targeted other species that were threatened as we expanded research and conservation possibilities. Creating a management plan for the endangered Central American river turtle (Figure 8.3) and the consequent creation of protective laws by the Belize Government was an offshoot of the ecotourism/research program, which was carried out with the cooperation of CBS villagers (Polisar & Horwich, 1994).

The CBS program also focused on voluntary local stewardship showing sensitivity and respect to villagers with the goal of empowering them. This was done by immersing the effort in the community's cultural, social, and economic conditions. The eventual goal was to instill and nourish a stewardship ethic in the landowners. The interim results are mixed; as in any community, some members are solely or primarily interested in the economic benefits whereas others show real conservation concerns for the monkeys and the environment. A number of examples document a change in ecological consciousness. These have included local discussions on the scarcity of wildlife, parents pointing the monkeys out to their children, farmers independently encouraging howler habitat on their lands and requesting suggestions on how to use shaded forests for additional crop use. These all indicate an emerging conservation consciousness that was not as prevalent as when the project began.

Community participation in the conservation process is not always a smooth operation, but local control of the process and of the revenues helps ensure that protection of habitat will continue because it builds local empowerment. Despite the fact that the CBS experiment has been successful in bringing economic incentives to the area (Hartup, 1989), it has suffered a number of problems (Horwich, Murray, et al., 1993). Many of these problems stemmed from competition for the ecotourism resource. Initially, competition was between local people and external tourist groups. Outside tour leaders would attempt to outskirt local guides to avoid the sanctuary guide fee and would bring in lunches from city hotels. Once the community sanctuary idea was accepted by outside tour groups, the competition was erased and tour leaders began working with CBS staff to arrange lunches in the villages. This economic arrangement has since been exported to other villages as well through more enlightened tour leaders. With increases in tourism income to the area, competition within the CBS communities emerged. Much of the economic benefit has settled into the central village of

Figure 8.3. Joe Herrera, of Isabella Bank, measuring endangered Central American river turtle.

Bermudian Landing, and a recent study indicates that this is felt by those in other
villages (Bruner, 1993).

Manatee Special Development Areas:
Private/Public Lands—Community and
Government Beginnings

The Manatee Area biodiversity project began with the idea of creating an ecologically diverse conservation area based on the Biosphere Reserve concept (Horwich
& Lyon, 1991). A main impetus was to build upon what we had learned in the CBS,

by deemphasizing mistakes and emphasizing the positive aspects of the CBS (Horwich, Murray, et al., 1993). The overall project encompasses four components: biodiversity research, conservation/management, ecotourism and development, and education. The ecotourism program under the auspices of the Gales Point Progressive Cooperative (Gales Point Progressive Cooperative and Manatee Advisory Team, 1992) includes a number of associations (bed and breakfast, guide, crafts, farming). Further details on some aspects of the Manatee project have been written about elsewhere (Greenlee, 1994; Horwich & Boardman, 1993; Horwich, Murray, et al., 1993). It has also been used as a study site for a recent ecotourism comparative study (Lindberg & Enriquez, 1994).

A major difference in integrating conservation of private and public lands as opposed to purely private lands is that the government must be a main participant in the process. Due to the success and publicity of the CBS and additional work that the Belize Audubon Society (BAS) was doing in integrating local people into the conservation process, many government officials and workers were interested in the possibilities of a liaison between communities and government. BAS, which had been given a mandate by the Government of Belize to organize some of the parks, had created positive situations in other communities through cross-pollination of ideas between various park staff under BAS (including CBS and Cockscomb Basin Wildlife Sanctuary).

When an initial proposal for management of the Manatee Area was submitted to the government, they responded with interest and began a dialogue by arranging a meeting of villagers, government staff from the Forestry and Archeology departments, political representatives from the Ministries of Natural Resources and Tourism and the Environment, and members from the tourism industry (Figure 8.4). Later, after we had meetings with government officials and had resubmitted an expanded proposal, the Government of Belize created two Special Development Areas (SDA), as interim protection for the area until a program for final protection can be worked out.

An important goal of the Manatee project was to develop a new management system whereby public and private lands can be managed under a cohesive system and to emphasize that landownership (i.e., public vs. private) is not necessarily the only way to view land use (Manatee Advisory Team, 1992). Gales Point, the only village within the two SDAs, has been the focal point of the conservation/ ecotourism project, promoting the idea that forests and wildlife in the region can become a resource well beyond that of a gathering or hunting ground. The Manatee project emphasizes that public and private lands can be linked together to maintain regional biodiversity and to ensure sustainable production of forests and wildlife.

To accomplish these goals, teams of researchers, students, and volunteers, including Peace Corps Volunteers, were organized to work with villagers to create a community-based program for the protection of the area. By involving local people in the research and conservation projects local conservation awareness is promoted. Community education occurs continuously due to the presence of re-

Figure 8.4. Meeting at Gales Point Community Building between villagers and Government of Belize staff and politicians.

searchers and conservation-minded tourists. Hiring local persons to assist in research efforts provides both local training and income as well as a conduit to transfer information and technology to the local community (Figure 8.5). For example, people involved in data collection on a species are better informed to talk about it and they see the conservation problems firsthand. Researchers also act as international advocates of projects and work to raise awareness of local needs in audiences of concerned organizations and peoples. Researchers also contribute to the local economy while living in an area and in essence become long-term "tourists" (Laarman & Perdue, 1989). A tourism research program has grown out of a hawksbill research/conservation program, which will support the local turtle conservation program (Smith, Eckert, & Gibson, 1992) (Figure 8.6).

Empowerment of local people was a main emphasis in our programs. We contend that if rural people are empowered with the ability and education necessary to manage their environment they will develop into true land stewards and thus add an extra multitude of conservation voices that reside specifically in the area to be protected. Empowering communities to control areas under their jurisdiction can lead to the development of a political voice that can directly influence decision making on public lands.

Local empowerment is enhanced and strengthened through encouraging participants of different community projects to interact with other like-minded communi-

Figure 8.5. Lindo Saqui with author (Horwich) tracking translocated howlers at Cockscomb Basin Wildlife Sanctuary.

ties to share information and boost morale. Our team, working with the Belize Enterprise for Sustainable Technology (BEST), stimulated and encouraged the transfer of ideas between the Gales Point Progressive Cooperative, the Association of Friends of Five Blues, and the Sandy Beach Woman's Cooperative, a very successful local tourism group. Earlier we had encouraged interactions between the staffs of the Community Baboon Sanctuary and the Cockscomb Basin Wildlife Sanctuary. BAS facilitated CBS staff interactions with Monkey River villagers. Monkey River village has since launched a conservation/ecotourism program with government support and legislation. We envision future programs to involve communities of similar cultures in different countries to interact. Such potential plans include

Figure 8.6. Dickey Slusher, of Gales Point, constructing
protective barrier against hawksbill turtle nest predation.

bringing together Creole communities from Belize and Nicaragua or Costa Rica
and involving experienced Mopan Maya staff of Cockscomb to work with a Mexican Yucatecan Mayan community at Punta Laguna.

In addition, we have encouraged interactions between different groups within the
Gales Point Progressive Cooperative. Agricultural and other associations (e.g.,
crafts, arts) are beginning to interface with the bed-and-breakfast and guide association programs to ensure that their voices, concerns, and ideas are heard (Figure
8.7). By working together, association participants can enhance sales of their
products to tourists or to host families, which provide meals and services for
tourists.

Figure 8.7. Visitors at a Gales Point "bed-and-breakfast" residence.

Cockscomb Basin Wildlife Sanctuary: Public Lands — Informal Community and Government Liaison

Cockscomb Basin Wildlife Sanctuary (CBWS) was initiated at about the same time as the CBS and both were formulated under the auspices of the Belize Audubon Society, which was designated by the Government of Belize to create a park system. The CBS was voluntarily placed under BAS auspices in order to give such an experimental idea a familiar structure. Consequently, the two reserves acted to influence each other in philosophy and the Belize Audubon Society began to embrace the idea of staffing the parks under their management with local people. This was especially important because a number of local Mayan families had moved into the Cockscomb Basin prior to the Cockscomb Basin's declaration as a park. These people were thus displaced from the area at the time of the park's creation, leaving a consequent conflict between the government and the local community.

Having the initial park staff administered by a U.S. Peace Corps volunteer allowed for the transition to the hiring of a local manager. As more staff were hired, it became a natural but pointed policy to hire other villagers. With a local manager, Ernesto Saqui, who continues to the present time as manager, and other staff, there was a concerted effort by BAS and the community to develop economic incentives

Figure 8.8. Research "tourists" at Maya Centre crafts cooperative building and registration area.

for other villagers to supplement the farming economy. Because the reserve is 10 km from the village and overnight accommodations are furnished by the park (Boo, 1990), the village bed-and-breakfast arrangement that has been possible in the CBS was not something easily accomplished, although some villagers hope to create guest houses at Maya Centre. These might be used as interim accommodations for travelers coming to and leaving the park.

A highly successful ecotourism enterprise was initiated by village women who began a crafts cooperative to sell local crafts at the park entrance (Boo, 1990; Lindberg & Enriquez, 1994) (Figure 8.8). They were also responsible for signing tourists in and out of the park and controlling the entrance gate. This introduced the tourists to their crafts, which were displayed in a building at the entrance. The economic impact of ecotourism at Cockscomb was studied along with the Manatee Area in a recent comparative study (Lindberg & Enriquez, 1994).

Future plans by villagers include other potential tourism services provided both within the park and within the village of Maya Centre. These include meal services for groups within the park, taxi services to the park (currently visitors without cars must walk 10 km to park headquarters from Maya Centre), bed-and-breakfast services within Maya Centre for visitors before entering the park and when leaving, a restaurant, gas station, and bicycle rentals. These services would provide a

Figure 8.9. Wisconsin Governor, Tommy Thompson, signs state legislation for the Kickapoo River Authority with local residents, state and county officials, and author (Horwich) looking on [photo by Broadcaster].

diversified economic base to supplement the current farm economy. The park staff has recently begun to investigate the possibilities of involving other villages on the park periphery in conservation and ecotourism. This involvement is important because there is some possibility of poaching within the park at those peripheries.

Five Blues Lake National Park: Public Lands—Formal Community and Government Agreement

The establishment of Five Blues National Park was influenced by publicity generated by other community conservation projects and the concern by Lee Wengrzyn and other members of St. Margaret's Village that the area surrounding their homes was rapidly being deforested. With the general political environment within Belize favoring ecotourism as an industry, the community was able to interest the Government of Belize in preserving the area. With that success, villagers formed the Friends of Five Blues Association to aid in the conservation process. This organization began to work closely with the government and was able to affect the addition of adjacent lands to the park. Later a formal liaison of local and national government was created to manage lands of Five Blues National Park for the benefit of local people (Anonymous, 1991). At this point there is no actual legal affiliation but the community/government liaison has become formal. Currently, they are developing an ecotourism program (Werner, 1994). A recent United Nations Global Environmental Fund grant awarded to the Friends of Five Blues Association has allowed for a formal staff to be created for the management of Five Blues. Recently, Wendy Gerlitz, a student working with Community Conservation Consultants and Friends of Five Blues Association, has created a preliminary management plan for the Park (Gerlitz, 1994).

Kickapoo River Community Reserve: Public Lands— Formal Community and Government Legislation

Dispute over control over the Kickapoo River valley lands north of La Farge, WI is an example of how state and federal government dealings with local communities can lead to conflict and animosity. Historically, there has been improper communication and a lack of sensitivity by government towards local people, and an accentuated rift between urban and rural views has developed. In the process, potential tourism development was held out to local people as an economic incentive without proper regard for the natural resources in the area. The result was that rural farmers were caught between the forces of government and urban environmentalists with no voice or empowerment in what was to happen to their lands.

In the 1960s, 144 farm families were displaced from their lands, covering 8,600 acres, for the creation of a flood control dam and the lands were placed under the control of the U.S. Army Corps of Engineers. The Corps actually spent millions of dollars on the project before it was stopped for environmental reasons due to pressure from outside environmental groups. The area was to become a lake, which rural residents were told would become a tourist attraction. However, the area to be flooded contained populations of threatened and endangered species as well as a large number of archeological sites. The lake, in retrospect, would have easily silted due to water runoff and consequent soil erosion. Thus, improper planning on the part of government placed rural residents in a no-win situation. This left the area in 25 years of turmoil, pitting neighbor against neighbor and most residents against the government, the Wisconsin Department of Natural Resources, and urban-based environmental organizations. Most of the river towns were left in an economically helpless position because building within the floodplain was tied to flood control plans, which were held hostage by this hopeless situation.

In 1991, when the Governor of Wisconsin publicly declared that the dam issue was dead, over 30 years after its first stirrings, we organized some valley residents and initiated a compromise proposal to utilize the lands for ecotourism without the building of the dam. The proposal blended a program of recreational activities with an ecotourism theme, with conservation and education. Because the social climate was still not good for such a program, we began giving talks to community groups who had interest in encouraging tourism in the area.

A committee of valley-wide representatives was coordinated by a University of Wisconsin extension agent appointed by the Governor. When this committee became interested in the proposal, we began working with a drafting committee under their auspices. Some state legislators also worked with this drafting committee. The drafting committee made presentations of the proposal to the surrounding communities with open discussions following. These open forums generated a good deal of positive feelings about the possibility of turning the dam site lands, which had been a cause for conflict, into a positive resource for tourism. What was most significant was that, despite the almost 25 years of conflict, virtually no negative comments were made against the proposal.

This seeming consensus to utilize the lands in conflict, for recreation and tourism, encouraged politicians to work in favor of it. With the help of local politicians and government lawyers, the drafting committee essentially wrote legislation for having the federal government turn the lands over to the Wisconsin Department of Administration and create a predominantly local Kickapoo Reserve Board to manage the lands (Figure 8.9). This Board, which was appointed by the Governor of Wisconsin in May, 1995, is composed of nine people, six of whom are local. Four members are from the townships and villages immediately surrounding the 8,600 acres of land, two additional members come from the Kickapoo River valley, and an additional three members are experts in conservation, archeology, tourism, or education. All local potential Board members were nominated by local government agencies or local school boards. The Governor then selected six members from these nominees and selected the other three from the state professional community.

Given the consensus reached by the general community, state bills submitted to the U.S. House of Representatives and the Senate passed overwhelmingly in mid-1994. Legislation passed in the federal House of Representatives in October, 1994 but similar legislation was held up in the Senate. Finally, in October, 1996, the legislation passed in both houses and $17 million was appropriated for the U.S. Army Corps to complete the land transfer. This money would be used to upgrade the existing roads passing through the lands and for restoration of the lands. This money did not include construction of a rural education center, which was proposed to blend conservation with the development of an ecotourism program that would have a broad-based education and research program. Additionally, the legislation called for up to 1,200 acres to be given to the Ho-Chunk Nation under the Department of the Interior to be protected for cultural reasons.

Although the Reserve Board has not received legal responsibility, they have been acting with the approval of the U.S. Army Corps, to oversee the management of the lands. They have also hired an Executive Director. They will continue to work with the Corps and attempt to establish an agreement with the Ho-Chunk Nation until the restoration has been completed and the lands have been officially turned over to the Wisconsin Department of Administration. The federal and state politicians have pledged to seek additional funds for the rural education center because the original legislation would not provide for it.

The reserve board has begun working with groups of local and other users of the land. These have included horesback riders, all terrain vehicle users, and bicyclists.

Under their guidance, the U.S. Army Corps have temporarily terminated use of all existing trails, which were created by users over time with no systematized methods. This was done in an effort to both rehabilitate eroded areas and to begin to superimpose some method of order in managing the area. However, because of the potential long-term process of turning over the lands and because of the economic importance of some of these user groups, local pressure is being put on the Board to reopen the trails to the public. Some user groups, such as the horesback riders, have been extremely cooperative in providing information and hands-on help in restoring the area. Because of their interest and cooperation, Board sentiment is leaning toward reopening the area for use to them with limited use for some other groups. In contrast, some all terrain vehicle users, during a trial period, left some major erosion problems, which has alienated both Board members and some local people to continued trail use for motorized vehicles. However, some snowmobile groups had already worked out an agreement with the U.S. Army Corps so they will continue to use some existing trails that they have created. The lands are still open to general use for walking, canoeing, and hunting during the hunting season.

Discussion and Conclusions

Rural ecotourism is a tool that can be used successfully to both support communities and help ensure protection of natural resources. However, ecotourism is not a panacea and it must be developed within a larger economic and environmental context. Although there are many reasons for concern about problems in ecotourism and reasons to monitor tourism, especially in developing countries (Cater, 1987), the examples noted in this chapter give reason for hope. These examples show that ecotourism in rural areas can be used as a tool to create and expand ecological consciousness through programs that integrate economic incentives with education, research, and conservation. However, such programs must emphasize safeguards on the supply side of ecotourism to protect the resources rather than the demand side alone, which is embraced by the tour operators who regard their main responsibility owed to their clients (Passoff, 1991).

Many persons can assist in the empowerment and development of communities under the banner of sustainable ecotourism development. Tour groups can be educated (voluntarily or mandated) to adopt local tourism "rules and regulations." Community development and conservation projects can be linked to the overall development goals of communities and local people should also be part of overall planning of ecotourism programs.

Although all of the projects described are experimental in nature, they display some similar characteristics that indicate their success in encouraging the conservation of natural resources. By interweaving economic incentives with research, education, and conservation, conservation issues become a part of community life and conservation topics come up increasingly in village discussions. Often such talk of fading resources is discussed between researchers and villagers as well. By adding local empowerment through involvement in all aspects of the project, pride in their area and natural resources also has become, increasingly, a topic for conversation. Despite the importance of discussion in raising conservation ethic consciousness, unless it is linked with some kind of empowering responsibilities for rural people, the discussions will just lead to discouragement with conservation issues. In most of the examples, the interest and support for the programs by most members of the community have led to support by government officials for their constituents. This government support in turn has led to a variety of important innovative liaisons between government and communities. These kinds of liaisons have the potential to further community empowerment and interest, while creating more cost-effective and democratic resource management.

Chapter 9

Managing Tourism-Induced Acculturation Through Environmental Design on Pueblo Indian Villages in the U.S.

Alan A. Lew

The Problem: Acculturation and Tourism

Acculturation and Adaptation

Acculturation is defined as the process of culture change that occurs when a society with superior technological sophistication comes into contact with one of inferior technological sophistication. The latter is most likely to become an acculturated society, experiencing dramatic shifts in social structure and world view. The North American experience has largely been one in which American Indians have experienced pressure to change under the expanding influence of European settlers (Bodine, 1972). Societies can react in a variety of ways under pressure of this kind (Lew, 1989). In general, these reactions can be classified into two types: *innovation diffusion* and *cultural adaptation*.

Innovation diffusion is the process by which one social group adopts practices that were originally developed by another social group. The degree of similarity or difference between the two groups is believed to have a bearing on the degree to which one group will adopt the practices of another. Some researchers focus on the characteristics of the "receiver" group. Of particular interest is the receiver group's perception of the innovation in terms of relative advantage, compatibility, complexity, experimentation (ability to try without adopting), and visibility of results. The adoption process is an ongoing one in which decisions to keep or reject the ways of the dominant culture occur at varying intervals and to different degrees.

Cultural adaptation has been defined as "the *process of change* in response to a change in the physical environment, or a change in internal stimuli, such as demography, economics, and organization" (Rogers, 1983, p. 401). Theories of cultural adaptation focus on changes that occur within a society in response to changes in the world it interacts with. In some cases resistance to change becomes increasingly more rigid and less flexible as environmental stress is prolonged. This form of adaptative response works to *preserve* against change. For example, it has been argued that pueblo Indians in the American Southwest have been able to preserve their traditional culture through *compartmentalization*—they have adopted clearly distinct spheres wherein traditional ways predominate and outside influences are prohibited (Dozier, 1964).

Cultural adaptations may also occur in a way that takes advantage of unanticipated changes. This reaction involves the exploitation of changing circumstances and it is sometimes described as the development or utilization of new ecological niches or opportunities.

Acculturation of Native Americans

Prior to European arrival, an estimated 5 million Native Americans lived in what is today the United States. These people adapted to their physical and social environment in a manner compatible with the population density and needs of their societies. Low-density populations throughout much of the precolonial U.S. put little pressure on natural resources and resulted in communal lifestyles and intertribal boundaries that were fluid.

On the other side of the Atlantic Ocean, European society was developing in a very different manner. European colonial expansion into North America arose in association with 16th century mercantilism and global economic expansion. By the 18th century the laissez faire doctrines of the French gave rise to the Classical School of economics in England. Classical economic theory, based on rational economic behavior and reliance on free market forces, came to prominence at the very founding of the United States as a country. It also helped to lay the foundations of the industrial revolution in both Europe and the U.S. (Cameron, 1975). More recent modifications of classical economic theory include Keynesian economics and monetarist theories. Through these adaptations, the U.S. has been relatively successful in the increasing competition for scarce global resources. Societies that have not adopted and adapted classical economic policies have been less successful in this competition.

Only a few aspects of the dominant American cultural system have deeply penetrated Native American society. Superficial "product" innovations, such as the ranch house and pickup truck, have been more readily adopted than have more intangible "soft" innovations (Vogt, 1951). The modern system of tribal government is a soft innovation that was forced upon reservation by the U.S. government, with mixed results (Smith, 1996a). Classical economic theory is a major soft innovation that many Native American reservations have been hesitant to adopt. This is because the basic assumptions of classical economic theory are at odds with the long-held beliefs of many Indian cultures (Trosper, 1995). For example, the common practice on most reservations of holding property communally, rather than individually, presents issues of usage and contract rights that are not present on off-reservation lands.

Reservations today are a perplexing mix of traditional and contemporary values (Bodine, 1972). Table 9.1 summarizes the competing values that are common on American Indian reservations. Most individual Indians fall somewhere in between the very traditional and very contemporary values indicated in this table. The less than complete adoption of classical economic principles by Native American societies results in the criticism that reservations require excessive expenditures of time, money, and effort to bring about minimal development progress (Kirst, 1987; Talbot, 1981). Such ethnocentricity is common among societies with comparatively greater technological sophistication. However, after a century of federal government efforts to eradicate Indian culture, it is now widely held that successful economic development on reservations requires a creative mix of traditional and classical economic beliefs (Cornell & Kalt, 1995.)

Tourism and the Acculturation Process

Tourism, as a form of economic development, is also influenced by the conflicting values found on reservations. Tourism, however, provides one of the major means of social contact between people from different societies. As such, it serves as a mechanism for innovation diffusion and acculturation. Although tourism is not the only force for change in traditional cultures, it is a major component of the entire milieu of relationships that exist between the more and less developed societies of the world.

Cultural tourism, or the curiosity about people and places who are in some way different, is one of the driving forces behind international tourism, a major segment of which consists of travel from the more developed countries of the world to the less developed countries. For a hefty price, tourists can take adventure trips to primitive Borneo, hidden Tibet, or deepest Africa.

Table 9.1. Competing Value Systems Common on American Indian Reservations

Traditional Indian Values	Dominant American Values
• Cooperation	• Competition
• Prestige and authority based on family, age, and religion	• Prestige and authority based on personal property, political position, education, and economics
• Education from elders	• Education in schools
• Animist religious beliefs	• Scientific rationalism
• Morality based on social conformity	• Morality based on good and bad
• Ceremonial activities	• Work activities
• Communal ownership and decision making	• Individual ownership and hierarchical decision making

Some have argued that this kind of tourism contributes to the homogenization of cultural differences and the decline of traditional societies (Britton, 1980). This is because wealthy tourists often demand, and receive, accommodations and services replicating their lives at home. Major hotel chains in India, for example, emphasize their modernity in the midst of an exotic society. The term "exotic" as used here may alternatively be interpreted as traditional and poverty-stricken.

Others argue that tourism is a modernizing force that brings about a better adjustment of traditional societies to the modern world (Bond & Ladman, 1980). By teaching people to adapt to modern ways of doing things, tourism can, in the extreme, save a culture from otherwise inevitable extinction. Cultural performances and other forms of "museumization" are a way of preserving cultures, just as zoos are used to save endangered species (Relph, 1976). In both the arguments for and against tourism development it is nevertheless seen as a major force for acculturation and culture change.

The tourism literature indicates two specific ways in which tourism contributes to the acculturation of a society: (1) the demonstration effect, and (2) the development of tourism management and development mechanisms (Mathieson & Wall, 1982). These correspond, respectively, to innovation diffusion and cultural adaptation, as discussed above.

The demonstration effect is the adoption of the behavior patterns of someone from another society. For example, youths on traditionally conservative South Pacific islands have been seen to adopt Western customs of holding hands and showing public affection whenever a cruise ship sails into port. Although they often revert back to traditional behavioral norms after the ship leaves, over time the impact will likely become more permanent. Critics of tourism argue that the demonstration effect is harmful because most tourists exhibit behavior that is far more affluent and carefree than they would if they were not on tour. Others hope that the demonstration effect will instill modern values and behavior patterns that are conducive to a global, cash-based economic system.

Of a more subtle nature is the way a society *adapts* to protect itself from the onslaught of new ideas and new ways of doing things. Some societies attempt to shield themselves from tourist influences by placing legal restrictions on tourists. Tourists may be restricted to visiting only certain cities, such as in China, or may be strongly encouraged to be part of an organized and tightly controlled tour group, as in the former USSR.

Another adaptation is the development of a commercial tourism industry. This can lead to a society becoming heavily dependent on tourism as a major sector of their economy, making it vulnerable to unanticipated shifts in tourist interests and travel patterns. It can also lead to a feeling that one's culture is being commercialized and commodified for sale.

A third option would be for a society to take no action at all in response to tourism. This approach could increase cross-cultural misunderstandings and conflicts. Both the hosts and guests are more vulnerable to exploitation when the rules of proper behavior and interaction are unclear.

Short of completely closing a society to outsiders, there is no out for traditional
cultures. Once tourists and the tourism industry designate a people and place as
being of interest, the people in that destination must come to terms with outside
visitors. The demonstration effect and the various means of cultural adaptation will
impact societies whether they like it or not, inevitably resulting in changes in their
traditional culture.

Tourism Issues on Pueblo Reservations

The pueblo reservations of the American Southwest are among the oldest sites of
continuous habitation and cultural continuity in the North America (Figure 9.1).
Minimal Spanish influence, as compared to Central America, and a long history of
cultural resistance to American domination have made the pueblo tribes among the
most traditional of all Native American cultures in the U.S. (Brew, 1979).

Early February marks the beginning of the weekend tourist season to pueblo
villages, such as those on the Hopi Reservation. Although some ceremonial dances
are held before this time, the Bean Dance is generally the first of the year to draw
large numbers of non-Hopi visitors. As the seasons change, so do the dances; and as
spring moves into summer, the number of tourists increases, both on the dance
weekends and during the more quiet midweek.

The exact numbers of annual visitors to the pueblo reservations of northern
Arizona and New Mexico is unknown. The Hopi Reservation is estimated to receive
between 75,000 and 100,000 non-Indian tourists a year. The Acoma Pueblo Reserva-

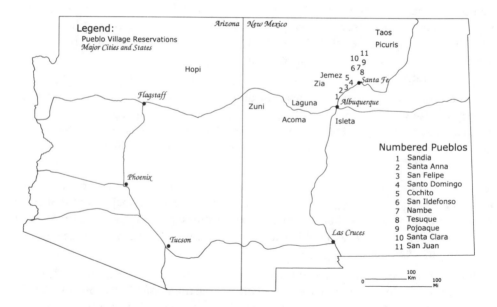

Figure 9.1. Map of pueblo village reservations in New Mexico and Arizona.

tion, which has better access to an Interstate freeway, receives between 300,000 and 400,000 visitors annually. This author has counted as many as 275 cars parked outside of a central plaza on the Hopi Reservation when a dance was in progress. Probably fewer than 10% of these vehicles brought non-Indian tourists to the dance. The others belong to:

- Hopis who came from other villages,
- Hopis who have briefly returned home from work in off-reservation cities,
- Indian visitors from tribes other than the Hopi.

Non-Indian tourists find an interest in the pueblo reservations primarily because of the strength of the traditional pueblo culture. A survey that this author conducted of 419 American tourists in the spring and summer of 1990 found 75% indicating that interests in seeing Native Americans was a major motivation for their coming to northern Arizona (Table 9.2). Surprisingly large numbers were particularly interested in American Indian culture and religious practices.

Traditional pueblo culture is "primal" in the sense that it is "not available for export." It is not possible for a nontribal member to become a pueblo Indian, although there are many pueblo "wannabes" who intentionally trespass onto sacred sites (Haederle, 1994). Nor can pueblo culture be replicated in anything but a contrived manner outside of the pueblo setting. The authenticity of the culture and its close integration with place are the essential elements in defining the attractiveness of the pueblo villages to visitors.

Pueblo Indians hold mixed opinions on tourists (Lujan, 1993). The traditional ways of the pueblo people are based primarily upon their religion and its relationship to the agricultural calendar (Harvey, 1972). Pueblo religion is organic in that it permeates every aspect of their society. Because of this, tourists visiting a village

Table 9.2. Major Motivations for Visiting Northern Arizona

	"Very" or "Extremely" Important	Mean Score
Seeing how Indians live	74.9%	4.07
Experience a natural setting	74.6%	4.02
New and different experience	72.0%	3.93
Develop deeper understanding of American Indian culture	71.7%	4.01
To explore new places	68.3%	3.89
Attend an American Indian religious ceremony	62.7%	3.69
Personally meeting American Indians	61.5%	3.72
Personal or spiritual values	48.9%	3.27
Shopping for American Indian arts and crafts	46.5%	3.34

N = 419 respondents. Mean score is based upon a Likert scale of 5 = "extremely important" and 1 = "not at all important." A score of 3 is midway on this scale.

cannot help but intrude upon pueblo culture in some manner. Some intrusions are actually welcome, whereas others can be the source of considerable tension.

A recent survey of pueblo Indians, conducted under the direction of the author, found that whereas most were warm and open to visitors, they still felt very protective of their religion (Table 9.3). Although there was some disagreement, most were keenly aware of the tourism situation on their reservations. Most felt that the tourism situation needed to be improved; and most approved of increasing signage to control visitors and expanding visitor services (such as providing public restrooms).

The shortcomings of tourism on pueblo reservations is directly related to the traditional qualities that tourists come to experience. The issue of how to maintain authenticity and traditional behavior patterns has been raised (Lew, 1990), but has yet to be adequately resolved. Sweet (1991) describes how pueblo Indians use secrecy about their religious practices as one way of maintaining cultural integrity against the onslaught of inquisitive tourists. She also discusses the establishment of regulations that govern tourist behavior and how they are enforced by religious

Table 9.3. Pueblo Indian Comments on Tourism

	Mean Score	SD
Comments Supportive of Increasing Tourism		
We need more motels and restaurants for tourists	4.88	0.47
Pueblos should provide public toilets for tourists at dances	4.85	0.60
Tourism is a good way of Indians to earn money	4.61	0.84
The tribe should provide professional tour guide training	4.48	0.77
The tribe should do more to promote tourism	4.39	1.03
Tourism is a good way to share our culture with others	4.36	1.13
Tourists have much to learn from the traditional Indian way of life	4.27	0.85
I enjoy sharing pueblo dances with tourists	4.24	1.16
Pueblo offices should be open on weekends to serve tourists	4.03	1.07
Comments Supportive of Protecting Pueblos from Tourists		
Pueblos should have specific parking areas for tourists	4.55	0.77
Pueblos should use more signs to control where tourists go and what they do	4.33	0.79
It is OK for a village to completely close itself to tourists	4.09	1.31
The tribe should educate tourists before they come to the pueblo	4.00	1.08
Tourists should be confined to certain areas to observe dances	4.00	1.26
Because tourists are too curious, they are offensive to Indians	3.64	1.08
Non-Indians should only be allowed at dances if they are guests of Indians	3.58	1.59

N = 31 respondents. Mean score is based upon a Likert scale of 5 = "Agree" and 1 = "Disagree" with the statement. A score of 3 is midway on this scale. A higher SD indicates less agreement among respondents.

leaders and tribal police on Acoma Pueblo—one of the better organized pueblos for tourism. The following discussion focuses specifically on the physical design aspects of pueblo villages and how these can influence tourist behavior and the impact of tourism on pueblo peoples.

Environmental Design and Tourism on Pueblo Reservations

Several authors have suggested models describing the functional design aspects of tourist attractions (Gunn, 1979; Leiper, 1989). These models generally involve a series of transition zones through which a tourist passes en route to the tourist attraction. These zones prepare the tourist for the attraction experience by providing information on (1) the significance of the attraction, and (2) proper behavior and attitude toward the attraction. Attractions for which these zones are poorly defined can cause a sense of uncertainty and disorientation in the tourist.

When tourists encounter culturally ambiguous environments, their immediate reaction is to search for environmental cues to help them define proper behavior. Culture shock results when such cues are difficult to detect or interpret. When the behavior of uninformed tourists negatively impacts the host society, the hosts may experience a *reflective culture shock*. Culture shock and reflective culture shock are most likely to occur in situations in which (1) cultural differences between hosts and guests are significant, and (2) mechanisms for managing tourist behavior are inadequate.

Most of the pueblo reservation today are puzzling environments for tourists. The lack of clear environmental cues for tourists results from a historic ambivalence toward tourism on the part of many pueblo residents. Pueblo residents sometimes interpret resulting tourist behavior as an affront to their culture, thereby further supporting antitourism opinions.

Semiotics and Environmental Design

Semiotics is the science of signs. The semiotic model includes a sender and a receiver who communicate information through one or more channels using some form of code (MacCannell, 1989, pp. 4-5). Although all forms of communication are subject to semiotic analysis, concrete informational and directional signs, such as those encountered in tourism, are particularly appropriate. Leiper (1989), drawing upon the earlier work of MacCannell (1976), defines a tourist attraction as: "... a system comprising three elements: a tourist or human element, a nucleus or central element, and a marker or informative element. A tourist attraction comes into existence when the three elements are connected."

This definition of a tourist attraction provides a framework within which we can come to understand the role and influence of environmental cues in tourism on pueblo reservations. In addition to this, there are essentially two types of environmental design cues (or informative elements) that can affect tourist behavior: overt and covert. Overt cues center on signage and other forms of tourist information and guidance. These are the "markers" in the MacCannell/Leiper model. Covert environmental cues consist of physical site characteristics associated with the "nucleus or central element" of the attraction system.

Because this current discussion focuses on environmental design, other types of overt cues, such as brochures and guidebooks, are not discussed. Similarly, covert cues concentrate on village design, excluding interpersonal forms of communication.

Overt Signage

Table 9.4 lists the signage considerations that can affect tourist behavior. Large, roadside billboard advertisements are the most common type of off-reservation signage. With some notable exceptions, there are very few billboards that actually promote visitation to any of the pueblo reservations. Most of the billboards that do exist promote visitation to shopping facilities and gaming casinos (or bingo halls) that are well removed from the residential areas of the pueblos.

The major exception in billboard use is Acoma Pueblo in New Mexico, which has several billboards along the nearby Interstate freeway promoting its tours of the "Sky City" village. Sky City sits majestically atop the cliffs of a formidable mesa, which allows the Acoma Reservation to maintain tight control over visitor access. The Acoma Reservation is also well marked by entrance signs, directional signs, building identification signs, signs indicating the visitor parking area, and restricted area signage. Exit signage, possibly the least important, is the only type in which Acoma is lacking. Acoma, however, is an exception. It is widely known to be a leader in its particular approach to tourism management (Smith, 1995). It has also been criticized by some Indians for being too commercialized and having lost its authenticity because of the way it has managed tourism. It is an example of what they do not want tourism to be on their reservation.

A less proactive, but equally effective, approach is used on Taos Pueblo. Taos is one of the better known pueblos in the Southwestern U.S. and does not need to rely on off-reservation signage to attract visitors. The design of the pueblo is such that a very large open plaza is situated in the middle of an area surrounded by adobe building complexes. This controlled open area is used for parking, for which visitors pay a fee. The high density of the surrounding adobe buildings allows the reservation to place only a few "no access" barriers at strategic locations to confine tourist movement to areas immediately adjacent to the plaza. Numerous arts and crafts shops and food stalls are found in buildings that face the open plaza area. Only modest window signs are used to distinguish a shop from a residence. Thus, the tourist space is clearly defined and separated from the nontourist space, helping to minimize (but not eliminate) intrusions into the lives of residents.

By contrast there is scant signage on most of the other pueblo reservations. For example, only one of the three major routes leading to the Hopi pueblos has a sign indicating that the visitor has passed from the surrounding Navajo Reservation onto the Hopi Reservation. Directional signage is virtually nonexistent, even to the visitor-oriented Hopi Cultural Center with its museum, motel, and restaurant facility.

Table 9.4. Signage Considerations for Village Design and Tourism Management

Sign Location
1. Generation markers (at the tourist's home location)
2. Off-site markers
    - Tribal
    - Nontribal
    - Billboard advertising
3. On-site markers
    - Entrance signage
        - Location confirmation
        - Welcome signs
        - Regulations
        - Further Information
    - Directional signage
    - Parking signage
    - Educational signage
    - Building identification
    - Restricted area signage
    - Exit signage

Sign Role and Meaning
1. Direction
    - Navigational
        - Commerical
        - Noncommercial
    - Behavioral
2. Significance
    - Importance or value
        - Societal benefit
        - Personal benefit

Sign Condition
1. Clarity
    - Size
    - Visibility or prominence
2. State of repair

Sign Role and Meaning

In most major tourist settings, visitors are looking for signs indicating appropriate direction and significance. Directional signs are of two types: *navigational* and *behavioral*. Navigational signs tell the newcomers where they are and indicate how to get to places they may wish to go. This information is helpful to the visitor and conveys a sense of local care for the visitor's well-being. Like the Hopi Reservation, most pueblo reservations lack any directional signs, parking signs, or restricted access signs. Without a good guide, map, or sense of direction it is easy for visitors to loose their way. Tourists visiting these pueblos for the first time are already likely to experience a high degree of culture shock and disorientation. Inadequate signage exacerbates these problems.

One type of directional sign that is prominent on many reservations are those that lead the tourist to arts and crafts shops, both within and outside of pueblo villages. However, the message of commercial directional signs is very different from noncommercial signs. Instead of feeling "cared for as a welcome guest," the visitor may feel even more alienated from the host society. The visitor's experience in this case is not one of a welcome guest, but of an exploitable outsider. This is particularly true when commercial signs exist to the total exclusion of noncommercial signs.

Individuals will respond to the message in different ways. Most tourists to pueblo villages have at least a vague preconception that the pueblo Indians are one of the most traditional Native American societies in the U.S., and therefore a general ambivalence toward tourism is understandable. Within this context, the lack of adequate directional signage may be accepted. However, the increasing prominence of commercial directional signs can stimulate a more reactionary response on the part of the visitor. If some Indians are willing and able to develop such a prominent display of commercial directional signs, why are the noncommercial navigational needs of the visitor not met in a similarly fashion?

Most tourists do not wish to intentionally violate the regulations and norms of the host society. However, unless those norms are clearly explained to them, unintentional violations are likely to occur. Signage is one means of identifying the proper behavioral role for the tourist. The lack of signage puts a greater onus on the tourists to formulate their own behavioral role models. Some tourists are better able to do this than others.

Many pueblo villages have entrance signs, which give behavioral guidance to the visitor. These tend to emphasize regulatory restriction on tourist behavior. They typically prohibit:

- alcohol and drug possession,
- photographing, sketching, and recording villages and ceremonies,
- visiting archeological sites,
- taking or purchasing cultural artifacts or antiquities.

These behavioral signs are effective for most visitors. Problems are encountered when the visitor does not notice the sign. The major reason that these signs may not be noticed is because they are often in a poor state of repair. Exposure to the elements causes deterioration and, from a distance, the list of restrictions can appear indistinguishable from a public notice bulletin board (which in some cases may be situated right next to it). Despite the poor state of repair of many of these signs, the overall message is clearly understandable, if read. Although mass tourists may resent restrictions such as these, the types of tourist who are drawn to the pueblos are generally more aware of their fragility and, therefore, are more inclined to appreciate the type of information provided by behavioral restriction signs.

They may not obey the restrictions, but at least they are aware of the risks involved in violating them.

Some pueblo village signs also state that visitors must register at the village administrative office. Because almost all of these offices are closed on weekends, few visitors abide by this requirement. Furthermore, pueblo administrative offices are sometimes poorly marked and difficult to find. This is an example of a situation in which the tourist receives mixed messages. Because the weekend tourist is unable to satisfy the stated registration requirement, the message becomes either (1) that the village is closed to visitors on weekends, or (2) that the stated regulations are not as serious a consideration as they might appear. In either case, the visitor is unsure of what constitutes appropriate behavior.

Another problem with signs that list rules of behavior is that they may not necessarily provide an accurate guideline for what is acceptable and proper tourist behavior in a village. A survey of pueblo Indians was conducted to determine which tourist behaviors are most resented (Table 9.5). This list indicates that there are several areas of tourist behavior that could be better defined for the tourist. This could be accomplished by not only advising tourists about improper behavior, but also by telling them what is acceptable.

Building and Site Design

In *The Image of the City*, architect Kevin Lynch (1960) defined five basic physical design elements that provide essential environmental cues for behavior in a place. These are:

- Paths: that people move along,
- Edges: between two different areas,
- Districts: clearly identifiable with common elements,
- Nodes: focal points, often at the junction of Paths,
- Landmarks: major points of reference.

Lynch's construct has provided a basis for understanding how people mentally and physically organize space. These elements are used to develop a sense of orientation and the ability to navigate through an environment. They are considered covert environmental cues because most people do not consciously think about their influence on behavior. Christopher Alexander and his colleagues have expanded upon Lynch's earlier work by contending that communities and buildings are physically organized into patterns that reflect and shape human use and behavior. In *A Pattern Language*, Alexander (1977) outlines a "language" of urban and architectural design that he believes to be effective in creating desirable places to live. For example, he states that "sacred sites" should be zealously protected by local government ordinance; and that their design elements should include:

- secluded and contemplative areas,
- special scenic views framed in a meaningful setting,
- trees situated in locations that contribute to the place experience,

Table 9.5. Acceptability of Tourist Behavior

Very Unacceptable Behavior
- Littering*
- Acting like an expert on pueblo culture
- Trying to act like an Indian
- Entering sacred areas knowingly
- Taking pictures of dances*
- Wearing shorts, halters, bathing suits, etc.
- Urinating behind a rock or house

Unacceptable Behavior
- Wandering around villages on their own
- Speaking loudly at dances
- Entering sacred areas without knowing it
- Not registering at the pueblo's administrative office*
- Asking questions about or at dances

Mixed Option
- Climbing on house roofs at dances
- Parking in villages

Acceptable Behavior
- Watching dances
- Bringing food (picnic) to eat at dances

Based on a survey of 31 pueblo Indian residents. *Normally indicated on a pueblo village rules sign.

- a semisecluded sitting area,
- access only by foot,
- some form of gateway indicating transition to a sacred ground.

Pueblo Village Design

The design and layout of the pueblo villages have been shaped by both the physical environment and the population dynamics of different villages. The narrow ridge top of Acoma's Sky City mesa forces a very compact and linear settlement. The broad hill on top of which the Zuni Pueblo has arisen allows for more dispersed settlement, although it still maintains the traditional clustering of adobe-style housing units set on an uneven grid street pattern. Lynch's landscape elements and Alexander's pattern language provide basic guidelines for understanding the relationship between the physical environment and tourist behavior and experience in pueblo villages. A summary of the basic design elements that may be used or manipulated in some manner to control tourist behavior and impacts is listed in Table 9.6.

Paths
Paths are one of the most important environmental design elements that influence tourism on pueblo reservations. Major paths between villages are generally well

marked, because most are part of a highway system managed by the states of Arizona and New Mexico. Once the visitor leaves these highway, however, the experience is very different. Few streets have names and only a handful are paved.

The visitor, therefore, must rely upon environmental cues to determine acceptable pathways. The most frequent cue is the degree of erosion evident along a given road or trail. Evidence that many others have driven the route is often interpreted to mean that anyone can drive the route. While this is often true, the survey of pueblo residents (Table 9.3) indicates that it may be in the best interest of some villages to try to control the degree of access that tourists have within a village. This problem is heightened by the arid environment in which the pueblos are located. Under these conditions, ruts in the ground are easily created by automobiles and foot traffic. Once created they remain for a long time and give the impression that entire villages are open to the public.

Villages wishing to confine tourist access to certain prescribed paths must clearly demarcate those routes for the visitor. This can be done most effectively through signage. However, it should also be supported by environmental design considerations. These could include barriers of wood or stone lining a path; color schemes that indicate path versus nonpath areas; the use of prominent buildings, viewpoints, and other landmarks around which to center visitor activity; and the use of pavement to make the acceptable route more prominent. Similar design considerations could also be used to distinguish acceptable visitor parking areas.

The organic layout of pueblo villages plays a major role in shaping the location of paths and the likely tourist use of them. Linear villages naturally have linear paths. Grid villages have grid paths. Plazas that are clearly demarcated with limited access points are more effective than those that are less obviously demarcated. The

Table 9.6. Pueblo Village Tourism Design Elements

1. **Paths** (which people move along)
   - Roads and trails: prominence; density; pattern/layout
   - Parking lots: size; location; surface
   - Viewpoints: off-site or on-site; interpretive information
2. **Edges** (between two different areas)
   - Walls, fences, and signs
   - Vegetation and ground markings
   - Building locations
3. **Districts** (clearly identifiable with common elements)
   - Tourist buildings and areas: visitors' centers; arts and crafts shops
   - Nontourist buildings and areas: private; sacred
4. **Nodes** (concentrated focal points, often at the junction of Paths)
   - Plazas: clearly demarcated entrance
   - Commercial centers: grocery, gas, and other services
5. **Landmarks** (major points of reference or interest)
   - Churches
   - Other site-specific features

protected plaza conveys the message that the community holds this place in special esteem. The limited or controlled access gives the visitor a sense of passage from a more profane space to a more sacred space. Such is often the case in those New Mexico pueblos that experienced the strongest Spanish influence. They typically have a controllable grid street layout with a plaza demarcated by the presence of an adobe Catholic church. Many of the pueblo Indians in these villages practice a mixture of traditional and Catholic religious rites.

Edges

Any area that has special meaning should be provided with an edge to demarcate it from the less meaningful world. Many of the design considerations that apply to paths actually involve the creation of edges between tourist space and nontourist space. This is similar to a fence, wall, or door demarcating the private home from the public community. There should also be a private community area that is protected from the public world. If there were no tourists, this would not be a problem. But there are, and there will probably be increasingly more for most pueblo villages in the future. Edges are not a part of pueblo culture to the same degree as in the dominant American culture with its fences and clearly demarcated property lines. However, unobtrusive edges, such as rock path boundaries, along with a couple of well-placed and maintained barriers or signs, might be all that is necessary to confine the majority of outsiders to acceptable public spaces.

Nodes and Landmarks

The presence of tourist-oriented businesses (even those operating out of an individual's home) provides the visitor with the sense of being in the proper place. The placement of these at certain strategic points could create nodes of visitor concentration. Such nodes within a village could become the focal point of visitor activities, where they would conceivably spend the majority of their time. Visitors would then be less likely to wander into more private back regions of the village. The First Mesa villages on the Hopi Reservation have such a node, which tourists are directed to. The village office is located there, as well as a small store and several households that sell arts and crafts.

A prominent landmark could provide the attractive element for the creation of tourist nodes. This could be the plaza (as discussed above), a distinctive cluster of buildings, or a scenic viewpoint. A visitors' center or museum could also serve this function. The landmark would catch the visitor's initial interest, whereas the associated tourist-oriented businesses and other activities could serve to maintain the visitor's longer interests.

Creating a Tourist District

The creation of a landmark-centered, nodal tourist district with a clearly defined path leading to it and well-marked edges would help the tourist in determining the acceptable way of visiting a pueblo village, and thereby lessen tourist–resident conflicts that occasionally arise (Table 9.7). Locating the village administrative office in this district would further enhance its importance in the eye of the visitor. This would also be an ideal location for public restrooms. If a village wished to allowing photography at a fee, which many New Mexico pueblos already do, the tourist district could provide the ideal location to introduce this concept. The advantage of this approach is that it would minimize the impact of tourism on a traditional village by making environmental cues as unobtrusive as possible through a mix of overt signs and covert physical design.

Other than Acoma and Taos, few pueblo villages have this type of tourist district. The only place on the Hopi Reservation that currently has a clearly defined "tourist district," somewhat similar to that suggested here, is on First Mesa. The First Mesa villages have an advantage because the physically narrow mesa on which they are located allows considerable vehicular control. All vehicular traffic is funneled through a single route where the cars can be intercepted and informed of village regulations. For most other pueblo villages, the first step would be to make the path leading to the tourist district more prominent. (Several pueblo reservations, including Hopi, have tourist districts located outside of the traditional villages. These types of facilities are easier to construct and identify than the village-based districts discussed here.)

According to MacCannell (1976) and others, one of the major motivations of tourists is to penetrate into the "back region" or "real world" of the place visited. For most tourists, the experience of a "tourist district" in a pueblo village is a sufficient back region experience. This, however, is not enough for some. A small minority will always try to go to places where they should not. No amount of environmental design or planning can prevent this. But the suggestions offered here could substantially reduce these types of occurrences.

Conclusions

Unlike many other tribes in the U.S., most of the pueblo Indians of the Southwest were not moved by military force from their homeland to a distant reservation. Although some dislocation occurred under Spanish rule, the pueblo villages of today reflect a cultural tradition dating back at least 1,000 years, with close links to cultures that are two to three times that old. Their villages are special places of

---

Table 9.7. Pueblo Village Tourism Design Prescriptions

1. Paths and edges should be clearly demarcated by use of distinct materials (rocks, wood, pavement) or color schemes. Some signage should be considered to supplement these. A tourist path that includes prominent landmarks, distinctive buildings, and attractive viewpoints should be developed and demarcated in some manner.
2. Tourist nodes should be allowed to develop at prominent locations, such as at viewpoints and near major landmarks. These nodes should be indicated by use of color schemes and signs. Tourist businesses and services should be isolated in the immediate vicinity of these nodes.
3. Private areas should be well protected by unobtrusive barriers and, where necessary, signs. A private, nontourist community area (or node) should be developed and protected from tourism.

which they are rightfully very protective. Smith (1996a, 1996b) refers to this as a habitat that is both available for exploitation as a tourist attraction, and in need of protection against improper use and abuse. For most Southwestern pueblo villages, the protection aspect has been a major concern with regard to tourism.

The present situation of tourism in the pueblo villages in the states of Arizona and New Mexico could be improved. One of the major problems from the tourist perspective is not knowing what is acceptable and unacceptable behavior. Minimal existing signage and the ambiguous physical design of villages results in confusion and disorientation. Most villages, however, were not designed with the needs of the tourist in mind. Nor should they have been. Now that the tourists are here, however, they must be accommodated in some manner. Using environmental design to both inform visitors (through signage) and to guide visitors (through physical design) could provide an unobtrusive means of managing the ever-increasing numbers of visitors to pueblo reservations.

The adaptation of environmental design concepts to the problem of pueblo village tourism management provides a potentially more positive diffusion of ideas than does unmanaged tourism-induced acculturation. This approach is highly compatible with existing village designs and lifestyles, it is not complex to understand, and it can and has produced visible results when implemented. By consciously controlling tourism, its negative impact on the acculturation of Native Americans can be lessened and tourism's more positive impact of enhancing cross-cultural understanding can be increased.

Chapter 10

Antarctica Tourism: Successful Management of a Vulnerable Environment

John Splettstoesser

Introduction

Antarctica was the last continent to be "discovered" (sighted in 1820), and for many years remained essentially unexplored. Its visitors in the 19th century included mainly those involved in commercial ventures such as sealing (for hides and oil) in the early 1800s, but by about 1830–1840 the population of fur seals, the primary target for this exploitation, had become commercially extinct and the activity ceased. Whaling began in 1904, with shore factories starting in South Georgia, and continued nearly uninterrupted until 1965, when the shore-based industry closed down. Adventurers and explorers appeared in Antarctica at various times during the 1800s, but in low numbers. The first documented wintering of anyone in Antarctica occurred in 1898, when the *Belgica*, expedition ship of a Belgian expedition headed by Adrien de Gerlache, spent the winter with its crew beset in ice in the Bellingshausen Sea. It was not until nearly the end of that century that scientific expeditions appeared, with efforts made toward an under-standing of the continent's geography, biology, atmosphere, geology, oceanography, and related studies common elsewhere in the world. It became evident relatively soon that indigenous humans were not living on this harsh and cold land mass, and probably never had. Political ambitions and territorial claims surfaced in the early 1900s, with the first formal claim being made in 1908 by Great Britain of the Antarctic Peninsular area. Other territorial claims followed, until, by the 1940s, a total of seven countries claimed parts of Antarctica. That situation persists to this day.

Antarctica After World War II

World War II curtailed interest and activity in Antarctica, although there were signs that Germany might use the continent as a base for ship activities in the Southern Hemisphere. Admiral Byrd's third expedition began in 1939, but was cut short by the onset of the war. Private expeditions resumed after the war, in the 1940s, and major expeditions by the United States ("Operation Highjump" and "Operation Windmill") in the late 1940s included large numbers of military vessels and personnel in efforts to survey and map coastal areas and conduct research programs. In the 1950s the United States and 11 other countries prepared for scientific studies of the entire continent as part of the International Geophysical Year (IGY), 1957–58, the first large-scale multidisciplinary and cooperative venture on the continent. Research stations were constructed along the coastline and a few on the ice sheet itself in efforts to study the atmosphere, ice sheet, and unknown parts of the interior, using aircraft, oversnow vehicles, and ships. For the first time, Antarctica began to yield many of its secrets. A world's record-low air temperature was recorded at the interior station Vostok (USSR), where –88°C was reached in mid-winter. (This record was exceeded in July 1983 when the temperature dipped to –89°C, also at Vostok.) Interesting and fascinating information on the continent's wildlife and plant life was revealed, new mountains were discovered, and the vast expanse of ice was mapped and measured. It was found that only a minor percentage of the entire continent was not covered by ice, and parts of the ice sheet were resting on bedrock below sea level. More recent analysis of the ice sheet by satellite imagery shows that less than 1% is exposed bedrock, and all the rest is ice bound. In one area of Wilkes Land, the ice is 4,776 m thick.

Antarctic Treaty

The IGY produced many more questions than were answered, and the countries active in Antarctica agreed that a formal document, such as a treaty, would resolve issues of territorial claims, potential resource exploitation, exchange of data, and the potential for military intrusion on a continent that had never seen conflict. The Antarctic Treaty of 1959 was thus born (ratified in 1961), in which these and other issues were addressed, including a ban on nuclear testing, radioactive waste disposal, and military maneuvers. The Treaty has since been amended many times, particularly as new issues surfaced. Mineral resources, for example, was not discussed or included in the 1959 Treaty because at that time very little was known about the occurrences of potentially valuable minerals, metals, or hydrocarbons. (In many respects, this is still the case, in 1997.) Nevertheless, the Treaty signatories, in negotiations in the 1980s, formulated a resolution that would permit prospecting and development of minerals, but only under extremely restrictive conditions in order to protect the environment. This resolution failed in later negotiations, and resulted in a ban on mining for a period of 50 years, which could be reviewed at that time for possible change or extension. This ban, and other significant environmental Annexes, have become part of the Environmental Protocol, signed in 1991 and ratified in 1998 (author's note: an assumption at the time of this writing). The message made clear by Antarctic Treaty signatories was established with the advent of the Treaty itself—that is, Antarctica is there as a laboratory for science, and anything else is secondary. No one can argue with that concept, but it can also be shown that nonscientific activities, such as tourism, can be conducted in Antarctica on a compatible, noninterference basis with science, and not adversely affect the pristine environment.

Onset of Tourism in Antarctica

Another subject that escaped the 1959 Treaty was that of tourism, which by that time had begun on a small scale but was hardly a controversial issue. Modern shipborne tourism in Antarctica began in 1958 (Headland, 1994), but trips on an annual basis did not start until about the mid-1960s. Tourism has continued uninterrupted until the present day. The concept of "expedition cruising," coupled with education as a primary theme of the cruise, began with Lars-Eric Lindblad in 1966. In 1969, Lindblad had the first ice-strengthened tourist vessel built, the *Lindblad Explorer*, and took her to Antarctica that austral summer. The ship has been to Antarctica every summer since, although under other ownerships and names (presently the *Explorer*). In the last few years, as many as 12 vessels and about 7,000–10,000 tourists have visited Antarctica annually. About 6,500 visitors are anticipated in the 1996-97 season (Table 10.1), although the total in 1995-96 was 9,200.

In addition to commercial tour vessels, ancillary aspects of tourism in Antarctica include private yachts, mostly in the Antarctic Peninsula because of the proximity to South American and Falkland Islands (Islas Malvinas) ports, and also because of the diversity of wildlife and spectacular scenery found in the Peninsula. Ten known yachts, some with fare-paying passengers, made 54 individual trips to Antarctica in the 1992-93 season (Enzenbacher, 1994, p. 109). The numbers of yachts and their passengers have increased somewhat since then. Because the activity of yachts is more difficult to regulate, or monitor, some Treaty signatories perceive yacht tourism as more of a potential threat to the environment than organized, commercial travel by tour vessels. In practice, this is not necessarily so. Nevertheless, yacht travel to Antarctica is popular, and will remain so, in some respects because it is more affordable than larger tour vessels, and it also does not have the time constraints of chartered cruise vessels with firm schedules and itineraries.

In addition to the more common means of visiting Antarctica, by ship, a private company has operated in Antarctica since 1985, providing logistics for visitors to the interior. Punta Arenas, Chile, is used as a base for flying visitors to the base camp at Patriot Hills (80° 20´S, 81°25´W) in the southern Ellsworth Mountains. The camp, constructed annually, is used as a staging area for mountaineering expeditions to the geographic South Pole, and other activities. (The highest peaks in Antarctica are found near the base camp, including Vinson Massif, at 4,897 m.) The total number of individuals involved in these private expeditions is about 150 annually, representing a minor complement of all visitors to Antarctica. A review of these operations in the interior is given by Swithinbank (1993).

Table 10.1. Estimate of 1996–97 Season Tourist Cruises to Antarctica

Vessel	Operator/Charter	Passenger Capacity	Probable No. Voyages	Estimated Average Load	Probable Total No. Passengers
Explorer	Explorer Shipping	96	9	75	675
Kapitan Khlebnikov	Zegrahm Expeditions	114	1	98	98
Kapitan Khlebnikov	Quark Expeditions	114	2	100	200
Professor Khromov	Quark Expeditions	38	8	30	240
Professor Molchanov	GMMS Pty. Ltd.	38	7	30	210
Professor Molchanov	Quark Expeditions	38	2	30	60
Akademik Shokalski	Southern Heritage Exp.	36	3	33	99
World Discoverer	Zegrahm Expeditions	138	1	125	125
World Discoverer	Society Expeditions	138	7	75	525
Bremen	Quark Expeditions	164	1	110	110
Bremen	Hanseatic Cruises	164	1	110	110
Hanseatic	Hanseatic Cruises	180	6	125	750
Akademik Ioffe	Quark Expeditions	79	3	75	225
Akademik Ioffe	Marine Expeditions	79	9	75	675
Akademik Sergei Vavilov	Marine Expeditions	79	10	75	750
Professor Multanovskiy	Marine Expeditions	36	5	32	160
Professor Multanovskiy	Mt. Travel—Sobek	36	4	33	132
Akademik Boris Petrov	Marine Expeditions	45	11	40	440
Alla Tarasova	Marine Expeditions	96	8	95	760
Alla Tarasova	Quark Expeditions	96	2	90	180
Totals			100		6,524

Based on information provided by members to the IAATO Secretariat as of April 22, 1996.

Other Types of Tourism and Impacts on Science Programs

In addition to shipborne tourism and the relatively minor aspect of airborne tourism conducted since 1985 in which a temporary summer camp is used as a staging area, another type of airborne tourism was popular in the 1970s. In 1977, Qantas airlines conducted overflights of the continent from Sydney, Australia, offering low-altitude views of the mainland in the Ross Sea sector, the

Transantarctic Mountains, and on to the geographic South Pole. Air New Zealand offered similar flights from New Zealand to the continent. No landings were made, however, and therefore no threats to wildlife or other potential environmental damage could result. These flights ended in the 1979-80 season when an Air New Zealand DC-10 crashed into Ross Island near Mount Erebus on November 28, 1979, killing all 257 aboard. The flight path was on a low-altitude heading in McMurdo Sound in conditions of poor visibility, and the pilot did not see the glacier-covered slopes of the island until it was too late.

This incident challenged the logistics resources of both McMurdo Station (U.S.) and Scott Base (New Zealand), located nearby on the southern part of the same island. Although in the midst of supporting active research programs in the early part of the summer season, U.S. helicopters and crews and New Zealand mountaineering personnel were recruited in search and rescue missions, and then collecting debris and bodies from the crash site. This perturbation in the relatively rigid logistics schedule for preplanned projects caused unexpected delays and possible cancellation of some of the ongoing research conducted at these stations and in remote areas on the continent.

The activity of scenic overflights was resumed by Croydon Travel, Victoria, Australia, using Qantas's Boeing 747 aircraft, and in the most recent seasons carried 2,128 passengers in 1994-95 and 2,958 in 1995-96. More flights are planned for the 1996-97 season.

A comparable situation occurred in 1989, when an Argentine supply vessel, *Bahia Paraiso*, ran aground on January 28 in Arthur Harbor, immediately after leaving Palmer Station (U.S.) on Anvers Island in the west side of the Antarctic Peninsula. The ship was on a resupply mission to Argentine stations in the Peninsula area, as well as exchanging base personnel, but there were also about 80 tourists aboard, a common practice for this ship in previous seasons. The ship stopped at Palmer Station for the benefit of the tourists. The grounding caused a rupture of the hull, resulting in leakage of 180,000 gallons of diesel fuel, which spread over the local area and affected primarily krill and intertidal organisms (limpets). Whether long-term effects resulted on other life in the area, such as penguins and shags, is unknown. Nevertheless, the potential for major environmental damage is obvious in the event of any future incident of this nature. The resources of the U.S. Antarctic Program, in particular, were taxed in the ensuing cleanup procedures, which began as soon as equipment could be brought to the site, a long and laborious process because suitable equipment was not at hand anywhere in the Antarctic. No human loss resulted, but the facilities of the small U.S. station were taxed to the limit, as well as those of the two tour vessels in the vicinity that assisted in transport of the *Bahia Paraiso's* passengers to Marsh Base (Chile) for evacuation to South America.

The outcome of these two incidents—the DC-10 crash in 1979 and the grounding of the ship in 1989—pointed to the need for better management controls on nongovernmental activities in Antarctica, particularly as the mishaps might affect scientific research programs. It also showed the need for contingency plans for both governmental and nongovernmental activities. As recently as the 1993-94 summer season, an accident and resulting death of a member of a private expedition in the interior initiated a search and rescue mission by U.S. and New Zealand personnel in a remote area of the continent, thus diverting support logistics from science programs.

The incidents discussed above are only a few of many that have occurred over the years since the IGY, some related to science programs, and a few to tourism activities. Because of the remoteness of the continent, and the potential for loss of life through accidents, all Treaty signatories are prepared and willing to assist in any distress call from any party. No one is immune from potential accidents, whether science or tourism related, but the mandate of the Antarctic Treaty requires that priorities be given to the conduct of science. Along with this treatise, it also means that the Treaty signatories have the sole authority to regulate activities of any of their citizens in Antarctica. Although there is as yet no "police force" in Antarctica, it is understood that the activities of anyone there are on the "honor system," and existing rules and regulations need to be observed, often voluntarily, because of the need for standardizing human conduct in a pristine environment (Splettstoesser, 1993, p. 7).

Environmental Impacts?

The issue of potential environmental impacts as a result of tourism in Antarctica must be viewed with a variety of factors in mind. Prior to the onset of tourism, there were numerous sporadic intrusions by humans in Antarctica, but until the IGY of 1957-58 (mentioned earlier) all those earlier visits constituted specific terms of occupation, such as an austral summer, a winter, or perhaps 2 years. These visitors included members of the private expeditions, for example, and a few government-sponsored expeditions. There were few instances of continuous occupation, and when a ship departed Antarctica at the end of a summer, the last person to step on the ship was the last on the continent. It is difficult to imagine that one of Earth's continents not only has never had human occupation during a period of modern human activity in all other parts of the world, but has not had continuous occupation until the last 40-50 years. Furthermore, the total numbers of individuals on the continent up to the IGY was far less than 100 annually, and since the IGY has probably not been more than 5,000 in its busiest time, in the austral summer (not counting tourists).

The few exceptions to continuous occupation occurred in the 1940s and 1950s, when a handful of bases were constructed in the Antarctic Peninsula and some offshore islands, including Laurie Island, South Orkney Islands, where the Argentineans have occupied Orcadas since 1904, thus providing the longest continuous period of meteorological observations anywhere in Antarctica. If the Antarctic Convergence delimits the northern boundary of Antarctica, then whaling activities at South Georgia (50° latitude) from 1904 to 1965 would also fall within the definition of continuous human occupation. (Antarctic Convergence is the zone in which cooler surface waters of the ocean around Antarctica descend

northward beneath the warmer waters of the other oceans.) The northern boundary of the area under the jurisdiction of the Antarctic Treaty is 60°S latitude.

However, until preparations began for the IGY and construction of some of the
stations in 1955, there was no large-scale continuous occupation of the continent.
The situation has changed, and may never be any different. There have been
humans on Antarctica ever since.

Environmental awareness was not foremost in the minds of planning of those
active in Antarctica in the last 40–50 years, and for this reason there has been some
criticism of site locations for stations, trash disposal, local pollution, and general
state of conditions of many of the pre- and post-IGY activities. In the U.S. Antarctic
Program, for example, McMurdo Station, an IGY facility, still in use today, has been
cited for abuse of environmental practices in common use in the U.S. today.
However, at the time of its inception and for some years after, the consciousness of
environmental practices as we know them today was not widespread, and not
implemented in Antarctica by most countries. It has taken some time for earlier
management procedures of the 1950s and 1960s to be brought into the modern
era of environmental management. McMurdo and other IGY stations might have
violated some of the current environmental regulations in their time, but if so it
occurred before the time of environmental awareness that exists today.

Comparisons of the estimated 5,000 individuals involved in the research programs
of the Antarctic Treaty countries with the 8,000 or so tourists in a given austral
summer shows that the "residence time" of tourists (Splettstoesser, 1992) is
insignificant with respect to that of the science programs. Headland (1994, p. 279)
estimates that tourist presence on the continent is about 0.5% that of all other
individuals. The reason for this is that shipborne tourism provides for the "hotel"
for all visitors, and there is no need for a shore-based facility, and thus no associated pollution, trash disposal, and other problems related to research stations. All
material that is brought into Antarctica by ship is disposed of according to interna-
tionally acceptable procedures at sea or disposed of at gateway ports.

The sole exception to the "residence time" of tourists is that of the private company (Adventure Network International) that flies its clients to the interior (the
camp at Patriot Hills, mentioned earlier), where a temporary summer camp is
erected. At the end of the summer activities, the camp is dismantled and all trash is
removed from Antarctica, including human wastes. As stated elsewhere
(Splettstoesser & Smith, 1994), an Antarctic cruise is the most comfortable and
least damaging travel mode, but Swithinbank (1993) presents a strong case for the
potential growth of airborne tourism. However, this would necessitate construction of hard-surface runways, hotels and other infrastructure, and provision for the
waste and trash disposal. On the other hand, the location of the present temporary
facility in the interior (Patriot Hills) is far away from wildlife areas, breeding birds
or other fauna, and no vegetation (minor lichen growth). As far as fauna, flora, and
the total environment are concerned, Patriot Hills and the satellite camps used by
the clients of Adventure Network produce no discernible environmental impact, as
illustrated in an Initial Environmental Evaluation conducted by an independent

consultant in 1994 (XVIII ATCM-Kyoto, Information Paper). This is also the case in
the IEE for one of the shipborne tour operators that conducts icebreaker and
helicopter activities in Antarctica (XVIII-Kyoto, Information Paper). Another advantage of the Patriot Hills operation is that of a natural, blue-ice runway on which
wheeled aircraft can land, a feature found in other parts of Antarctica where
potential tourism to the interior might be contemplated.

This kind of environmental record in Antarctica is commendable, inasmuch as the
tour industry has not been regulated to date, except for its own self-imposed
practices. The formation of IAATO in 1991 (see below) to provide a central organization that speaks for the entire industry, to coordinate and standardize acceptable
environmental guidelines for visitors and tour operators, and assist Treaty signatories in their science missions, is a milestone in the history of humans in Antarctica.
The Bylaws of IAATO provide further details on its objectives, but overall the
organization is unique with respect to the management of a commercial industry
in one of the critical environments of the world (Splettstoesser, in press).

Butler (1991), among others, discusses the relationship between tourism, the
environment, and the kinds of tourists that might be found in a place like Antarctica. Unlike "mass tourism," the type of tourist normally found in Antarctica appreci-
ates nature and ecotourism, green tourism, or other labels commonly associated
with the environment (Butler, 1991, pp. 205–206). Butler also points out, however,
that these kinds of visitors are rarely repeat visitors; for example, having visited the
Canadian Arctic, their next destination might well be Antarctica, and after that the
Andes, etc. However, this author's personal experience has shown that visitors to
Antarctica are commonly repeaters because there is a considerable amount of
variety in what it has to offer, and it cannot be seen or enjoyed in a single trip.

State of Today's Tourism in Antarctica:
Formation of Environmental Guidelines and IAATO

As mentioned earlier, modern shipborne tourism in Antarctica began in 1958,
although the intensity and numbers of ships and tourists has become most active
only within the last 10 years. This has resulted in a number of developments,
virtually all of them self-imposed by the tour operators.

The guidelines for tour operators and for visitors were compiled in the late 1980s,
consisting of a code of practices that the operators had been using for many years.
The only change was that they were put into writing and distributed to all existing
operators at the time. Much of the content was excerpted from Antarctic Treaty
Recommendations, and elaborated on with regard to some of the guidelines. The
primary theme of the guidelines related to the environment, and protection of
wildlife and vegetation.

In 1991 the active tour operators founded the International Association of Antarctica Tour Operators (IAATO) as a means of pooling resources and knowledge, as
well as promoting legislation that is compatible with the type of tourism that the
operators had exhibited in their history. A Spokesperson was appointed to monitor

the activities of U.S. and other Treaty signatories with regard to legislation that might affect the tourism industry in Antarctica. Other responsibilities include attending Consultative Meetings of the Antarctic Treaty as an invited delegate and representative of IAATO, tabling papers related to tourism, and advising when legislation is drafted; testifying at Hearings of the U.S. House and Senate for bills that include language on tourism; and generally keeping the IAATO members informed of proceedings pertaining to the industry. All these responsibilities require maintaining a vocal and aggressive stance in support of the tourism industry and its successful record of environmental management of visits to Antarctica.

IAATO members immediately adopted the existing Guidelines that had been compiled by the operators in 1989, distributing them widely to all tour operators in ensuing seasons in order to ensure that all passengers were informed of these as-yet unofficial documents. IAATO also had these Guidelines made available in all four of the Treaty languages (English, French, Russian, Spanish), plus German and Japanese, in efforts to reach as wide an international audience as the industry clientele would normally include. IAATO members also continue the practice of "educational programs" as part of "expedition cruising," much as Lars-Eric Lindblad began in the 1960s (Splettstoesser, 1996). A staff of naturalists/lecturers on a cruise ship normally includes individuals with considerable experience on tour ships to Antarctica, as well as many with research experience under the auspices of some of the Treaty Parties' national programs. Zodiac Drivers, Expedition Leaders, and other key tour staff provide a wealth of experience and expertise in "expedition cruising," a critical factor in educating visitors about the fragile and vulnerable ecosystem found in Antarctica.

Original IAATO membership consisted of the seven active tour operators in 1991, and invitations for others to join are issued as new operators schedule their activities in Antarctica. Membership for the 1996–97 season consisted of 12 members from six countries (Table 10.2). Full text of the Guidelines and Bylaws, with membership lists, has been published elsewhere (Splettstoesser, 1992; Splettstoesser & Folks, 1994; Splettstoesser & Smith, 1994). Copies of the current membership list and information about IAATO membership is available from the Secretariat in New York (Table 10.2).

Protocol on Environmental Protection to the Antarctic Treaty

At the XVth Antarctic Treaty Consultative Meeting (ATCM) in Madrid, Spain in 1991, a major step was taken toward a consensus to protect the environment in Antarctica, formally known as the "Protocol on Environmental Protection to the Antarctic Treaty" (also known as the Madrid Protocol). This document covers the activities of virtually any visitor to Antarctica (scientist or support staff, tourist, or anyone else) with regard to planning for station construction, site management for scientists, environmental impact assessment of prospective field areas, protection of fauna and flora, marine pollution, and reclassification of protected areas. It also

Table 10.2. Membership of International Association of Antarctica Tour Operators (IAATO) (as of May 1998)

Office of the Secretariat
111 East 14 Street, Suite 110
New York, NY 10003 USA
Darrel Schoeling
Tel: 212 460 8715
Fax: 212 529 8684
IATTO@aol.com

Spokesperson
John Splettstoesser
Rockland, ME, USA
Tel/Fax: 207 594 7594
jspletts@midcoast.com

Members

Abercrombie & Kent/Explorer Shipping Corp.
Oak Brook, IL, USA
Victoria Underwood
Tel: 630 954 2944
Fax: 630 572 1833
vunderwood@compuserve.com
www.abercrombiekent.com

Adventure Network International
Beaconsfield, Bucks, UK
Anne Kershaw
Tel: 44 1494 671808
Fax: 44 1494 671725
adventurenetwork@compuserve.com
www.adventurenetwork.com

Aurora Expeditions
Sydney, NSW, Australia
Greg Mortimer
Tel: 61 2 9252 1033
Fax: 61 2 9252 1373
auroraex@world.net

Hapag-Lloyd Cruiseship Management GmbH
Hamburg, Germany
Bärbel Krämer
Tel: 49 40 3001 4600
Fax: 49 40 3001 4601
baerbel_kraemer@hanseatic-cruises.ccmail.compuserve.com
or info@hapag-lloyd.com
www.hapag-lloyd.com

Heritage Expeditions
Christchurch, New Zealand
Rodney Russ
Tel: 64 3 359 7711
Fax: 64 3 359 3311
hertexp@ibm.net

Marine Expeditions
Toronto, Ontario, Canada
Patrick Shaw
Tel: 416 964 9069
Fax: 416 964 2366
ops@marineex.com

Mountain Travel.Sobek
El Cerrito, CA, USA
Olaf Malver
Tel: 510 527 8105
Fax: 510 525 7710
olaf@mtsobek.com
www.mtsobek.com

Quark Expeditions
Darien, CT, USA
Denise Landau
Tel: 203 656 0499
Fax: 203 656 6623
quarkexpeditions@compuserve.com
www.Quark-expeditions.com

Society Expeditions
Seattle, WA, USA
John Tillotson
Tel: 206 728 9400
Fax: 206 728 2301
Societyexp@aol.com

Travel Dynamics
New York, NY, USA
Jim Smith
Tel: 212 517 7555
Fax: 212 517 0077
jim@travdyn.com
www.travdyn.com

Wildwings
Bristol, Avon, UK
John Brodie-Good
Tel: 44 117 9848040
Fax: 44 117 9674444
wildinfo@wildwings.co.uk
www.wildwings.co.uk

Zegrahm Expeditions
Seattle, WA, USA
Werner Zehnder
Tel: 206 285 4000
Fax: 206 285 5037
zoe@zeco.com
www.zeco.com

Provisional (New) Members

Adventure Associates
Sydney, NSW, Australia
Dennis Collaton
Tel: 61 2 9389 7466
Fax: 61 2 9369 1853
mail@adventureassociates.com
www.adventureassociates.com

Clipper Cruise Line
St. Louis, MO, USA
Kristen Deeg
Tel: 314 727 2929
Fax: 314 727 5246
smallship@aol.com
www.clippercruise.com

Plantours & Partner
Bremen, Germany
Brigit Ernstmeier
Tel: 49 421 1736927
Fax: 49 421 1736935

Pelagic Expeditions
Hamble, Hants, UK
Skip Novak
Tel/Fax: 44 1703 454120
skipnovak@compuserve.com
www.pelagic.co.uk

Special Expeditions
New York, NY, USA
Sven-Olof Lindblad
Tel: 212 765 7740
Fax: 212 265 3770
travel@specialexpeditions.com
www.specialexpeditions.com

Associate Members

Japan Euro-Asia Service Co.
Tokyo, Japan
Matsui Sadaaki
Tel: 81 3 3221 9121
Fax: 81 3 3221 9120

LaTour Chili
Santiago, Chile
Mike Gallegos
Tel: 56 2 225 2883
Fax: 56 2 225 2545

addresses the issue of mineral resources by placing a ban on prospecting and exploitation of minerals and hydrocarbons for a period of 50 years. The Madrid Protocol thus covers not only the activities of those involved in science programs, but tourists as well. Still to be ratified (put into effect) in January 1998, each of the consultative (voting) signatory countries passed its own national legislation as a follow-up to the Protocol in order to have jurisdiction over its citizens. Thus, national laws in one country may differ slightly from those of another with respect to the Protocol, but the overall content must reflect the specific intent of the Protocol.

Until the Protocol was ratified, and a system of monitoring observers was implemented in order to ensure compliance with its regulations, tour operators agreed to follow the Recommendation XVIII-1, the official version of many of the self-imposed tour operator guidelines. For the last few years, since the Madrid Protocol was enacted, the U.S. National Science Foundation (NSF) instituted a system of shipboard monitors for selected tour vessels as a means of observing actions of tour operators that relate to potential environmental impacts. This system was welcomed by the tour operators, partly because it provided independent confirmation of their minimal impact operating procedures. The NSF observer program will probably become a model for the U.S. and other countries to follow in a formal Treaty-wide management plan for observers under the auspices of the Protocol.

Several programs in the last few austral summers have provided site analyses of the areas commonly visited by tourists in the Antarctic Peninsula. Project Antarctic Conservation (PAC), conducted by Dr. Bernard Stonehouse of the Scott Polar Research Institute, Cambridge, England, and another by Oceanites, headed by Ron Naveen (U.S.), collected field information from commonly visited sites in efforts to provide base data for methods of monitoring Antarctic tourism, and to assist in preparation of environmental assessments. The International Centre for Antarctic Information and Research (ICAIR), located in Christchurch, New Zealand, is currently the repository of all data collected under these monitoring programs. The Council of Managers of National Antarctic Programs (COMNAP) is involved in a process of setting up standards for expedition ships, plus related requirements for tourism activities, and assists in coordinating and compiling statistics for tourism.

ATCM — Kyoto, 1994

The XVIIIth Antarctic Treaty Consultative Meeting in Kyoto, Japan in April 1994 produced a significant document on the subject of Antarctic tourism. After laboring through several annexes on the subject at previous ATCMs, none of which was approved, the Kyoto meeting resulted in passage of "Recommendation XVIII-1, Tourism and Nongovernmental Activities," which includes sections on Guidance for Tour Operators and Visitors. This document incorporates many of the former, self-imposed guidelines that the tour operators had been practicing for some years. Now formalized under the Treaty System, the text has been printed by IAATO and is distributed to all tour operators and visitors in each austral season.

Future of Antarctic Tourism

With the ratification of the Madrid Protocol, and subsequent probable cumbersome requirements for permit applications, environmental impact studies, restrictions imposed on types and sizes of ships, authorized site visits, and other barriers, tour operators in Antarctica will face new and occasionally insurmountable problems in continuing their programs. Those operators who have markets in other parts of the world and can operate there successfully without regulatory problems might elect to move out of Antarctica. Adventure, or expedition tourism in Antarctica, however, will continue, for the market will continue to be there, providing travel to an unusual and unique place on Earth. The numbers of visitors will probably decline, which is probably a positive outcome for the future in the event of a possible shrinking industry and for the fragile environment found in Antarctica. But for the remaining tour operators, those who continue to conduct conscientious and environmentally sound trips to Antarctica, the continent will attract and provide the ultimate trip for the adventurous tourist.

A final note is worth mentioning with regard to the recent history of IAATO as an organization. Because of its importance in coordinating industry activities in Antarctica, and its acceptance by the Antarctic Treaty community, IAATO should be viewed as a prospective analogue for a comparable organization for Arctic tourism. Although the geographic and political conditions are different, an "Arctic IAATO" should be considered as a viable tool for successful tourism management in the Arctic, and development of an Arctic visitor's code (Mason, 1994).

Acknowledgments

Assistance by Melissa Folks, former IAATO Secretariat, Kent, WA, USA, is appreciated in all aspects of compiling data and providing general support in the preparation of this chapter. Follow-up assistance was provided by Darrel Schoeling, current IAATO Secretariat. Dr. Valene Smith, California State University, Chico, CA, USA, provided support in many ways and collaborated many times in our studies of Antarctic tourism. Kim Crosbie assisted with the manuscript as reviewer and for clarification of parts of the content.

Author's Note

Tables 10.1 and 10.2 and other dated parts of this chapter are superseeded annually by new statistics. The article by Splettstoesser (in press) should be consulted for some of these changes.

Chapter 11

Tourism in Sensitive Environments: Three African Success Stories

Charlotte M. Echtner

Introduction

There is tremendous potential to develop tourism in Africa. The continent offers diverse scenery, fascinating cultures, and unspoiled wilderness and wildlife. Despite these assets, Africa currently captures just over 3% of the world tourism market (World Tourism Organization [WTO], 1996). Kenya, a tourism leader in Africa, attracts about one thousandth of the global tourism market (WTO, 1996). However, as tourists increasingly seek out authenticity and adventure, Africa's exotic offerings will undoubtedly be particularly appealing. As a result, the African tourism industry will continue to grow and penetrate new, highly sensitive areas of the continent.

The following discussion highlights the successes and challenges of tourism development in Africa via an examination of three exemplary case studies. These cases have been chosen to provide a sampling of the sensitive issues and environments that exist throughout the continent. The first case study examines village tourism in the country of Senegal in western Africa. This is an example of tourism occurring in a highly sensitive sociocultural setting. The second case explores gorilla tourism in the central African country of Uganda. In this example, a sensitive ecological system must be held in balance. Finally, the third case outlines tourism development in the country of Namibia in southern Africa. This case examines how this new nation intends to develop sustainable tourism that is sensitive to both the cultural and natural environments.

These three "success stories" involve alternative forms of tourism. Alternative tourism refers to "small-scale, non-conventional, non-mass specialized forms of tourism that are socially and environmentally sensitive and respectful, as opposed to conventional forms of mass tourism" (Inskeep, 1991, p. 166). As will be illustrated throughout the discussion, such forms of tourism are especially appropriate in situations where traditional cultures and sensitive natural environments must be preserved.

Senegal: Village Tourism in a Sensitive Cultural Environment

Background

Village tourism in Senegal is not a recent innovation. It was introduced in the mid-1970s by a French ethnologist named Christian Saglio (Bilsen, 1987). After extensive field studies in Senegal, Saglio suggested that tourist facilities could be developed on the outskirts of certain existing Senegalese villages. He proposed that the villagers, themselves, could build a small-scale tourist complex, using only local materials and replicating the traditional style of village architecture. Upon completion, the villagers could then manage the facility. Tourists visiting the complex could experience the village way of life. He maintained that, if properly designed and managed, this form of tourism would encourage villagers to maintain their traditional lifestyle.

The Senegalese government was impressed by Saglio's concept, and between the period of 1974 and 1991, 13 tourist villages with a total capacity of 500 beds were built. The initial investment required (approximately US$170,000) was very minimal because all of the manpower and most of the materials were supplied by the villagers (Government of Senegal, 1991). Most of the initial, start-up funds were solicited from foreign aid agencies, including the Canadian University Service Overseas and the French Agency of Cultural and Technical Cooperation.

One of the tourist villages is located near the capital of Dakar and another in the eastern region of the country adjacent to a national park (refer to Figure 11.1). However, the majority of the villages, 11 out of 13, are located in the southern Casamance region of Senegal. This is an isolated region of Senegal, separated from the capital of Dakar by the country of Gambia. Because of this isolation, the

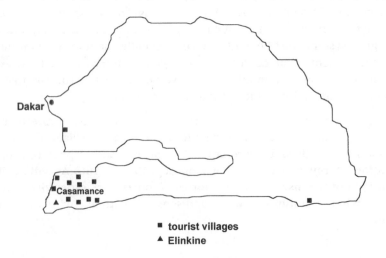

■ tourist villages
▲ Elinkine

Figure 11.1. Location of tourist villages in Senegal.

residents of the Casamance maintain a very traditional lifestyle, creating a fascinating setting for village tourism.

The latest statistics available (1990) indicate that 20,000 visitors came to the 13 tourist villages (Government of Senegal, 1991; Knights, 1993). About three quarters of the tourists were French, probably due to the traditional ties between Senegal and France (Senegal was formerly part of French West Africa). The total revenue generated from village tourism in 1990 was US$253,000. Although at first glance this revenue seems minimal, these funds have been able to bring noticeable, positive benefits to the local area. This is because there is no economic leakage—that is, all of the revenue is funneled directly back into the local village economy.

A Typical Example

The first tourist village was built in Elinkine in 1974. Elinkine is a small, traditional fishing village located along a very beautiful beach in the Casamance region of Senegal. The tourist complex is built on the outskirts of Elinkine, within easy walking distance of the village. Visitors are accommodated in traditional-style buildings, consisting of mud brick walls with straw roofs. A large oblong building, of the style normally used to accommodate an extended family, houses dormitory-style accommodation for groups. There are also smaller round huts that are suitable for two to four people. The total capacity is 50 beds. The facilities are very basic—no electricity and a communal amenities block with toilets and cold showers. The meals are cooked by the village women in the traditional manner and are eaten family-style in an open pavilion. The cost of accommodation and three meals is US$17.00 per person per day. The revenue generated has been used to build a maternity clinic, a school extension, and to purchase new motorized fishing boats (Knights, 1993).

There are very few preplanned activities in the tourist village. The main activity is to observe and experience the lifestyle of the villagers. In Elinkine, opportunities are available to accompany local fisherman on fishing trips. Boat trips can also be arranged to nearby beaches or to view wildlife in the extensive estuaries in the surrounding area.

Successes

Village tourism in Senegal has proven its sustainability—socially, environmentally, and financially—over a period of more than 20 years. One of the primary reasons for the success of this type of tourism is the in-depth participation of the local villagers. They are involved in each step of the development from planning, to construction, to the management and operation of the tourist complex. In each location, a council of elected village members oversees the entire tourist operation and decides on the allocation of profits. In addition, there is a team of about six people responsible for the day-to-day running of the tourist village. This includes registering guests, providing meals, and housekeeping. These "employees" are paid monthly by dividing up 30% of the total receipts (Government of Senegal, 1991).

As mentioned previously, in this form of tourism there is no economic leakage—100% of the profits get channeled back into the villages. Examples of the projects that have been funded by village tourism include the construction of health clinics, schools, and mosques; installation of water and sewage systems; the purchase of new agricultural or fishing equipment; and the start-up of new industries such as furniture making, market gardening, and indigenous crafts. Another very interesting, locally initiated concept is the use of profits to provide interest-free loans to villagers facing financial difficulty (Knights, 1993).

Besides these obvious economic benefits, village tourism has also had several positive sociocultural impacts. Most significantly, it has helped to preserve the local lifestyle by attracting tourists that are interested in the village way of life. Villagers are encouraged to preserve and share with tourists the traditional architectural styles, food, and customs. In this manner, the contrasts between the tourist and resident, in terms of lodging and lifestyle, are reduced to a minimum. This encourages more earnest and equitable host–guest interactions (Inskeep, 1991).

Another positive social effect is the curbing of the migration of young people to the cities. Employment is not only provided directly within the tourist village, but opportunities are also created for providing other services to the tourists, such as guiding. In addition, revenues from the tourism venture are often used to build and run other facilities in the villages, creating further, indirect employment opportunities.

One of the main reasons for the success of this form of tourism is the strict limitations that are placed on the location and scale of development. Only villages that have a population of over 1,000 are chosen because a tourist development would likely be overwhelming for a village of a smaller size. The tourist facilities are built on the periphery of the village in order to accommodate the privacy of villagers and guests. In addition, the number of beds in each tourist village is restricted to a maximum of 50. As a result of these limitations on development, the tourist villages in Senegal have not infringed too dramatically on day-to-day village life.

Challenges

Of course, village tourism in Senegal has not occurred without significant challenges. Initially, this type of tourism was met with a great deal of local skepticism and suspicion (Bilsen, 1987). Villagers had previously been marginalized by tourism development and, therefore, were unconvinced that any of the benefits would actually accrue to them. As such, it took considerable effort to motivate villagers to participate in the project.

Once the initial skepticism was overcome, a significant amount of training was required. Villagers needed to obtain the skills necessary to manage the facility and to receive and handle visitors. These initial stages required considerable investment in well-qualified experts and trainers, many of whom needed to be imported from foreign countries and regions.

Village tourism has produced several negative sociological impacts. In any form of cross-cultural interaction, it is difficult to control the "demonstration effect," and village tourism is no exception. After being exposed to tourists, certain villagers, especially younger people, have imitated foreign behaviors and forms of dress. The demonstration effect has been evident in most of the villages, especially among the young men who commonly act as tourist guides. In addition, begging for favors and money has become more pronounced, especially among the children.

Tourism has also introduced a degree of competitiveness into a normally coopera- tive village structure. In most villages, several enterprising and entrepreneurial locals have set up small businesses, such as restaurants or craft shops, within their homes. Others offer guiding services or excursions to nearby attractions. As a result, there is competition for tourist dollars, and this has caused some animosity between the normally cooperative inhabitants of the villages.

The philosophy of village tourism dictates that as problems arise (such as those outlined above), they should be dealt with by the villagers through the existing council and/or other locally instigated mechanisms. To date, however, there have been few studies to determine how effectively these social problems have been handled.

In the Casamance region of Senegal, there have been clashes between village tourism and mass tourism. Along the coastal region, village tourism is located in close proximity to mass tourism complexes, such as Club Med and other large resort developments. As a result, the villages have become day excursion destina- tions. This has caused considerable friction because the attitudes, behaviors, and volume of these "day-trippers" are not compatible with the village tourism concept. Unfortunately, up to this point, villagers have had difficulty controlling these touristic incursions. It is evident that if these two kinds of tourism are to coexist within a country, there must be a more effective means of separating them, either through distance or more controlled access.

Transportation infrastructure is another challenge in the development of village tourism. Although Senegal has a fairly well-developed network of roads, it is still quite difficult to access the villages in the Casamance region. Locations for village tourism must allow relatively easy access for the tourists while still providing a traditional village experience. However, most traditional villages tend to be quite remote. Therefore, the development of successful village tourism requires balanc- ing the need for authenticity with ease of accessibility.

Finally, appropriate and controlled marketing must accompany village tourism development. In the case of Senegal, promotion has been accomplished mainly through government brochures, select tour operators, and word of mouth (Bilsen, 1987; Senegal Tourist Office, 1991; Sy, 1991). However, up to this point, occupancy rates have been relatively low at about 20%. The challenge, in this case, is to increase appropriate tourism. In other words, not only the quantity of tourists but also the quality of tourists is important. Although some form of brochure may be effective in this endeavor, the format and distribution must be carefully controlled to attract a particular kind of tourist. Village tourism is designed to appeal to those visitors who want to understand the local culture and closely interact with the local people. Appropriate marketing must not only promote but must also educate and inform potential tourists as to appropriate behavior while at the village.

Uganda: Gorilla Tourism in a Sensitive Natural Environment

Background

Up to the late 1960s, Uganda had a well-developed tourism industry. However, political instability, beginning in the 1970s, caused considerable disruption in tourism. During this period, much of the tourism infrastructure and wildlife in Uganda were destroyed. Presently, Uganda is attempting to rebuild its tourism industry. There has been some success. From 1990 to 1994 tourism in Uganda increased over 70%, from 69,000 to 119,000 visitors (WTO, 1996).

National parks and game reserves are Uganda's primary attractions. There are about one dozen of these scattered throughout the country, featuring a large variety of scenic natural attractions. The largest and most well-known of the parks are Queen Elizabeth II National Park and Murchison Falls National Park. However, this discussion will focus on the two national parks that feature gorilla tourism: Bwindi Impenetrable Forest and Mgahinga.

At present, there are only about 600 gorillas remaining in the mountainous area that straddles the three countries of Zaire, Rwanda, and Uganda. About half (300) of the gorillas are located in Uganda, with the remainder scattered in Zaire and Rwanda. Recently, political instability has severely hampered gorilla tourism in both Rwanda and Zaire. Uganda, therefore, is poised to exploit a unique opportunity in terms of developing its gorilla tourism.

As Figure 11.2 illustrates, the Ugandan gorillas are located in two small preserves in the southwest corner of the country. The Bwindi Impenetrable Forest National Park contains the largest concentration of gorillas in the world with about 50 troops. Mgahinga National Park contains only about three troops but has the advantage of easier accessibility.

Gorilla tourism can be a very lucrative endeavor. Currently, visitors are charged US$120.00 per person (David Abura-Ogwang, head of Planning Unit, Uganda Ministry of Tourism, Wildlife and Antiquities, personal correspondence, 1994). The viewing excursion takes anywhere from 2–4 hours, depending upon the location of the gorillas. Only a set amount of time (usually 1 hour) is spent with the gorillas once they have been located—the remaining time is spent hiking through the rainforest searching for the gorilla troop. If there are several troops in an area, revenue could easily reach thousands of dollars per day.

Successes

Uganda has exercised admirable constraint in developing gorilla tourism, especially when the urgent need for foreign currency is considered.

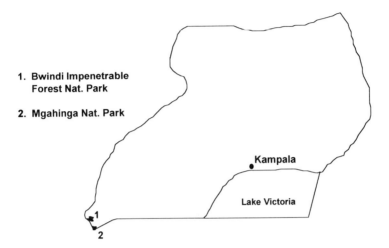

Figure 11.2. Location of gorilla tourism in Uganda.

One of the most impressive aspects of the management of gorilla tourism is the use of scientific expertise. Uganda actively allows and supports field research facilities for primate zoologists from the international scientific community. In the past, the government has relied heavily on the advice of these experts. Tourists are only allowed to visit those troops that have been carefully habituated to human presence by the scientists. This process is lengthy, taking up to 18 months to complete. Initially, three troops were habituated in Mgahinga and six in Bwindi. After a period of visitation, areas are sometimes closed to allow the gorillas some reprieve. In fact, in 1989, gorilla tourism was temporarily halted in Uganda based on the scientists' fears that monitoring was inadequate, and that the gorillas might be introduced to human diseases (Uganda Ministry of Tourism, Wildlife & Antiquities, 1990).

Very strict tourism carrying capacities have been established. Each habituated troop of gorillas is only visited by one group for 1 hour each day. There is a maximum of six persons per group, and the visitors must be over the age of 15. Tourists are carefully briefed by the guide and/or park naturalist before visiting the gorillas. Strict guidelines for behavior are outlined including no flash photography, conversing only in low tones, and keeping a specified distance from the gorillas. Tourist behavior is very closely monitored by guides during the visit with the gorillas. Only officially trained park guides may accompany tourists—no private sector operators are permitted unless specially authorized (Uganda Ministry of Tourism, Wildlife & Antiquities, 1990).

A portion of the revenue from gorilla tourism is redistributed directly into local communities in order to demonstrate the value of gorilla preservation. In this case, 20% of the profits are channeled into local project development funds, with the remaining 80% earmarked for expenses and scientific research.

Challenges

In Uganda, as in many developing nations, a balance must continually be struck between the preservation of pristine natural resources and the need for hard currency. Tensions have arisen over the use of the gorillas for purely scientific study versus their use as a tourism attraction and revenue generator. Up to this point, the Ugandan government has managed to balance both goals by allowing scientists and tourists controlled access to the gorillas. Bwindi and Mgahinga were recently designated as national parks to ensure the protection of the gorilla habitat. However, the continued commitment of the government is required to prevent the future destruction of the gorilla habitat. Adequate staff must be hired and trained to patrol the national parks and to protect against poaching, encroachment, and illegal visitation.

Although efforts have been made to train local individuals as guides and patrol guards, this has not always been as effective as relying on more professional scientific personnel. Successful guiding requires considerable knowledge of gorilla behavior and movement. Guides must also be able to speak the language of the tourists and to deal with tourist behavior (often more unpredictable than that of the gorillas!). Therefore, few opportunities have been created for the employment of local people.

In order to gain the commitment of the local inhabitants, efforts need to be made to provide other, indirect employment opportunities. The general populace must also be educated as to the economic and environmental importance of preserving the gorillas. Without local support, the preservation of the gorillas and their habitat will be much more difficult to maintain.

Lack of infrastructure in Uganda is a significant challenge. Although the road system is fairly well maintained, other services, such as water, electricity, and telecommunications, are intermittent. With regard to tourism infrastructure, the majority of the 4,000 rooms in Uganda are of low standard. Kisoro, the nearest town to Bwindi National Park, has only 70 beds (Uganda Ministry of Tourism, Wildlife & Antiquities, 1993). At this point, Uganda attracts mainly "backpacker" tourists due to this lack of facilities and infrastructure. However, if gorilla tourism is to be successful, there is tremendous work that needs to be done in terms of developing and upgrading the infrastructure of the country. Currently, the government is planning to improve the access roads to the gorilla sanctuaries. There are also plans to build small rest camps in the national parks, as well as to upgrade and expand the accommodation facilities in nearby towns.

Finally, with regard to marketing, Uganda faces a severe image problem. Most commonly the country is associated with instability, military strongmen, AIDS, and other negative characteristics. Uganda has a tremendous challenge ahead in communicating to potential tourists that it is now a safe place to visit. At this point, some care is required to create realistic expectations in terms of facilities and infrastructure. The first steps in a marketing initiative are outlined in several documents produced by the Ministry of Tourism, Wildlife & Antiquities (1990,

1993). Packages that combine the gorillas with other attractions in the area—
including mountains, lakes, flora and fauna (chimpanzees, Golden monkeys,
birds)—are proposed. However, currently very little funding is available for this
challenging marketing task.

Namibia: Tourism in a "New" Country

Background

Namibia was formerly called Southwest Africa and was first administered by the
Germans and later by the South Africans. Independence was finally gained in 1990
after several decades of turbulence. However, unlike many other African countries,
this new country has enjoyed consistent political stability since its independence.

Namibia is endowed with many attractions, including astounding landscapes, abundant wildlife, unique flora, and diverse cultures. The population of the country is low
(about 2 million), resulting in large tracks of unspoiled wilderness. Notable natural
features include Fish Creek Canyon (the second deepest canyon in the world),
Etosha National Park (abundant wildlife), and the Namib Desert (world's oldest
desert and highest sand dunes). Cultural attractions include the German influence in
the major urban centers and various indigenous tribes throughout the country.

Tourism is currently the fourth most important sector of the economy after mining,
agriculture, and fisheries (Frank, 1992). There were about 290,000 visitors to
Namibia in 1993. Just over 60% of these visitors were from South Africa and about
11% were from Germany, reflecting the close traditional ties with these countries.
The remaining visitors came from a variety of countries, including neighboring
African countries, the United Kingdom, Italy, France, and North America (Namibia
Ministry of Environment and Tourism, 1995). Tourism is predicted to increase at a
rate of 8.5% per annum over the next decade (Namibia Ministry of Trade and
Industry, 1992).

The formation of a new country in Africa provides a unique case study in terms of
tourism policy development and implementation. To date, Namibia has set an
impressive example and several of the factors for its success are outlined below.

Successes

Namibia's approach to tourism development is cautious and well planned. Upon
independence, the importance of conservation and sustainable development was
enshrined in Namibia's constitution. This document outlines the conservation
policy for the new country, including protection of the natural environment and
sustainable utilization of wildlife. Over 15% of the land area has been designated
for national parks (Namibia Ministry of Wildlife, Conservation and Tourism, 1994).

In terms of tourism development, the first step undertaken was the completion of
a comprehensive tourism master plan in September, 1992. This document outlines
a detailed 5-year strategy for the tourism industry. It includes suggestions for
product development, organizational structure, the establishment of a tourism

management information system, manpower education and training, marketing and financing (Namibia Ministry of Wildlife, Conservation and Tourism, 1994).

Currently, the Green Plan study is under way and when completed will provide an environmental assessment policy to control the negative environmental impact of various forms of development, including tourism. Investors will be subject to an environmental assessment study (EAS), which will examine how their proposed project contributes to sustainable development and minimizes detrimental environmental effects (Namibia Ministry of Trade and Industry, 1992).

In order to provide well-trained personnel for the tourism industry, a hotel school is planned near the capital city of Windhoek. Professional consultants from South Africa will be used to assist in the initial establishment of the school, and trainers will be supplied by Namib-Sun Hotels, a Namibian hotel chain. Courses of 2–3 weeks are planned for chefs, waiters, room service, housekeeping, and front desk personnel ("Namibia to Get Hotel School," 1993/1994). It is envisioned that eventually the school will also be able to provide training at the management level. Recently, the Namibian Academy for Tourism and Hospitality (NATH) has been established and offers training in tour guiding. Eventually, diploma and degree courses will be offered at this institution ("Tour Guide Courses," 1994/1995).

The tourism industry is quite well organized in Namibia. In the private sector, there are a number of organizations, such as associations for tour operators, hotels, travel agencies, and car rental companies. There is also an umbrella group called FENATA, the Federation of Namibian Tourism Associations. This organization has been established to facilitate communication between the public and the private sector. The organization consists of representatives from private sector tourist associations and from public organizations and ministries. FENATA has been one of the major sounding boards for the challenges and issues that face the Namibian tourist industry.

Although the infrastructure in many African countries presents a significant challenge to tourism development (as was illustrated in the previous discussions concerning Senegal and Uganda), this is not the case for Namibia. Transportation systems and communication systems are relatively well developed. There is a well-maintained system of roads reaching all corners of the country. Water, electricity, and telecommunications are dependable in most areas.

The accommodation infrastructure is also well organized and well regulated. The South African one- to five-star classification system has been used in the past, but the Ministry of Environment and Tourism is currently setting up a new classification/grading system to suit the Namibian situation. In addition, detailed licensing and regulation criteria have been put in place (Shackley, 1993). There are some 4,500 accommodation rooms with approximately 10,400 beds. About 65% of these are privately owned. The remainder consist of government-run facilities, mostly located within the national parks. Various kinds of accommodation are available from tented safari camps to air conditioned bungalows. However, a shortage of "upmarket" accommodation facilities has been identified (Frank, 1992). The public and private sectors have recognized this need and are working towards developing

Chapter 12

Developing Tourism in the Environmentally Sensitive North West Cape Region, Western Australia

Ross K. Dowling

Introduction

The North West Cape region is situated on Western Australia's (WA) coast approximately 1200 km north of the state's capital city, Perth. It is an area of outstanding natural beauty, with a coastline marked by a large marine embayment, Exmouth Gulf, separated from the Ningaloo reef, a fringing barrier coral reef, by the Cape Range peninsula (Figure 12.1). The whole area is exceptionally rich in scientific, cultural, scenic, and recreational features (Humphreys, 1993; May, Lenanton, & Berry, 1983). Protected natural areas include Ningaloo Marine Park and Cape Range National Park, as well as several reserves on the off-shore islands, all administered by the WA Government's Department of Conservation and Land Management (CALM).

The Ningaloo Marine Park is acknowledged as having major significance as a conservation and education resource because of the biological organisms it contains (CALM, 1988). It also has high local (Western Australian) recreation value, and is becoming increasingly recognized as a tourism resource of national and international standing because of its relative wilderness character (Shea & Sharp, 1993). In recognition of the outstanding environmental attributes of the region WA state environmental groups are urging for its World Heritage listing.

The Park contains an extensive fringing coral reef system and protected, relatively shallow, back reef lagoons. These habitats support marine communities that are as diverse and complex (if not as abundant) as those of the Great Barrier Reef on Australia's east coast. The Ningaloo Reef is much more accessible as it varies from a few hundred meters to a few kilometers offshore.

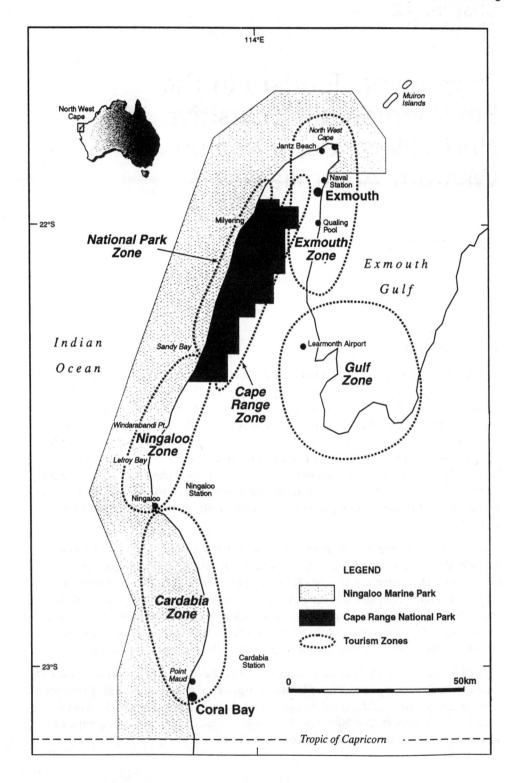

Figure 12.1. North West Cape, Western Australia.

Seagrass beds within the lagoons are important feeding grounds for endangered animals such as green and hawksbill turtles, and dugong. Some beaches also provide nesting grounds for these turtles during the summer. Tidal flats are also important habitats for international migratory wading birds during the summer. A unique feature is the presence of whalesharks, the world's biggest species of fish.

To protect these resources and allow for recreational use of the Park, a management plan has been developed by CALM (1989) that is based on three use zonings as follows:

- **General Use Zone**: commercial and recreational uses consistent with conservation of natural resources;
- **Recreation Zone**: recreation uses consistent with the conservation of natural resources;
- **Sanctuary Zone**: use consistent with the protection of natural resources.

The Marine Park is managed by CALM according to the management goals and objectives outlined in the management plan. Many of these goals are complementary to developing the tourism and recreational use of the Park's waters. The aim of the goals is to:

- Provide tourism consistent with the maintenance of resources;
- Provide recreational opportunities and facilities that maximize the quality of experience sought by visitors;
- Manage fishing without adverse effects on target populations;
- Ensure that all development and activities are consistent with the maintenance of species populations, habitats, natural features, and cultural and social values;
- Conduct research into understanding how the impacts of use and natural processes affect the maintenance and management of the Park.

The Built Environment

The town of Exmouth (2,600 people), which serves the area, has been economically dependent on a joint United States–Australian Naval Communications Station since 1967. However, in 1992 the Americans withdrew from the partnership and, although the station has continued to operate under the Royal Australian Navy, there has been a large reduction of personnel and income for the town. With Exmouth's future relatively uncertain, tourism is viewed as a potential economic savior. The existing tourism infrastructure includes a range of moderate and budget accommodations and the nearby jumbo jet-capable Learmonth air strip.

In 1992 the WA State Government touted the area worldwide in a bid to encourage developers to build an international resort based on the local natural attractions. Although there were three developers interested in entering negotiations for a marina and resort development, so far nothing has been finalized. The State's Department of Environmental Protection (DEP) has refused to make public a report that "is scathing of the way WA authorities have handled development issues on the North West Cape." The report's authors say they have serious reservations about some of the tourist, mining, and residential projects that the State Government has approved in the area (Capp, 1996).

Tourism

The Department of Regional Development and the North West (DRDNW) has stated that tourism is the fastest growing industry in the region. Because this industry is almost entirely dependent on natural areas there is increasing concern for the region's environment. In 1993, over 100,000 tourists generated more than $10 million in revenue. Most visitors (70%) come from other parts of WA, 22% from elsewhere in Australia, and the remainder (8%) from overseas (Dowling, 1992).

The main reasons for visiting the region are its pleasant climate, opportunities for fishing, and natural attractions, especially the reef and the range (Dowling, 1993). The peak tourist season is June to September (the cooler winter period). Tourist accommodation in the region consists of approximately 500 hotel/motel bedspaces, over 600 chalets and vans, and 1,400 caravan and camping sites. In 1993 the five caravan parks recorded approximately 14,000 guest arrivals and their takings were about $1 million (Western Australian Tourism Commission, 1993). The local office of CALM estimates that well over half of the region's visitors visit Ningaloo Marine Park.

A rapidly growing ecotourism industry is being established around the whalesharks. The reef is the only readily accessible place on earth where the sharks gather annually in large numbers and can be readily viewed (Lent, 1995). The reef's proximity to land, as close as 200 m to shore, means tourists have easy access to the whalesharks and in 1996 seven tour operators took approximately 3,000 people out to swim with the sharks ("Ningaloo's Giants the Focus," 1996). To manage the increasing number of, largely international, tourists the Department of CALM has developed a Code of Conduct for whaleshark watching (CALM, 1996) and a Whaleshark Research Foundation has been established (Medcraft, 1996).

With the continued growth of tourism in the region and the need to replace the economic benefits of the Communications Station, the Australian Federal and Western Australian State Governments commissioned a Tourism Development Study of the region in 1993. Subsequently, the Government appointed the international real estate company Jones Lang Wootton (JLW) to carry out the study, which was completed in mid-1993. This chapter reports on their approach to the task and findings as well as the subsequent developments over the last 5 years.

Methodology

JLW's approach to the study stemmed from its commitment to balance the competing needs of profitable development, tourism values, community lifestyles, and environmental protection (Figure 12.2). Its underlying philosophy derived from the need to find options and solutions by the application of an open methodology. This was based on understanding the inputs, letting land assets and natural re-

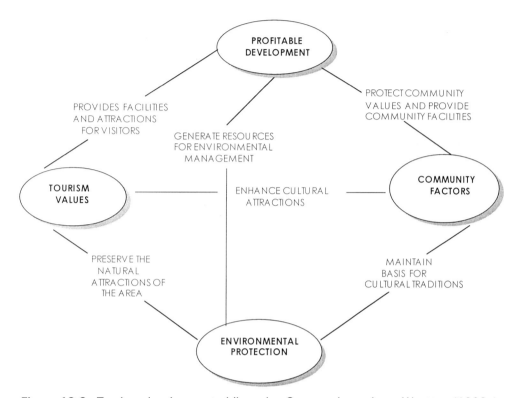

Figure 12.2. Tourism development philosophy. Source: Jones Lang Wootton (1993a).

sources speak, gaining expert and public input, and formulating recommendations that emanated clearly from the information base.

By applying this methodology, it was possible to "grow" a long-term strategy that is sustainable:

- **politically**—because the various viewpoints are properly and objectively analyzed;
- **commercially**—because the development models are tested for long-term profitability;
- **ecologically**—because the impacts of the development models are examined in relation to known resource data;
- **socially**—because the economic, demographic, and cultural impacts are established in consultation with local people;
- **technically**—because the scope of the use of appropriate technologies is demonstrated in the evaluation process. (Jones Lang Wootton, 1993a, p. 4)

In order to translate this philosophical base into practical application, JLW devised a methodology incorporating three phases: analysis, formulation, and reporting (Figure 12.3). The analysis phase included site visits and local consultations, the formulation phase included an evaluation of options, and the reporting phase included a review with local decision makers.

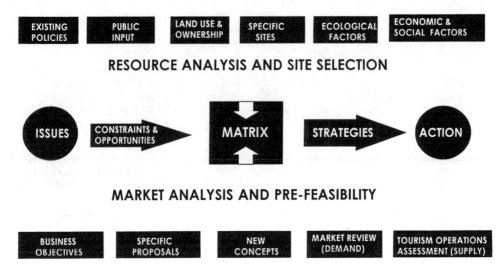

Figure 12.3. Plan methodology. Source: Jones Lang Wootton (1993a).

The focus was on the formulation stream of action in the center of the diagram, where the information was brought together after analyses. Each information source was tested for relevance and processed as necessary to operate the methodology.

The field work was carried out in February and March 1993 by both ground and low-level aerial surveys. Detailed inspections were made of 102 sites, which were classified according to a number of environmental and tourism values (Jones Lang Wootton, 1993a). Analysis of the values led to the classification of each site with regard to its suitability of tourism development.

Findings

The principal findings of JLW's study were twofold. They included the need to align tourism demand and natural resource management in the region as well as the proposal that the government work toward achieving a minimum level of tourism sustainable development while allowing the decision on whether to implement maximum development to be made at a later date (Jones Lang Wootton, 1993b).

The Minimum Sustainable Development Approach

This approach represents a "bottom-up" approach based on immediate need. This approach is considered the minimum requirement to bring the management of the natural resources into line with tourism demand. It represents a management response to trends, and the approach can be considered as "a maintenance of the resource" policy.

This approach envisages that the existing tourist accommodation could be approximately doubled over the next 5-7 years (Table 12.1). It incorporates a range of accommodation generally represented by local capital investment types.

It also envisages the doubling in size of Cape Range National Park through the incorporation of Ningaloo Station to the south. This expansion and reorientation of the management of the area is considered the minimum essential to sustain the resource under foreseeable tourism pressures. It also represents an opportunity to obtain revenues to support the necessary rationalization and ongoing resource management.

The northern section of the extended park would primarily consist of nature-based tourism with some recreational use whereas the southern section of the park would comprise mainly recreational use with some nature-based tourism.

The number of sites suitable for development is reasonably few (three major, seven minor) in a study area of some 2,000 km^2. If these sites were to be released for suboptimal development there would be no practical possibility of moving to a higher level and quality of inventory at a later stage. For this reason, the minimum scenario also includes measures to set aside and protect these sites for future decisions.

The Maximum Carrying Capacity Approach

This approach is considered the maximum level at which management of the natural resources would be comfortably in line with tourism provision. It represents a purposeful economic development initiative and the approach can be considered as "a resource development" policy.

Table 12.1. Minimum Sustainable Development Approach

Locality	Current Inventory	Maximum Scenario Bedspaces	Tourism Potential Concept
Learmonth	—	300	Caravan Park
Jantz Beach	—	180	Small resort
Milyering	—	1,000	Wilderness Caravan Park
National Park	170	—	Rationalized camping
Sandy Bay	—	200	Annex to Milyering
Winderabandi	—	—	Site reserved
Lefroy Bay	—	1,000	Wilderness Lodge, Caravan Park
South of National Park	400	300	Interim camping control
Ningaloo	—	—	Site reserved
Coral Bay	750	750	No expansion assumed
Exmouth	2,360	2,360	No expansion assumed
Total	3,680	6,390	

Source: Jones Lang Wootton (1993c).

It represents a "top-down" approach based on constructing a tourism industry for economic reasons, including wealth generation and employment creation, that is nevertheless environmentally sustainable. The fundamental premise is that provision of tourism accommodation inventory up to this level will be within the carrying capacity of the region in the sense that the few specific sites available for development have natural growth limitations. In other words, if this maximum level were to be exceeded, tourism pressure would not be manageable at a sustainable level, with consequent dangers of resource degradation and the erosion of economic benefits.

A further underlying premise is that the tourism accommodation inventory must be located according to a specific strategy to enable management of the resource and maximize income from the users. Purposeful, planned growth of tourism development in the region, fostered by priority at both the state and national levels, is assumed in this scenario. It seeks to achieve the highest sustainable level of accommodation inventory and to provide the greatest spread of accommodation types.

Under this approach the existing tourist accommodation will grow to a peak of approximately 13,000 bed spaces over the next 15–20 years (Table 12.2). There would be a purposeful strategy to protect and then develop selected sites and provide infrastructure to support this level of inventory.

Tourism Zones

Six tourism zones have been identified in the region. Each zone has been inventoried and assessed with recommendations being made in regard to the conservation

Table 12.2. Maximum Carrying Capacity Approach

Locality	Current Inventory	Maximum Scenario Bedspaces	Tourism Potential Concept
Learmonth	—	300	Caravan Park
Qualing Pool	—	300	Caravan Park
Jantz Beach	—	180	Small resort
Milyering	—	1,000	Wilderness Lodge, Caravan Park
National Park	170	—	Rationalized camping
Sandy Bay	—	200	Annex to Milyering
Winderabandi	—	1,000	Wilderness Lodge, Caravan Park
Lefroy Bay	—	2,500	High inventory development
South of National Park	400	300	Rationalized camping
Ningaloo	—	2,500	High inventory development
Coral Bay	750	750	No expansion assumed
Exmouth	2,360	4,000	Expansion assumed
Total	3,680	12,730	

Source: Jones Lang Wootton (1993c).

of natural environmental values as well as the types and levels of tourism developments. The six zones are: Gulf, Cardabia, Cape Range, National Park, Ningaloo, and Exmouth.

The Gulf Tourism Zone is a low-lying area of ancient sand dunes, swampland, and mangroves at the southern end of Exmouth Gulf. It is relatively remote, inaccessible station country that is also the home to a few fishermen on the coast. Activities that could be developed in this zone include terrestrial and marine-based nature tourism such as camping, fishing, canoeing, and yachting.

The Cardabia Tourism Zone comprises a 50-km-long stretch of coast in the southern part of the region. It includes Coral Bay, a small coastal settlement, whose economy is totally reliant on reef tourism. During peak times the township swells from 50 people to over 2,000. Already the town's resources are stretched to the limit and further development will require considerable additional service infrastructure.

A site in this zone is under consideration for the development of a marina-based settlement. If this proposal is implemented it will have significant impacts on the Coral Bay township. The Coral Coast Resort proposed for Point Maud, just north of Coral Bay, is a AUD$400 million new town including a 400-room club resort, 250-room hotel and convention center, a 175-bay caravan park, 75 chalets, and a 120-bed backpackers hostel. It will be built at Point Maud, immediately north of Coral Bay. However, the proposed development has drawn considerable flak from local and state environmental groups who argue that it will provide no real benefits for the community and will put the area's fragile ecosystem under enormous pressure (Capp, 1995).

The Cape Range Tourism Zone comprises the heavily dissected limestone anticline of Cape Range. Although no tourism development sites were identified in this zone, the area has considerable potential as a day-visitation area. Longer stay visits such a backpacking or mountain-bike camping would be encouraged by the establishment of walk and mountain cycle trails. This would help establish the nature focus of the area and connect its many viewpoints.

The National Park Tourism Zone comprises the seaward side of Cape Range National Park. It is proposed that the current policy of numerous small coastal camping sites be rationalized and replaced with two accommodation complexes built in the northern and southern parts of the park (Figure 12.4). Each site would consist of a range of accommodation types from tent sites to wilderness lodges.

The Ningaloo Tourism Zone extends southwards from Cape Range National Park along the coast. Currently the land is leased to station owners who permit camping along the coast. The zone is used extensively for camping and fishing and is under considerable pressure during the peak visitor season. There are over 200 informal campsites at the peak season accommodating approximately 1,000 people. The natural environment is heavily degraded and there is urgent need of control and management. Therefore, it is recommended that the land be brought into national park status and hence given some form of protection.

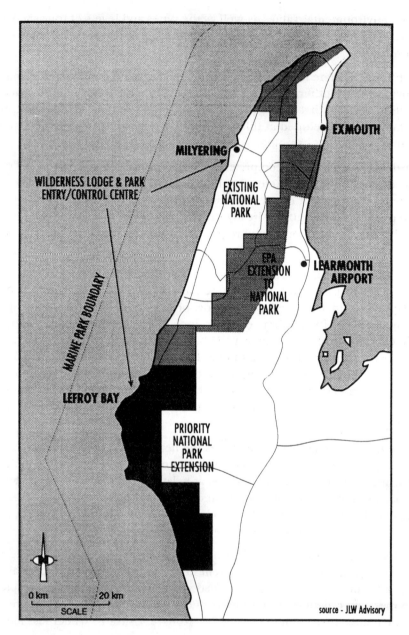

Figure 12.4. Proposed accommodation complexes in Cape Range
National Park. Source: Jones Lang Wootton advisory.

Three major tourism development sites have been identified in the southern part
of this zone. The sites comprise superb sheltered unspoiled beaches backed by
sufficient land for substantial built tourism infrastructure. Together they represent

a unique opportunity for Western Australia to develop a tourism region of international standard.

The Exmouth Tourism Zone comprises the area around the town of Exmouth. It acts as a tourism base for the region due to its roles as an administrative center, service center, and staging point. As tourism grows in the region so too will the town. The Western Australian Government is currently developing a $10 million marina complex immediately south of the town, which includes areas for a large-scale resort and associated residential subdivision.

Levels of Accommodation Development

A number of different types of accommodation and levels of inventory have been proposed for the region. They include wilderness lodges, camping and caravan parks, together with large-scale resorts.

For each type of facility it is assumed that the design, development, and operation embodies the general principles of environmentally sensitive design and sustainable development. The underlying premise in the development of these facilities is that they should provide comfortable lodgings with low ecological impacts. Such facilities should also serve as "windows" to the natural world and as vehicles for learning and understanding (Andersen, 1993).

Wilderness lodges are accommodation facilities designed to provide a comfortable and relaxing base for visitors to explore and enjoy the surrounding natural environment. In the context of this region, however, an important principle is made in relation to the lodges. Underscoring the introduction of new tourism accommodation inventory in the area is the idea that there is a need for a nonelitist mix of accommodation types. This is not fostered as a social idea, but is promoted mainly on the grounds of economic survival. This approach recognizes that income sources should be diversified. This can be achieved through marketing to existing and emerging tourist segments.

Another successful marketing approach is through the promotion of special events to broaden the tourist season. This event-driven occupancy comprises natural events (coral spawning, whale watching, whaleshark watching) and organized events (festivals, diving, sporting competitions, windsurfing, and fishing).

To accommodate the market mix and extend the season a wilderness lodge should provide for a range of accommodation levels. These include campgrounds, caravans, hostel, chalets, and lodge units.

Recent Developments

Tourism development in the environmentally sensitive North West Cape Region of Western Australia has been proposed at two levels. Both are based on a conservation-oriented, sustainable development path, shaping and directing the prevalent informal tourist use of the area by advocating a marked increased in the size and management of the national park as well as the concentration of accommodation facilities at a selected number of appropriate sites.

Following the publication of the Report on Tourism Development in the North West Cape Region, a number of developments have taken place. First, an advisory committee has been established to advise CALM on the implementation of the management plans for the Ningaloo Marine Park and Cape Range National Park. Second, oil and gas exploration drilling immediately outside the park boundary has focused environmental concern for the region from around Australia. Although the WA Government and mining companies have supported the test drilling, the environmental groups such as Greenpeace, the Conservation Council of WA, and the Ningaloo Preservation Association have suggested that the reef has qualities to be included on the World Heritage Register.

In 1995 a Parliamentary Select Committee was convened on Cape Range National Park and Ningaloo Marine Park in order to address the growing resource development–environment preservation tension. The bipartisan committee found that the precious natural resources of North West Cape are rare and priceless assets that must be preserved at all costs (Western Australian Government, 1995). The report advised that although the initial impetus for its establishment emerged from the discussion relating to exploration for oil on Ningaloo Reef, other issues had since evolved. The most critical one was how to control tourism development, and indeed, whether or not there should be any development at all on the west coast.

The committee endorsed the earlier JLW (1993) plan by supporting its recommendations to:

1. Negotiate the extension of Cape Range National Park to include Ningaloo Pastoral Station to the south.
2. Prevent major tourist development occurring on the west coast within the National Park.
3. Examine the potential of converting Milyering Visitor Centre to a wilderness/camping tourism area.
4. Encourage a high standard of commercial operations to ensure ecologically sustainable development of tourism-based activities within the two parks.
5. Carefully examine the social and environmental impacts of the proposed Coral Coast Resort.

However, one of the report's recommendations, which is at variance with the earlier study, is the advocacy that there should be no shore-based resort development on the western side of Cape Range on coastal land abutting Ningaloo Marine Park. The JLW (1993c) study suggested that while there should be no major developments within the National Park, they advocated such proposals for the coastal strip immediately south of the park in the Ningaloo Tourism Zone. This then remains a contentious issue.

Recently a regional coastal strategy was prepared by the State's Ministry for Planning (Ministry of Planning, 1996). The strategy proposed the vision for the area as being to develop the coast into a tourism region of international significance, focusing on its unique natural features. This is to be achieved in a manner that is ecologically sustainable, retains the sense of wilderness, and provides local and regional economic and social benefits. It also affirms the key tourist development sites suggested by the JLW (1993) report.

Other initiatives in the region include the state's four public universities investigating the establishment of a Tropical Research Centre, the development of an underwater observatory, and the establishment of a camel safari operation and an ostrich farm to complement the seasonal events of whaleshark and coral spawning watching in the region. In addition, a number of direct tourist charter flights have been made from Singapore to Exmouth by a Singapore-based travel agency.

The WA Museum, WA Tourism Commission, and Department of Conservation and Land Management have jointly funded a study to find ways of developing access to selected caves in Cape Range National Park in order to promote nature-based tourism. In 1994 a Nature Based Tourism Strategy for the whole of the Gascoyne Region was prepared by the Gascoyne Development Commission and CALM (Gascoyne Development Commission, 1995).

The Future

The next phase in the tourism development of the region incorporates the plan being approved by the Western Australian Parliament so that a comprehensive approach to the region's development can be made in a sustainable manner. Although this has not yet been carried out the WA Government has prepared an overall *Western Australian Tourism Infrastucture Strategy* (Western Australian Tourism Commission, 1995) as well as a *Nature-Based Tourism Strategy* (Western Australian Tourism Commission & CALM, 1997). Both reports have identified the region as one of 11 state "Zones of Opportunity" for tourism development. Obviously, the future of tourism in the region looks bright; however, the key to its success will rely on the continued protection of the environmentally sensitive range and reef.

Acknowledgments

This chapter is derived from a number of reports compiled during 1993 as part of the North West Cape Tourism Development Study. The study was undertaken by Jones Lang Wootton's International Investment and Development Division, Perth, Western Australia, by its Director, Dusan Mills, and Manager Patrick Dick. The author of this chapter was contracted by JLW as an Ecotourism Consultant for the 6-month duration of the study. He wishes to thank JLW for permission to publish information compiled in the original report.

Contributors

Ray E. Ashton, Jr. is Vice President for Sustainable Tourism and Natural Resource Development Services, Principal Scientist and Director of Biological Services of ATM, a consulting firm with eight U.S. and an international office. He has published over 100 articles and books in the fields of biology and sustainable tourism (ecotourism), including the three-volume *Handbook of Reptiles and Amphibians of Florida* and *An Introduction to Sustainable Tourism (Ecotourism) in Central America* that he co-authored with Patricia S. Ashton. He is also the series editor of the Rare and Endangered Biota of Florida series. He brings to sustainable tourism his uniquely practical perspective from 30 years as a biologist and museum educator blended with his hands-on experiences in the international tourism industry and his understanding of business and governmental practices. Ray often works for local and international governments, governmental agencies, and private developers in creating sustainable tourism plans, ecolodges, resorts, and national parks.

Ralf Buckley is Director of the International Centre for Ecotourism Research and Professor in the Faculty of Engineering and Applied Science at Griffith University in Queensland, Australia. He is also an adjunct professor in business, and Director of the Centre for Environmental Management. He has worked in over 40 countries worldwide, and has over 15 years' experience in commercial consulting and private industry. He has written over 100 consultant reports in a wide range of industry sectors, over 100 articles in refereed journals including the international science journal *Nature*, and 6 books, including 3 on environmental planning, audit and management. He has run or contributes to over 30 exectuve short courses in environmental management, and acted as consultant or expert witness to government agencies and parliamentary inquiries into tourism, biodiversity, overseas aid, coastal development, and sustainable development. He has also been nominated as Director of the proposed national Cooperative Research Centre in Sustainable Tourism.

Peiyi Ding is a graduate student of the Department of Geography and Planning, University of New England, Armidale, Australia. He recently completed doctorate research in environmental auditing for tourism development, in particular for coastal resorts, under the supervision of Professor John Pigram. He has extensive experience in ecologically sustainable development and environmental management in China and Australia.

Ross K. Dowling is an international speaker, researcher, planner, and consultant on ecotourism. He is Treasurer of the Ecotourism Association of Australia and Vice Chairperson of The Forum Advocating Cultural and Ecotourism in Western Australia. While planning the Ningaloo Reef, Dr. Dowling was employed in Jones Lang Wootton's international Investment & Development Division as an Ecotourism Consultant. He is currently Associate Professor of Tourism, School of Marketing and Tourism, Faculty of Business, Edith Cowan Univeristy, Western Australia.

T. David Dougherty is a Senior Consultant in the Environmental Management Services Practice of Consulting and Audit Canada. He has specialized in assessment and remediation of environmental impacts in private industry during the 1980s, and in the 1990s has moved into sustainable development policy issues in the public sector. He is the author of over a dozen publications and over 100 consulting reports.

Charlotte M. Echtner has a Ph.D. in Tourism from the University of Calgary, Canada. Presently she is Assistant Professor, James Cook University, Townville, Australia. Her research interests include Third World tourism issues, destination image, tourism marketing, and the application of semiotics to tourism. She has published in many of the leading tourism journals, including *Annals of Tourism Research, Journal of Travel Research, Journal of Tourism Studies,* and *Tourism Recreation Research.* Currently her research focuses on the representation of the Third World in tourist brochures.

Alison Gill is an Associate Professor at Simon Fraser University and a member of the Centre for Tourism Policy and Research. Dr. Gill teaches graduate level courses in community tourism development and tourism systems in the School of Resource and Environmental Management. She also delivers tourism courses in the University's Geography program. Her research interests are closely aligned to the study of single industry and small community development processes and issues. Dr. Gill currently is specializing in research related to planning and development processes in resort communities.

Robert G. Healy is Professor of Environmental Policy at the Nicholas School of the Environment, Duke University, Durham, NC. An economist by training, he has written seven books on land use policy and on environmental policy in developing countries. Currently he is working on the relationship of tourism to national parks and local economic development. He is particularly interested in the role of handicrafts, artisanal food products, and other tourist merchandise in providing economic development opportunities for the rural poor in Brazil and Mexico.

Robert H. Horwich received his Ph.D. in 1967 from the University of Maryland and then worked in India with the Smithsonian Institution. Based on his research on infant development, he developed a method for reintroducing cranes. Having studied primates in India and Central America since 1967, he developed a method for translocating howlers. Since 1984, he initiated community projects in Belize, Mexico, the United States, and Russia. He founded and is Director of Community Conservation Consultants.

Alan A. Lew is an Associate Professor of Geography and Public Planning at Northern Arizona University, where he teaches courses in geography, planning, and tourism. He conducts research and consults on tourism in East and Southeast Asia, and in rural areas and Indian reservations in the western U.S. He is a member of the American Institute of Certified Planners and was the co-editor of the book *Tourism in China* (1995).

Jonathan Lyon received a Ph.D. in ecology from Pennsylvania State University in 1995. He then accepted a postdoctoral fellowship position at the University of Arkansas studying the impacts of soils and disturbance on riparian vegetation in the Ozarks of Missouri. He is currently Assistant Professor of Biology at Edgewood College in Madison, WI. He also is Assistant Director of Community Conservation Consultants. His research interests include: plant community ecology, disturbance ecology, conservation biology, and community-based conservation initiatives.

Edward W. Manning is Principal in the Environmental Management Services Practice of Consulting and Audit Canada and Associate Director of the Centre for a Sustainable Future. He has served as a consultant on environmental, tourism, and resource development issues to more than a dozen nations, the World Tourism Organization, and the Global Environmental Facility. He is the author of 21 books and over 70 articles on sustainable development, regional planning, and tourism.

John J. Pigram is Associate Professor in Geography and Planning and Executive Director of the Centre for Water Policy Research at the University of New England, Armidale, Australia. Dr. Pigram teaches and undertakes research in Recreation Geography and Tourism and is the author of *Outdoor Recreation and Resource Management*. He is a Charter Member of the International Academy for the Study of Tourism and has held visiting appointments at several universities in North America.

Shalini Singh is Professor at the Centre for Tourism Research & Development (CTRD), Lucknow, India. She is editor for the Centre's journal, *Tourism Recreation Research*. Dr, Singh has published books on: *Cultural Tourism and Heritage Management* (1994) and *Profiles of Indian Tourism* (1996). She is visiting Professor to Indian Universities and Management Institutes. She serves on the Editorial Board of *Tourism Management*, and is a member of the Asia Pacific Tourism Association, South Korea.

Tej Vir Singh is Professor and Director of the Centre for Tourism Research & Development (CTRD), Lucknow, India. He is the founder and publisher of the Centre's International Journal, *Tourism Recreation Research*. A specialist in Himalayan Tourism, Dr. Singh has produced 15 international titles and 100 technical papers on tourism development and impacts. He was Sr. Fellow Ford Foundation at ICIMOD, Kathmandu in 1988. Dr. Singh is a member of the International Academy for the Study of Tourism (Madrid) and Chapter Chair–Asia Pacific Tourism Association, South Korea. He consults for the UNEP and Green Globe.

John Splettstoesser is a geologist with field experience in Antactica that began in 1960. His work there has included studies on wind erosion, mineral resources evaluation, and ice-drilling for paleoclimatic information. In addition to geological consulting and part-time college teaching, he has been a part-time lecturer on tour vessels to Antarctica (more than 70 cruises since 1983) and to the Arctic. He is editor of 5 books on polar subjects, including *Antarctic Tourism* (with Valene Smith, 1994). He is Spokesperson for the International Association of Antarctica Tour Operators (IAATO), and has two geographic features named for him in Antarctica.

Peter W. Williams is Director of Simon Fraser University's Centre for Tourism Policy and Research. He teaches graduate level tourism policy, planning, and development courses in the School of Resource and Environmental Management. His research interests are centered on issues related to growth management strategies in tourism settings and behavioral dimensions of tourism product development. Dr. Williams is particularly involved with research addressing issues of sustainability in tourism development.

Bibliography

Albuquerque, T. (1988). *Anjuna: Profile of a village in Goa*. New Delhi: Promilla & Co.

Alderman, C. L. (1990). *Study of the role of privately owned lands used for nature tourism, education, and conservation*. Washington, DC: Conservation International.

Alexander, C., et al. (1977). *A pattern language*. New York: Oxford University Press.

Alito Siqueira. (1991). Tourism and the drama of ethnicity. *Bangkok Post*.

Alvar, J., & Alvar, J. (1979). *Guaraquecaba: Mar e Mata*. Curitiba: Universidade Federal do Parana.

Alvares, C. (1993). *Fish curry and rice*. Mapusa, Goa: The Other India Press.

Andersen, D. L. (1993). A window to the natural world: The design of ecotourism facilities. In K. Lindberg & D. E. Hawkins (Eds.), *Ecotourism: A guide for planners and managers* (pp. 116-133). North Bennington, VT: The Ecotourism Society.

Anderson, E. (1994). Towards self-regulation for sustainable tourism. In *Proceedings of Ecodollars Tourism Conference*. Brisbane: Environmental Management Industry Association of Australia.

Anonymous. (1991, April 28). Conservation-it did not start overnight in Belize. *Belize Times*, 3738, pp. 1, 13.

Ashton, R. E., Jr. (1991). The financing of conservation: The concept of self-supporting ecopreserves. In *Ecotourism and resource conservation* (Vol. 2, pp. 547-556). First International Symposium: Ecotourism and Resource Conservation Project, Berne, NY.

Ashton, R. E., Jr., & Ashton, P. S. (1993). *An introduction to sustainable tourism (ecotourism) in Central America*. Paseo Pantera: Regional Wildlands Management in Central America, USID.

Askey, E., & Williams, P. E. (1992). *Tatshenshini Alsek River use study*. Burnaby, B.C.: Simon Fraser University, Centre for Tourssm Policy and Research.

Australia, Commonwealth Department of Tourism. (1991). *National ecotourism strategy*. Canberra: AGPS.

Australian Tourism Industry Association. (1990). *Environmental guidelines for tourism developments*. Canberra: Author.

Baez, A. L., & Ashton, R. E., Jr. (1992). Programa de Ecoturismo Para Centro America: Una Experiencia sin precedentes. Ponecia presentada en al. 1.12 Workshop. *The role of ecotourism*. IV Congreso Mundial De Parques Nacionalessy Areas Protegidas Caraca, Caracas, Venezuela.

Barnett, P. (1992). *Beyond the green horizon*. London: WWF and Tourism Concern.

Bilsen, F. (1987). Integrated tourism in Senegal: An alternative. *Tourism Recreation Research, 13*(1), 19-23.

Biswas, K., & Geping, Q. (Eds.). (1987). *Environmental impact assessment for developing countries* (Natural Resources and the Environment Series, Vol. 19). London: Tycooly International, United Nations University.

Bodine, J. J. (1972). Acculturation and population dynamics. In A. Ortiz (Ed.), *New perspectives on the pueblos* (pp. 257-285). Albuquerque: University of New Mexico Press.

Bond, M. E., & Ladman, J. R. (1980). International tourism: An instrument for third world development. In I. Vogeler & A. R. de Souza (Eds.), *Dialectics of third world development* (pp. 231-240). Totowa, NJ: Allanheld, Osmun.

Boo, E. (1990). *Ecotourism: The potentials and pitfalls*. Washington, DC: World Wildlife Fund.

Brandon, K. (1993). *Paper prepared for International Conference on Ecotourism and Local Communities.* Bellagio, Italy: The Rockefeller Foundation.

Braun, T. A., & Winston, J. T. (1986). The Vail Village urban design guide plan: A framework for guiding development. *UD Review, 4*(4), 12–18.

Brew, J. O. (1979). Hopi prehistory and history to 1850. In A. Otiz (Ed.), *Handbook of North American Indians, Vol. 9, Southwest* (pp. 514–523). Washington: Smithsonian Institution.

Bridel, L. (1984). Forms and trends in tourist development. In E. A. Brugger, G. Furrer, G. Messerli, & P. Messerli (Eds.), *The transformation of Swiss mountain regions.* Bern, Switzerland: Haupt.

British Airways. (1992). *Annual report.* London: Author.

Britton, R. (1980). Shortcomings of third world development. In I. Vogeler & A. R. de Souza (Eds.), *Dialectics of third world development* (pp. 241–248). Totowa, NJ: Allanheld, Osmun.

Bruner, G. (1993). *Evaluating a model of private-ownership conservation: Ecotourism in the Community Baboon Sanctuary in Belize.* M.S. thesis, Georgia Institute of Technology.

Buckley, R. C. (1991a). *Perspectives in environmental management.* Berlin: Springer-Verlag.

Buckley, R. C. (1991b). When is an activity unsustainable? *EIA News, 17,* 5.

Buckley, R. C. (1991c). Environmental planning and policy for green tourism. In R. C. Buckley, *Perspectives in environmental management* (pp. 226–242). Berlin: Springer-Verlag.

Buckley, R. C. (1991d). Environmental impacts of recreation in parks and reserves. In R. C. Buckley (Ed.), *Perspectives in environmental management* (pp. 243–258). Berlin: Springer-Verlag.

Buckley, R. C. (1994a). A framework for ecotourism. *Annals of Tourism Research, 21,* 661–665.

Buckley, R. C. (1994b). Cumulative environmental impacts: Problems, policy and planning law. *Environmental Plannning Law Journal, 11,* 317–320.

Buckley, R. C. (1994c). Strategic environmental impact assessment. *Environmental Planning Law Journal, 11,* 166–168.

Buckley, R. C. (1995a). Environmental audit. In F. Vanclay & D. Bronstein (Eds.), *Environmental impact assessment.* New York: Wiley.

Buckley, R. C. (1995b). Ecolodges in Australia. In D. Hawkins (Ed.), *Ecolodges. Proceedings First World Ecolodge Forum.* Washington, DC: George Washington University.

Buckley, R. C. (1996). Sustainable tourism issues and management tools. *Annals of Tourism Research.*

Buckley, R., & Araujo, G. (1997). Environmental management performance in tourism accommodation. *Annals of Tourism Research 24,* 465–469.

Buckley, R. C., & Warnken, J. (1996). Tourism EIA. In A. Porter & R. Fittipaldi (Eds.), *Environmental methods review 1996.* Tampa, FL: AEPI.

Butler, R. W. (1980). The concept of a tourist area cycle of evolution: Implications for management of resources. *The Canadian Geographer, 14*(1), 5–12.

Butler, R. W. (1991). Tourism, environment, and sustainable development. *Environmental Conservation, 18*(3), 201–209.

Cameron, R. (1975). The diffusion of technology as a problem in economic history. *Economic Geography, 51*(3), 217–230.

Canadian Pacific Hotels. (1993). *Green partnerships.* Montreal: Author.

Capp, G. (1995, May 8). Tourist boom or enviro-doom? *The West Australian.*

Capp, G. (1996, October 14). The report they wanted to hide. *The West Australian.*

Cater, E. A. (1987). Tourism in the least developed countries. *Annals of Tourism Research, 14,* 202–226.

Checkley, A. (1992). Accommodating the environment: Greening of Canada's largest hotel company. In *Proceedings of ISEP Conference on Strategies for Reducing the Environmental Impact of Tourism* (pp. 178–189), Vienna.

Chung, C., & Hildebrand, L. (1994, January). A multinational assessment of coastal zone management in OECD countries. *Ecodecision,* 44-49.

Cientistas descobrem diversidade recorde. (1993). *Journal da Mata Atlantica, 1*(1), 1.

Clark, E. (1992). Whale sharks: Gentle monsters of the deep. *National Geographic, 182*(6), 120-139.

Cleveland, S., & Hansen, C. (1994). Growth management and public participation: A small town approach works for Sedro-Woolley, Washington. *Small Town, 24*(4), 4-13.

Coastal Committee of New South Wales. (1994). *Draft revised coastal policy for NSW.* Sydney.

Cohen, E. (1978). The impact of tourism on the physical environment. *Annals of Tourism Research, 5*(2), 215-237.

Cornell, S., & Kalt, J. P. (1995). Reloading the dice: Improving the chances for economic development on American Indian reservations. In S. Cornell & J. Kalt (Eds.), *What can tribes do? Strategies and institutions in American Indian economic development* (pp. 1-59). Los Angeles: American Indian Studies Center, UCLA.

Cornwall, G., & Burns, B. (1992). The greening of Canada. In F. Edwards (Ed.), *Environmental auditing. The challenge of the 1990s* (pp. 1-6). Calgary: Banff Centre for Management, University of Calgary Press.

Culbertson, K. S., & Kolberg, J. (1991). Worker housing in resorts: Aspen's experience. *Urban Land, 50*(4), 12-15.

Culbertson, K., Jackson, S., & Kolberg, J. (1992). Loving the mountains to death: Toward a definition of sustainable development in the Roaring Fork Valley of Colorado. In A. Gill & R. Hartman (Eds.), *Mountain resort development, Proceedings of The Vail Conference* (pp. 41-52). Burnaby, B.C.: Simon Fraser University, Centre for Tourism Policy and Research.

D'Amore, L. J. (1983). Guidelines to planning in harmony with the host community. In P. E. Murphy (Ed.), *Tourism in Canada: Selected issues and options.* Victoria, B.C.: University of Victoria.

Daltabuit, M., & Pi-Sunyer, O. (1990). Tourism development in Quintana Roo, Mexico. *Cultural Survival Quarterly, 14*(1), 9-13.

De Groot, R. S. (1983). Tourism and conservation in the Galapagos Islands. *Biological Conservation, 26,* 291-300.

De Groot, R. S. (1986). *A functional ecosystem evaluation method as a tool in environmental planning and decision-making.* Wageningen, The Netherlands: Nature Conservation Department, Wageningen Agricultural University.

De Groot, R. S. (1988). Environmental functions: An analytical framework for integrating environmental and economic assessment. In *Workshop on Integrating Environmental and Economic Assessment.* Ottawa, Canada: Canadian Environmental Advisory Council.

Dean, W. (1996). *With broadaxe and firebrand.* Berkeley: University of California Press.

Department of Conservation and Land Management. (1988). *Range to reef: Discover Cape Range National Park and Ningaloo Marine Park.* Perth: Author.

Department of Conservation and Land Management. (1989). *Ningaloo Marine Park management plan.* Perth: Author.

Department of Conservation and Land Management. (1996). *Experiencing whalesharks in Ningaloo Marine Park: A guide for passengers of commercial tours.* Perth: Author.

Diario do Grande ABC. (1994, February 25-27). Diario na Praia: Ilha do Cardoso (No. 10). Sao Paulo.

Ding, P., & Pigram, J. (1995). Environmental audits: An emerging concept in sustainable tourism development. *Journal of Tourism Studies, 6*(2), 2-10.

Dorward, S. (1990). *Design for mountain communities.* New York: Van Nostrand Reinhold.

Dowling, R. K. (1992). Public view on natural area tourism: North West Cape, Western Australia. *Australian Parks and Recreation, 28*(2), 28-32.

Dowling, R. K. (1993). Tourist and resident perceptions of the environment—tourism relationship in the Gascoyne Region, Western Australia. *GeoJournal, 28*(3), 243-251.

Doxey, G. (1975). A causation theory of visitor-resident irritants: Methodology and research inferences. *Proceedings of Travel and Tourism Research Association Annual Conference* (pp. 195-198). San Diego, CA/Salt Lake City, UT: TTRA.

Dozier, E. P. (1964). The Pueblo Indians of the Southwest. *Current Anthropology, 5*(2), 79-97.

Drake, S. (1991). Local participation in ecotourism. In *Nature tourism.* Washington, DC: Island Press.

Draper, W. H., III. (1991). *Human development report 1991.* New York: United Nations Development Program.

Echtner, C. M. (1995). Tourism education in developing nations: A three-pronged approach. *Tourism Recreation Research.*

Edwards, J. R. (1987). The U.K. Heritage Coast: An assessment of the ecological impact of tourism. *Annals of Tourism Research, 14*(I), 71-87.

Enzenbacher, D. J. (1992). Antarctic tourism and environmental concerns. *Marine Pollution Bulletin, 25*(9-12), 258-265.

Enzenbacher, D. J. (1994). Antarctic tourism: An overview of 1992/93 season activity, recent developments, and emerging issues. *Polar Record, 30*(173), 105-116.

Evers, W. R. (1989). A strategic tool for sustainable development. In *Strengthening environmental cooperation with developing countries.* Brussels, Belgium: Organization for Economic Cooperation and Development (OECD).

Federal Environmental Assessment Review Office. (1989). *Initial environmental assessment procedures and practices* (instructor's manual). Ottawa, Canada.

Filion, F. L. (1988). Managing for sustainable development: The strategic role of economic and social aspects of wildlife. In *Proceedings, Second International Wildlife Symposium.* Mexico City, Mexico: The Wildlife Society of Mexico.

Folha de Sao Paulo (1994, February 17). P. 20.

Frank, A. (1992, April). Namibia's tourist industry: Overcoming constraints to growth. *Namibia Review,* 15-19.

Friends of Pulau Redang. (1992). *Save Pulau Redang.* Penang, Malaysia: Jutaprint.

Fundacao O Boticario. (1996). *Descriptive brochure distributed at World Conservation Congress, Montreal.* Curitiba: Author.

Fundacao SOS Mata Atlantica. (1992). *Dossier: Atlantic Rain Forest.* Sao Paulo: Author.

Gadja Mada University and University of Waterloo. (1992). *Sustainable development strategy for Bali.* Yogyakarta, Indonesia: University Consortium on the Environment, Gadja Mada University.

Gales Point Progressive Cooperative and Manatee Advisory Team. (1992). *Management plan for the development of community based tourism in Gales Point, Manatee.* Gales Point: Author.

Gantzer, H. cited in Lobo, J. (1991). *Repercussions of luxury tourism in Goa.* Bangalore: Mirithu.

Gascoyne Development Commission. (1995). *Gascoyne regional ecotourism strategy.* Prepared by David Wood for the Gacoyne Development Commission, Perth.

Gerlitz, W. (1994). *Five Blues National Park Management Plan* (draft).

Getz, D. (1982). A rationale and methodology for assessing capacity to absorb tourism. *Ontario Geography, 19,* 92-101.

Gill, A. (1992). Issues and problems of community development in Whistler. In A. Gill & R. Hartman (Eds.), *Mountain resort development, Proceedings of The Vail Conference* (pp. 27-31). Burnaby, B.C.: Simon Fraser University, Centre For Tourism Policy and Research.

Gill, A., & Williams, P. W. (1993). Tourism growth management in mountain communities. *Expanding Responsibilities: A Blueprint for the Travel Industry, Conference Proceedings of The Travel and Tourism Research Association, Whistler B.C., 1993* (pp. 179-185). Wheatridge, CO: TTRA.

Government of Prince Edward Island. (1987). *A conservation strategy for Prince Edward Island*. Charlottetown, Canada.

Government of Senegal. (1991). *Presentation du Tourisem Rural Integre*. Dakar: Author.

Greenlee, D. (1994, April). Community based ecotourism in Gales Point, Belize. *Belize Currents*, 10-11.

Gunn, C. A. (1979). *Tourism planning*. New York: Crane Russak.

Haederle, M. (1994, May 14). Homage of Hokum?—Wanna-bes are intruding on Native American Ritual. *The Arizona Republic*, pp. B6-7. (Originally published by the *Los Angeles Times*.)

Harrison, D., & Price, M. (1996). Fragile environments, fragile communities? An introduction. In M. Price (Ed.), *People and tourism in fragile environments* (pp. 1-18). Chichester: John Wiley & Sons.

Hartup, B. (1989). *An alternative conservation model for tropical areas: The Community Baboon Sanctuary*. M.S. thesis, University of Wisconsin-Madison.

Hartup, B. K. (1994). Community conservation in Belize: Demography, resource use, and attitudes of participating landowners. *Biological Conservation, 69*, 235-241.

Harvey, B., III. (1972). An overview of pueblo religion. In A. Ortiz (Ed.), *New perspectives on the pueblos* (pp. 197-217). Albuquerque: University of New Mexico Press.

Hawkes, S., & Williams, P. (1993). *The greening of tourism*. Burnaby: Centre for Tourism Policy and Research, Simon Fraser University.

Hawkes, S., & Williams, P. (1993). *The greening of tourism: From principles to practice*. Ottawa, Canada: Centre for Tourism Policy Research, Simon Fraser University, and Tourism Canada.

Hawkins, A. E. (1987). *A carrying capacity model for resort planning and management with preliminary application to Whistler, Canada*. Unpublished Master of Natural Resources Management Research Project, Burnaby, BC, Simon Fraser University.

Headland, R. K. (1994). Historical development of Antarctic tourism. *Annals of Tourism Research, 21*(2), 269-280.

Healy, R. G. (1988). *Economic considerations in nature-oriented tourism: Latin American case studies* (FPEI Working Paper No. 39). Research Triangle Park, NC: U.S. Forest Service. Southeastern Forest Experiment Station.

Healy, R. G. (1994). Tourist merchandise as a means of generating local benefits from ecotourism. *Journal of Sustainable Tourism*.

Helber, L. (1985). The resort development planning process. In J. Dean & B. Judd (Eds.), *Tourist developments in Australia* (pp. (37-45). Canberra: Royal Australian Institute of Architects.

Hill, C. (1990). The paradox of tourism in Costa Rica. *Cultural Survival Quarterly, 14*(1), 14-19.

Horwich, R. H. (1990). How to develop a community sanctuary—an experimental approach to the conservation of private lands. *Oryx, 24*, 95-102.

Horwich, R. H., & Boardman, B. (1993, April). Community conservation and ecotourism—Gales Point, Manatee. *Belize Review, 14*-15, 18-20.

Horwich, R. H., Koontz, F., Saqui, E., Saqui, H., & Glander, K. (1993). A reintroduction program for the conservation of the black howler monkey in Belize. *Endangered Species Update, 10*, 1-6.

Horwich, R. H., & Lyon, J. (1988). Experimental technique for the conservation of private lands. *Journal of Medical Primatology, 17*, 169-176.

Horwich, R. H., & Lyon, J. (1990). *A Belizean Rainforest—The Community Baboon Sanctuary*. Gay Mills, WI: Orang-utan Press.

Horwich, R. H., & Lyon, J. (1991). *Proposal for a multiple land use system for the Community Manatee Reserve*. Manuscript.

Horwich, R. H., & Lyon, J. (in press). Multi-level conservation and education at the Community Baboon Sanctuary, Belize. In: K. Jacobson (Ed.), *Wildlife conservation: International case studies of education and communication programs.* New York: Columbia University Press.

Horwich, R. H., Murray, D., Saqui, E., Lyon, J., & Godfrey, D. (1993). Ecotourism and community development: A view from Belize. In: K. Lindberg & D. E. Hawkins (Eds.), *Ecotourism: A guide for planners & managers* (pp. 152-168). North Bennington, VT: The Ecotourism Society.

Humphreys, W. E. (Ed.). (1993). *Biogeography of Cape Range, Western Australia.* Perth: WA Museum.

Ilhas de Tesouro. (1990, December 5). *Veja,* 74-75.

Inskeep, E. (1991). *Tourism planning: An integrated and sustainable development approach.* New York: Van Nostrand Reinhold.

Inskeep, E. (1994). Tourism carrying capacity of Goa. In *National and regional tourism planning methodologies and case studies.* London: Routledge.

Inskeep, E., & Kallenberger, M. (1992). *An integrated approach to resort development.* Madrid, Spain: World Tourism Organization.

Instituto Brasiliero para Meio Ambiente e Recursos Naturais. (1996). Private natural heritage reserves: Expanding conservation areas. Brasilia: Author.

International Hotels Environment Initiative. (1994). *Environmental management for hotels.*

International Union for the Conservation of Nature and Natural Resources. (1980). *World conservation strategy.* Gland, Switzerland: Author.

International Union for the Conservation of Nature and Natural Resources. (1991). *Caring for the world: A strategy for sustainability.* Gland, Switzerland: World Conservation Union (IUCN), United Nations Environment Program (UNEP), and the World Wide Fund for Nature (WWF).

Jacobs, P., & Munro, D. A. (1987). *Conservation with equity: Strategies for sustainable development.* Cambridge, England: IUCN.

Jha, L. K. (1963). *Report Adhoc Committee on Tourism.* New Delhi.

Johnson, B. (1990). Introduction: Breaking out of tourist trap. *Cultural Survival Quarterly, 14*(1), 2-5.

Johnstone, A. I. (1986). *An introduction to environmental impact assessment.* Paper presented at the Environmental Impact Assessment Workshop, Environmental Institute, University of Salford, 15-17 October.

Jones Lang Wootton. (1993a). *North West Cape tourism development study: draft report—part one.* Perth: Author.

Jones Lang Wootton. (1993b). *North West Cape tourism development study: draft report—part two.* Perth: Author.

Jones Lang Wootton. (1993c). *North West Cape tourism development study.* Perth: Author.

Jungk, R. (1979). *The nuclear state.* London: John Calder.

Kamat, U. D. (1993). Development of tourism. *Tourism development and management of coastal areas* (Technical Papers). Institute of Town Planners, India, New Delhi.

Kamat, U. D. (1996). Development of tourism in Goa. In S. Singh (Ed.), *Profiles of Indian tourism.* New Delhi.

Kelleher, G. (1993). Sustainable development of the Great Barrier Reef. In S. Hawkes & P. Williams (Eds.), *The greening of tourism.* Burnaby: Centre for Tourism Policy and Research, Simon Fraser University.

King, B., & Whitelaw, P. (1992). Resorts in Australian tourism. *Journal of Tourism Studies, 3*(2), 41-48.

Kirst, L. (1987). American Indian economic development policies. *Journal of Planning Literature, 2*(1), 101-110.

Knights, P. (1993). *Tourism for discovery in Senegal*. Washington, DC: Environmental Investigation Agency.

Laarman, J. G., & Perdue, R. R. (1989). Science tourism in Costa Rica. *Annals of Tourism Research, 16*, 205-215.

Lawerence, R. A., Hafer, H. R., Long, P. T., & Perdue, R. R. (1993). Rural residents' attitudes toward recreation and tourism development. *Journal of Travel Research, 31*(4), 27-33.

Lawrence, A. M. (1990). Seeking the optimum point. *Ski Area Management, 29*(1), 75.

Lea, J. P. (1993). Tourism development ethics in the third world. *Annals of Tourism Research, 20*, 701-715.

Leiper, N. (1989). Tourist attraction systems. *Annals of Tourism Research, 16*, 367-384.

Lent, L. (1995). A whale of a time on Ningaloo reef. *Ranger—A Journal for Conservation Managers, 31*, 9-10.

Lew, A. A. (1989). *Innovation diffusion and cultural adaptation: Geography and social change*. Paper presented at the 52nd annual meeting of the Association of Pacific Coast Geographers, 20-24 September, Fairbanks, AK.

Lew, A. A. (1990). *Acculturation and tourism on Native American reservations*. Paper presented a the 86th annual meeting of the Association of American Geographers, 19-22 April, Toronto, Ontario, Canada.

Lindberg, K. (1991). *Policies for maximizing nature tourism's ecological and economic benefits*. Washington, DC: World Resources Institute.

Lindberg, K., & Enriquez, J. (1994). *An analysis of ecotourism's economic contribution to conservation and development in Belize* (Vol. 1 and 2). Washington, DC: World Wildlife Fund.

Lindberg, K., Enriquez, J., & Sproule, K. (1996). Ecotourism questioned: Case studies from Belize. *Annals of Tourism Research, 29*(3), 543-562.

Lobo, J. (1991). *The repercussions of luxury tourism in Goa*. Bangalore: Mirithu Publishing House.

Lujan, C. C. (1993). A sociological view of tourism in an American Indian community: Maintaining cultural integrity at Taos Pueblo. *American Indian Culture and Research, 17*(3), 101-120.

Lynch, K. (1960). *The image of the city*. Cambridge, MA: MIT Press.

MacCannell, D. (1976). *The tourist: A new theory of the leisure class*. New York: Schocken Books.

MacCannell, D. (1989). Introduction (to special issue on the Semiotics of Tourism). *Annals of Tourism Research, 16*, 1-6.

Manatee Advisory Team. (1992). *Manatee Special Development Area (MSDA) Recommendations submitted to the Lands Utilization Authority MSDA subcommittee*.

Manning, E. W. (1992). *Indicators for the sustainable management of tourism: Report of the International Working Group on Indicators of Sustainable Tourism*. Madrid, Spain: World Tourism Organization.

Manning, E. W. (1993). Managing sustainable tourism: Indicators for better decisions. In *Proceedings of the 1992 World Congress on Adventure Travel and Ecotourism*. Whistler, Canada.

Manning, E. W. (1996, Spring). Tourism: Where are the limits? *Ecodecision, 35-39*.

Manning E. W., Clifford, G., Dougherty, T. D., & Ernst, M. (1995). *What tourism managers need to know: A practical guide to the development and use of indicators of sustainable tourism*. Madrid: World Tourism Organization.

Manning, E. W., & Dougherty, T. D. (1995). Sustainable tourism: Preserving the golden goose. *Cornell Hotel and Restaurant Administration Quarterly, 29-42*.

Manning, E. W., Rizzo, B., & Wiken, E. (1990). Conservation strategies, sustainable development, and climatic change. In G. Wall & M. Sanderson (Eds.), *Climate change: Implications for water and ecological resources.* Waterloo, Canada: Department of Geography, University of Waterloo.

Martin, B. S., & Uysal, M. (1990). An examination of the relationship between carrying capacity and the tourism lifecycle: Management and policy implications. *Journal of Environmental Management, 31*(4), 327–333.

Mason, P. (1994). A visitor code for the Arctic. *Tourism Management, 15*(2), 93–97.

Master plan for tourism development in Goa, 2001 AD. (1987). Town & Country Planning, Goa, Panaji.

Mathieson, A., & Wall, G. (1982). *Tourism: Economic, physical and social impacts.* New York: Longman.

May, R. F., Lenanton, R. C. J., & Berry, P. F. (1983). *Ningaloo Marine Park: Report and recommendations by the Marine Park Working Group* (Report No. 1). National Park's Authority, Western Australia.

McIntyre, G., & Hetherington, A. (1991). *Sustainable tourism development: Guidelines for local planners.* Madrid, Spain: World Tourism Organization.

Medcraft, T. (1996). *Ningaloo Reef: Australia's best kept secret of the sea.* Exmouth, WA: Whaleshark Adventures Ltd.

Mercer, D. (1972). *Planning for coastal recreation* (Monograph 1). Melbourne: Combined Universities Recreation Research Group.

Meyer-Arendt, K. (1990). Modelling environmental impacts of tourism development along the Gulf Coast. *The Compass, 67*(4), 272–283.

Miller, L. M. (1987). Tourism in Washington's coastal zone. *Annals of Tourism Research, 14*(1), 58–70.

Ministry of Planning. (1996). *Gascoyne Coast regional strategy.* Perth: Western Australian Planning Commission.

Moulin, C. L. (1980). Plan for ecological and cultural tourism involving participation of local population and associations. In: D. E. Hawkins, E. L. Shafer, & J. M. Rovelsted (Eds.), *Tourism planning and development issues* (pp. 199–211).

Munasinghe, M. (1993). Key issues in sustainable development. In M. Nazim & N. Polunin (Eds.), *Environmental challenges: From Stockholm to Rio and beyond* (pp. 171–207). Lahore, Pakistan: Energy and Environmental Society fo Pakistan and Geneva, Switzerland: Foundation for Environmental Conservation.

Murphy, E. (1985). *Tourism: A community approach.* New York: Methuen.

Namibia Ministry of Environment and Tourism. (1995). *Annual visitor arrival statistics 1993.* Namibia: Author.

Namibia Ministry of Trade and Industry. (1992). *The investor: Investing in Namibia* (Vol. 1, No. 3). Windhoek: Author.

Namibia Ministry of Wildlife, Conservation and Tourism. (1992). *Namibia tourism development study.* Windhoek: Author.

Namibia Ministry of Wildlife, Conservation and Tourism. (1994). *Namibia: Africa's gem.* Windhoek: Author.

Namibia to get hotel school. (1993, December/1994, January). *Travel News Namibia,* 1.

National Institute of Oceanography. (1977). *Report on studies of the environment and stability condition of the Sinquerim Beach, Panaji* (Report No. 811).

Nelson, J. G. (1991). *Tourism and sustainable development with special reference to monitoring.* Waterloo, Canada: Heritage Resources Centre.

Neufeldt, V. (1988). *Webster's new world dictionary of American English* (third college edition). New York: Simon & Shuster, Inc.

Ningaloo's giants the focus of forefront research. (1996, Autumn). *Murdoch News,* 8 (Newsletter of Murdoch University, Perth).

O'Reilly, A. M. (1986). Tourism carrying capacity. *Tourism Management, 7*(4), 254-258.

Organisation for Economic Cooperation and Development. (1986). *Environmental assessment and developing assistance* (OECD monograph No. 4). Brussels, Belgium: Author.

Organisation for Economic Cooperation and Development. (1993a). *Coastal zone management: Selected case studies.* Paris: OECD Document Series.

Organisation for Economic Cooperation and Development. (1993b). *Coastal zone management: Integrated policies.* Paris: Author.

Orlande, T., Laarman, J., & Mortimer, J. (1994). *White gold: Palmito sustainability and economics in Brazil's Atlantic Forest* (FPEI Working Paper No. 55). Research Triangle Park, NC: U.S. Forest Service.

Passoff, M. (1991). Ecotourism re-examined. *Earth Island Journal, 6*(2), 28-29.

Pearce, D. (1989). *Tourism development* (2nd ed., pp. 25-26). New York: John Wiley & Sons.

Pearce, D., & Freeman, S. (1991). *Informational requirements for policy decision-makers* (Theme Paper One, Environmental Information for the Twenty-first Century). Montreal, Canada: International Forum.

Pigram, J. (1977). Beach resort morphology. *Habitat International, 2*(5/6), 525-541.

Pigram, J. (1989). *Outdoor recreation and resource management.* London: Croom Helm (reprinted).

Pigram, J. (1995). Resource constraints on tourism: Water resources and sustainability. In R. Butler & D. Pearce (Eds.), *Change in tourism. People places process* (pp. 209-228). London: Routledge.

Pigram, J. J. (1990). Sustainable tourism—policy considerations. *Journal of Tourism Studies, 1*(2), 2-8.

Plog, S. C. (1991). *Leisure travel: Making it a growth market again!* New York: John Wiley & Sons.

Polisar, J., & Horwich, R. H. (1994). Conservation of the large economically important river turtle *Dermatemys mawii* in Belize. *Conservation Biology, 8,* 338-342.

Poon, A. (1993). *Tourism, technology and competitive strategy.* Wallington, UK: CAB International.

Price, M. F. (1985). Impacts of recreational activities on alpine vegetation in Western North America. *Mountain Research and Development, 5*(3), 263-278.

Price, M. (Ed.). (1996). *People and tourism in fragile environments.* Chichester: John Wiley & Sons.

Queensland Department of Tourism, Small Business and Industry. (1997). *Queensland ecotourism plan.* Brisbane: Author.

Queensland Tourism and Travel Corporation. (1993). *Queensland tourism bulletin.* Brisbane: Author.

Reardon. D. (1995, February 14). Coral Bay resort plan draws fire. *The West Australian.*

Rees, W. E. (1990). The ecology of sustainable development. *The Ecologist, 20*(1), 18-23.

Regional Plan Goa 2000 AD. (1987). Town & Country Planning Goa, Panaji.

Relph, E. (1976). *Place and placelessness.* London: Pion.

Resort Municipality of Whistler. (1988). *Comprehensive development plan.* Whistler, B.C.: Author.

Resort Municipality of Whistler. (1993). *Comprehensive development plan.* Whistler, B.C.: Author.

Roderjan, R. (1981). *Focolore Brasileiro: Parana.* Rio de Janeiro: FUNARTE.

Rogers, E. M. (1983). *Diffusion of innovations* (3rd ed.). New York: The Free Press.

Ruschmann, D. v.d.M. (1992). Ecological tourism in Brazil. *Tourism Management, March,* 125-128.

Scace, R. C., Grifone, E., & Usher, R. (1992). *Ecotourism in Canada.* Ottawa, Canada: Canadian

Environmental Advisory Council.

Schiffman, I. (1989). *Alternative techniques for managing growth.* Berkeley, CA: Institute of Government Studies, University of California at Berkeley.

Secretaria do Meio Ambiente. (1991). *Educacao Ambiental em Unidades de Conservacao e de Producao.* Sao Paulo: Governo do Estado do Sao Paulo.

Senegal Tourist Office. (1993). *Senegal is always in season: Information and travel guide.* Dakar: Author.

Shackley, M. (1993). Guest farms in Namibia: An emerging accommodation sector in Africa's hottest destination. *International Journal of Hospitality Management, 12*(3), 253-265.

Shea, S., & Sharp, J. R. (1992). *Emerging tourism opportunities—Western Australia's natural advantage.* Paper presented to the Into Asia Conference, Perth, Western Australia, November, 1992.

Sinclair, T. K. (1983). *A content analysis of six Wisconsin newspaper's coverage of the La Farge dam controversy.* M.S. thesis, University of Wisconsin-Madison.

Singh, S. (1994). Problem of tourism development in coastal Goa. *Tourism Recreation Research, 19*(1), 65-72.

Singh, T. V., & Kaur, J. (1985). In search of holistic tourism in the Himalayas. In T. V. Singh & K. Jagdish (Eds.), *Integrated mountain development.* New Delhi, India: Himalayan Books Ltd.

Smith, G. W., Eckert, K. L., & Gibson, J. P. (1992). *Sea turtle recovery action plan for Belize* (WIDECAST Technical Report No. 18). Caribbean Environmental Program, Kingston, Jamaica.

Smith, V. L. (1995). *The 4 H's of tribal tourism: Acoma—A pueblo case study.* Paper presented at the biennial meeting of the International Academy for the Study of Tourism, Cairo, Egypt, 24 June to 1 July.

Smith, V. L. (1996a). Indigenous tourism: The four Hs. In R. Butler & T. Hinch (Eds.), *Tourism and indigenous peoples* (pp. 283-307). London: International Thomson Business Press.

Smith, V. L. (1996b). The Inuit as hosts: Heritage and wilderness tourism in Nunavut. In M. F. Price & V. L. Smith (Eds.), *People and tourism in fragile environments* (pp. 33-50). Chichester/New York: John Wiley and Sons.

Southern African tourism: Cooperation can make the difference. (1995, April-May). *Travel News Namibia,* 1.

Splettstoesser, J. (1992). Tourism in Antarctica—guidelines for a low-impact presence. *Proceedings of the First International Symposium, Tourism in Polar Areas,* Colmar, France, 21-23 April.

Splettstoesser, J. (1993). Antarctica: the last outpost of the honor system. *Insights on Global Ethics, 3*(6), 7.

Splettstoesser, J. (1996). Education of visitors to Antarctica. In *Opportunities for Antarctic Environmental Education and Training: Proceedings of SCAR/IUCN Workshop* (pp. 75-86), Gorizia, Italy, April 26-29, 1993. Cambridge: IUCN.

Splettstoesser, J. (in press). IAATO's stewardship of the Antarctic environment. In *Progress in tourism and hospitality research.* New York: John Wiley and Sons.

Splettstoesser, J., & Folks, M. (1994). Environmental guidelines for tourism in Antarctica. *Annals of Tourism Research, 21*(2), 231-244.

Splettstoesser, J., & Smith, V. J. (1994). Antarctic tourism: A successful union for tourism and the environment. *Proceedings of Symposium on Sustainable Tourism Development,* presented at IITP Conference, Building a Sustainable World Through Tourism, Montreal, Canada, 12-16 September.

Srisang, K. (1987). A Goan army against five star tourism. *Contours, 3*(3), 9-13.

Stachowitsch, M. (1992). Tourism and the sea. In *Proceedings of ISEP Conference on Strategies for Reducing the Environmental Impact of Tourism* (pp. 30-36), Vienna.

Stillwell, H. D. (1987). Environmental impacts and site constraints of mountain resort developments. *Applied Geography Conferences, 10*, 297-305.

Swamy. M. C. K. (1993). Conservation and protection of coastal belt. *41st ATCP Seminar on Development and Management of Coastal Areas*, Institute of Town Planners India, New Delhi.

Sweet, J. D. (1991). "Let 'em loose": Pueblo Indian management of tourism. *American Indian Culture and Research Journal, 15*(4), 59-74.

Swithinbank, C. (1993). Airborne tourism in the Antarctic. *Polar Record, 29*(169), 103-110.

Sy, A. (Ed.). (1991). *Annuaire Touristique du Senegal*. Dakar: Nouvelles Imprimeries du Senegal.

Talbot, S. (1981). Economic plunder of American Indians. *Today's Political Affairs, 60*(10), 29-37.

Tour guide courses offered by NATH. (1994, December/1995, January). *Travel News Namibia*, 13.

Tourism Concern. (1993, January 26). *Sweet Poison*. Press Release.

Townley, P. (1995). Is 'green marketing' worthwhile? In *Waste management and environment sourcebook* (p. 165). Sydney: Minnis Business Press.

Trosper, R. L. (1995). Mind sets and economic development on Indian reservations. In S. Cornell & J. Kalt (Eds.), *What can tribes do? Strategies and institutions in American Indian economic development* (pp. 301-333). Los Angeles: American Indian Studies Center, UCLA.

Troyer, W. (1992). *The green partnership guide*. Toronto: Canadian Pacific Hotels and Resorts.

Uganda Ministry of Tourism, Wildlife & Antiquities. (1990). *Uganda tourism development: Tourism rehabilitation & development planning for Uganda*. Kampala: Author.

Uganda Ministry of Tourism, Wildlife & Antiquities. (1993). *Integrated tourism master plan*. Kampala: Author.

Veeryya, M. (1978). *Studies on the geological aspects of beaches of Goa in relation to some meteorological and physical oceanographic factors*. Unpublished Ph.D. thesis, University of Goa. Panaji.

Vogt, E. Z. (1951). *Navaho veterans, a study of changing values*. Papers of the Peabody Museum of American Archeology and Ethnology, Harvard University, Vol. XLI, No. 1.

Wall, G. (1982). Cycles and capacity—incipient theory or conceptual contradiction? *Tourism Management, 3*(3), 188-192.

Werner, L. (1994, March/April). Pondering "parks vs. people" in Belize. *Americas*.

Western Australian Government. (1995). *Parliamentary Select Committee on Cape Range National Park and Ningaloo Marine Park*. Perth: Author.

Western Australian Tourism Commission. (1993). *Western Australian Tourism Monitor 1992/93*. Perth: Author.

Western Australian Tourism Commission. (1995). *Western Australian tourism infrastructure strategy*. Prepared by Coopers & Lybrand for the Western Australian Tourism Commission, Perth.

Western Australian Tourism Commission & CALM. (1997). *Nature-based tourism strategy*. Perth: Author.

Williams, M. V. (1993). *Growth management in tourism communities*. Unpublished Master of Natural Resource Management research paper, Burnaby, B.C., School of Resource and Environmental Management.

Williams, P. W., & Dossa, K. B. (1994). *B.C. skiers in profile 1993-1994*. Burnaby, B.C.: Simon Fraser University, Centre for Tourism Policy and Research.

World Commission on Environment and Development (Brundtland Commission). (1987). *Our common future*. New York: Oxford University Press.

World Tourism Organization. (1989). *Report—tourism carrying capacity Goa, India*. Madrid: Author.

World Tourism Organization. (1996). *Yearbook of tourism statistics.* Madrid: Author.

World Tourism Organization, World Travel and Tourism Council, and Earth Council. (1995). *Agenda 21 for the travel and tourism industry.* London, England: Author.

World Travel and Tourism Council. (1990). *Environmental impact assessment and audit guidelines.* Brussels, Belgium: Author.

World Travel and Tourism Council. (1992, revised 1993). *Statistical indicators needed to monitor sustainable travel and tourism development.* Oxford: World Travel and Tourism Environment Research Centre.

Ziffer, K. (1989). *Ecotourism, the uneasy alliance.* Washington, DC: Conservation International.

Zimmerman, F. (1992). Issues, problems, and future trends in the Austrian Alps: The changes within traditional toursim. In A. Gill & R. Hartman (Eds.), *Mountain resort development: Proceedings of the Vail Conference* (pp. 160-170). Burnaby, B.C.: Simon Fraser University, Centre For Tourism Policy and Reserach.

Zurick, D. N. (1992). Adventure travel and sustainable tourism in the peripheral economy of Nepal. *Annals of the Association of American Geographers, 82*(4), 608-628.

Index

tourism dynamics

Cognizant Communication Corporation
New York • Sydney • Tokyo

Martin Oppermann

Sex Tourism and Prostitution

Aspects of Leisure, Recreation, and Work

Cognizant Communication Corporation
New York • Sydney • Tokyo

tourism dynamics

Softcover	$30.00	ISBN 1-8882345-15-0
Hardcover	$38.00	ISBN 1-8882345-14-2

Paul F. Wilkinson

Tourism Policy & Planning:
Case Studies from the Commonwealth Caribbean

Cognizant Communication Corporation
New York • Sydney • Tokyo

Choice Review

Softcover	$26.00	ISBN 1-8882345-13- 4
Hardcover	$35.00	ISBN 1-8882345-12-6

Edited by:
Klaus Meyer-Arendt
Rudi Hartmann

Casino Gambling in America:
Origins, Trends, and Impacts

Cognizant Communication Corporation
New York • Sydney • Tokyo

tourism
dynamics

Softcover	$30.00	ISBN 1-8882345-17- 7
Hardcover	$38.00	ISBN 1-8882345-16-9

Edited by:
Alan A. Lew
George A. Van Otten

Tourism and Gaming on American Indian Lands

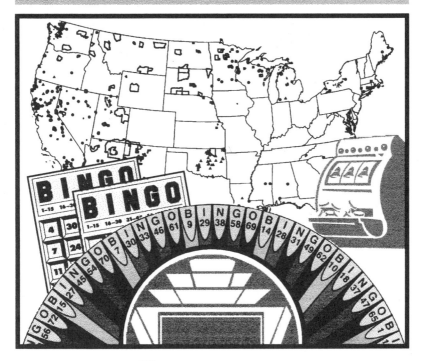

Cognizant Communication Corporation
New York • Sydney • Tokyo

Softcover $30.00   ISBN 1-8882345-21-5